LESSONS FOR
DECIMALS AND PERCENTS

GRADES 5-6

THE TEACHING ARITHMETIC SERIES

San Diego Christian College
2100 Greenfield Drive
El Cajon, CA 92019

LESSONS FOR
DECIMALS AND PERCENTS

▲▲▲▲▲

GRADES 5–6

CARRIE DE FRANCISCO
MARILYN BURNS

MATH SOLUTIONS PUBLICATIONS
SAUSALITO, CA

Math Solutions Publications
A division of
Marilyn Burns Education Associates
150 Gate 5 Road, Suite 101
Sausalito, CA 94965
www.mathsolutions.com

Library of Congress Cataloging-in-Publication Data

Francisco, Carrie De.
  Teaching arithmetic : lessons for decimals and percents, grades 5–6 /
Carrie De Francisco, Marilyn Burns.
     p.   cm.—(Teaching arithmetic)
Includes index.
     ISBN 0-941355-44-6 (alk. paper)
    1. Decimal fractions—Study and teaching (Elementary)   2.
Percentage—Study and teaching (Elementary)   I. Burns, Marilyn, 1941–
II. Title.   III. Series.
   QA117 .F69825   2002
   372.7'2—dc21
                                                         2002007472

Editor: Toby Gordon
Production: Melissa L. Inglis
Cover & interior design: Leslie Bauman
Composition: Cape Cod Compositors

Printed in the United States of America on acid-free paper
06 05   ML   2   3   4   5

A Message from Marilyn Burns

We at Math Solutions Professional Development believe that teaching math well calls for increasing our understanding of the math we teach, seeking deeper insights into how children learn mathematics, and refining our lessons to best promote students' learning.

Math Solutions publications share classroom-tested lessons and teaching expertise from our faculty of Math Solutions Inservice instructors. Our publications are part of the nationwide effort we've made since 1984 which now includes:

- more than 500 face-to-face inservice programs each year for teachers and administrators in districts across the county;
- annually publishing professional development books, now totaling more than fifty titles and spanning the teaching of all math topics in Kindergarten through grade 8;
- four series of videotapes for teachers, plus a videotape for parents, that show math lessons taught in actual classrooms;
- on-site visits to schools to help refine teaching strategies and assess student learning;
- free online support, including grade-level lessons, book reviews, inservice information, and district feedback, all in our quarterly Math Solutions Online Newsletter.

For information about all of the products and services we have available, please visit our web site at *www.mathsolutions.com*. You can also contact us to discuss math professional development needs by calling (800) 868-9092 or by sending an e-mail to *info@mathsolutions.com*.

We're always eager for your feedback and interested in learning about your particular needs. We look forward to hearing from you.

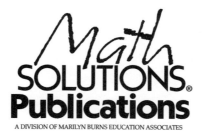

A DIVISION OF MARILYN BURNS EDUCATION ASSOCIATES

CONTENTS

LINKING MONEY AND DECIMALS

ADDITIONAL ACTIVITIES 161

ASSESSMENTS 169

BLACKLINE MASTERS 179

ACKNOWLEDGMENTS

I would like to thank all of my students—past and present—for being my inspiration.

I would like to thank my husband for his constant love and support, my parents for their bountiful confidence in me, and my family for their continuous assistance and patience with me as I worked on this project.

I would like to offer a special thanks to Mrs. Sue Arnold, Mrs. Josie Sheatsley, and Mrs. Karen Ventura and their students for opening up their classrooms and for sharing their classwork with me. And a special thanks to my niece, Misha, for also taking part in the book by contributing her ideas and student work as well.

INTRODUCTION

Before beginning instruction about decimals, I gave the class a writing assignment. "Today we'll start to study about decimals," I told them. "But first I'd like to find out what you already know about decimals. So think for a moment about decimals and how they're used, and then write down everything you can think of. If you aren't sure about what to write, try recording a few decimal numbers you've seen and write about where you've seen them." The students in my class were used to writing assignments in math class. As they got out paper for this assignment, I wrote prompts on the board to direct the students' writing:

1. *Write everything you already know about decimals.*
2. *Where might you have seen these numbers used?*
   .369
   1.75
   .5
3. *Where else have you seen decimal numbers used?*

Typically when I give this direction to a class, at first many students aren't quite sure what to write. Although they've had experiences with decimals, they usually have a hard time describing them and explaining the meanings of the numbers. Even so, I like to give students a chance to reflect in writing first before initiating discussion. Writing helps students focus and I find that they bring more to a lesson when they've reflected individually first.

After the students had time to record some ideas, I said, "Share with your partner what you wrote. Discuss with your partner where you might have seen the decimal numbers I listed and what each of them might mean. Listen carefully to each other's ideas. When we come together as a class to share our different ideas, you should be ready to share your partner's ideas as well as your own."

I think that it's extremely valuable for students to share ideas in pairs or small groups. Talking about ideas supports students' learning, and when students talk among themselves, many more of them have the chance to voice their thinking. Also, some students are shy or lack mathematical confidence and don't volunteer ideas in class discussions. These students are typically more willing to talk with just one or a few classmates.

When I called the class back to attention, I said, "I'm interested in hearing everything you already know about decimals and perhaps where you've seen them used or displayed."

Justin went first. He said, "I see decimals all the time on receipts. Rory agreed with me that decimals are used with money."

"My mom's checkbook has decimals in it and that has to do with money, too," Chen added.

Crystal said, "Whenever we write dollars and cents we use decimals, like two dollars and fifty-eight cents or that number on the board—one point seventy-five. That could be a money amount, too. It could mean a dollar seventy-five."

Madison said, "I see them in sports all the time. In track, they use decimals to keep track of how fast they go or how high they jump."

Jenny, Madison's partner, added, "They use them in other sports, too, like in gymnastics."

Misha added, "It's in Olympic figure skating, too. The judges give scores and then they average them. The final score usually has a decimal in it."

I continued with the sports theme and asked, "Has anyone else seen decimals used in sports?"

Frank responded, "Batting averages use decimals all the time. It's like that number on the board—point three sixty-nine. That could be a batter's hitting average."

"Would that player be considered a good hitter?"

"Yeah, he's very good. The closer the number is to one, the better the hitter."

Kim asked, "Then why would he be considered good? That number isn't close to one at all."

"It's impossible to hit every ball in every game. They pitch too fast. A player is lucky if he gets a hit or two a game," Frank responded.

"So could a player have an average of five hundred?" I asked. I wrote on the board:

.500

Matthew answered, "That would be like getting a hit half the time. That's almost impossible in major league baseball, so a three hundred average is pretty good. It's like getting a hit one-third of the time."

Hunter added, "I've seen decimals in football and basketball, too."

"Have you seen decimals anywhere else besides in sports?" I asked. Students had various ideas.

Blaire said, "I've seen them at the grocery store when the checker scans the fruits and veggies. I'm not quite sure what the decimals mean but I've seen them there."

Kendra said, "I've seen them on the meat packages in the weight and money sections."

Jose said, "Our scale at home measures me with decimals."

I then asked, "Can you tell me what five-tenths means or when it might be used?"

Elaine answered, "It means one-half, like half of a dollar or half of a pizza."

Misha said, "You can write it like 'point five' or 'point fifty,' which means fifty cents or one-half, which is a fraction."

"Does anyone have another way to explain this?"

Luis said, "Point five is more than zero but not one whole. It's right in the middle."

I ended the discussion by collecting the students' papers (see Figures 1–4). I planned to have the class write again in several weeks. Then I'd return these papers so that students could compare what they wrote both times and see what they learned.

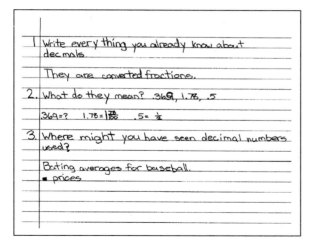

1. Write every thing you already know about decimals.

They are converted fractions.

2. What do they mean? .369, 1.78, .5

.369=? 1.78=1$\frac{78}{100}$ .5=$\frac{1}{2}$

3. Where might you have seen decimal numbers used?

Batting averages for baseball.
• prices

▲▲▲▲▲▲Figure 1   *Frank's paper showed that he had some understanding of decimals as converted fractions.*

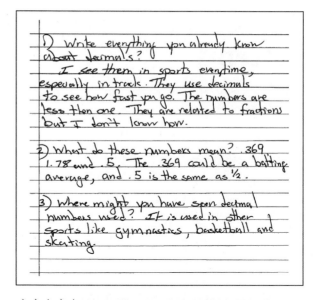

1) Write everything you already know about decimals?
   I see them in sports everytime, especially in track. They use decimals to see how fast you go. The numbers are less than one. They are related to fractions but I don't know how.

2) What do these numbers mean? .369 1.78 and .5. The .369 could be a batting average, and .5 is the same as ½.

3) Where might you have seen decimal numbers used? It is used in other sports like gymnastics, basketball and skating.

▲▲▲▲▲▲Figure 2   *Madison related decimals to sports, but wasn't sure about how they relate to fractions.*

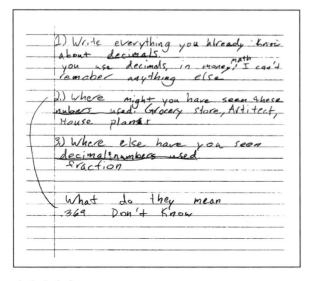

1.) Write everything you already know about decimals.
   you use decimals, in money, math I can't remember anything else.

2.) Where might you have seen these numbers used? Grocery store, Artitect, House plans.

3.) Where else have you seen decimal numbers used? fraction

What do they mean
.369   Don't Know

▲▲▲▲▲▲Figure 3   *Rory's paper revealed his limited understanding about decimals.*

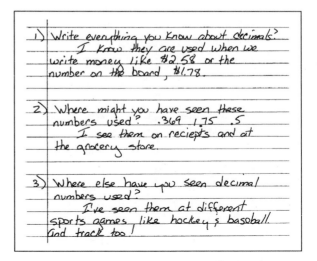

1.) Write everything you know about decimals?
   I know they are used when we write money like $2.58 or the number on the board, $1.78.

2.) Where might you have seen these numbers used? .369 1.75 .5
   I see them on reciepts and at the grocery store.

3.) Where else have you seen decimal numbers used?
   I've seen them at different sports games like hockey & baseball and track too!

▲▲▲▲▲▲Figure 4   *Crystal saw how decimals are used to represent amounts of money.*

Goals for Instruction About Decimals and Percents

Our goal in introducing decimals and percents in grades 5 and 6 is to give all students the chance to

▲ extend their understanding of our place value system to include decimals;

▲ learn how decimals relate to fractions;

▲ represent, read, and interpret decimal numerals;

▲ compare decimal numerals; and

▲ learn what percents are and how they relate to fractions and decimals.

By the end of middle school, students are expected to use decimals and percents in both science and mathematics applications. Because of this charge, teachers in the upper elementary grades often focus instruction on building students' skills by emphasizing teaching procedures for computing. Often, not enough time is given to creating a foundation of understanding of decimals and percents on which skills can build. Learning procedures without a firm foundation of understanding runs the risk of preparing students to deal mechanically with decimals and percents and can limit their ability to use them in problem-solving situations.

The emphasis of instruction in these lessons is to build on students' prior knowledge and extend their understanding. The lessons in this book assume that students have studied fractions and are comfortable representing, interpreting, and comparing fractions. The instructional ideas presented build on this understanding and present decimal numerals as different representations for certain fractions, those whose denominators are a power of ten—ten, one hundred, one thousand, and so on. In this light, students aren't expected to learn new concepts about numbers in their initial study of decimals but to learn a new standard symbolism for representing numbers they already understand.

Of course, there is a good deal of complexity in understanding the new notation. Students need to extend their understanding of our place value system to understand the logical structure of decimal notation. Also, they need to learn how to relate decimals to fractions with denominators other than a power of ten. And they need to connect their understanding to include percents as well.

The lessons use a variety of approaches. They draw on base ten blocks to provide concrete representations of decimals, real-world contexts to ground students' learning in practical applications, problem-solving explorations to support students in learning to reason with decimals and percents, and games to extend learning and provide practice. Also, calculators are used in several of the lessons to support students' learning and help them investigate patterns, improve their ability to estimate, and verify computations.

PEDAGOGICAL RATIONALE

Learning doesn't occur in a vacuum, and the process of learning calls for connecting new ideas to existing ones. New learning may expand previous understanding or cause students to revise or rethink ideas, but the anchor of existing knowledge is essential to the process of making sense of new concepts. It's for this reason that we connect instruction about decimals and percents to what students already understand about fractions.

It's also important to consider when teaching decimals and percents two aspects of the learning required by students. One involves the social conventions of representing decimal numerals and percents. Decimal numerals, for example .4 or .23, are alternate ways for representing the fractions $\frac{4}{10}$ and $\frac{23}{100}$. Also, four-tenths of something can be represented as 40%. The decimal point and the percent sign are agreed-upon social conventions, just as the fraction bar for writing four-tenths as $\frac{4}{10}$ is another social convention. There is no meaning in the symbols themselves other than the meanings that we give to them. (In Great Britain, for example, the decimal numerals above are written as ·4 and ·23, with the decimal points raised.)

It's appropriate to teach these standard representations by showing them to students and telling them that they are other ways to represent fractions. "Showing" and "telling" are appropriate because the source of knowledge about social conventions is outside the students, not something they could discover for themselves other than being introduced to the idea from a source outside them—another person, a book, or some other resource.

However, it's important to keep in mind that learning about decimals and percents calls for more than learning the social conventions for representing them. While there isn't a logic in the particular symbols we use, there is an important logical structure to the meaning of the numbers. To understand why, for example, .2 and .20 are equivalent, students have to apply and extend their understanding of our place value system and make sense of the meaning of these numerals. To support learning about the logic of numbers, "showing" and "telling" are not appropriate instructional choices. We can "show" students how to line up decimal points in a column of numbers and "tell" them how to add the columns, but this doesn't necessarily ensure that students understand the reason for the procedure. Rather, we have to provide students ways to interact with ideas so that they can make sense of them. This is the essence of teaching for understanding.

Of course, social knowledge and logical knowledge do not exist in isolation from each other. We rely on our conventions for representing decimals and percents to communicate about them and operate with them. The lessons in this book offer a balance of presenting information to students and giving them experiences through which they can build understanding.

ABOUT REPRESENTING AND READING DECIMALS

When we see decimal numerals such as .4 and 2.37, it's common for us to read them as "point four" and "two point thirty-seven." While this usage is acceptable, we're careful throughout the lessons in this book to read decimals such as these as "four-tenths" and "two and thirty-seven hundredths." Reading decimals in this way takes a bit of discipline if you're not used to it, but we think it's worth the effort. It helps connect the decimal numerals to their meanings and clarifies how they relate to our number system.

Also, for decimal numerals less than one, we alternate between placing a zero before the decimal point and omitting it. For example, it's appropriate to represent four-tenths as .4 and as 0.4. Because students will see both representations, we feel it's valuable to use them interchangeably.

The Structure of the Lessons

In order to help you with planning and teaching the lessons in this book, each lesson is organized into the following sections:

Overview   To help you decide if the lesson is appropriate for your students, this is a nutshell description of the mathematical goal of the lesson and what the students will be doing.

Materials   This section lists the special materials needed along with quantities. Not included in the list are regular classroom supplies such as pencils and paper. Worksheets that need to be duplicated are included in the Blackline Masters section at the back of the book.

Time   Generally, the number of class periods is provided, sometimes with a range allowing for different-length periods. It is also indicated for some activities that they are meant to be repeated from time to time.

Teaching Directions   The directions are presented in a step-by-step lesson plan.

Teaching Notes   This section addresses the mathematics underlying the lesson and at times provides information about the prior experiences or knowledge students need.

The Lesson   This is a vignette that describes what actually occurred when the lesson was taught to one or more classes. While the vignette mirrors the plan described in the teaching directions, it elaborates with details that are valuable for preparing and teaching the lesson. Samples of student work are included.

Extensions   This section is included for some of the lessons and offers follow-up suggestions.

Questions and Discussion   Presented in a question-and-answer format, this section addresses issues that came up during the lesson and/or have been posed by other teachers.

While organized similarly, the lessons here vary in several ways. Some span one class period, others take longer, and some are suitable to repeat over and over, giving students a chance to revisit ideas and extend their learning. Some use manipulative materials, others ask students to draw diagrams, and others ask students to rely on reasoning mentally. And while some lessons seem to be more suited for beginning experiences, at times it's beneficial for more experienced students to engage with them as well. An activity that seems simple can reinforce students' understanding or give them a fresh way to look at a familiar concept. Also, a lesson that initially seems too difficult or advanced can be ideal for introducing students to thinking in a new way.

How to Use This Book

Teaching the lessons as described in the nineteen chapters requires a minimum of twenty-six days of instruction, not including time for repeat experiences as recommended for some lessons or for the seven individual assignments suggested. While it's possible to spend a continuous stretch of weeks on these lessons, we don't think that is the best decision. In our experience, time is required for students to absorb concepts, and it can be more supportive to spend a three-week period and then wait two months or so before returning for another three-week period, or arrange for three chunks of time, each two weeks or so, spaced throughout the year. When students return to ideas after a break, they bring not only the learning they've done in other areas but also a fresh look that some distance can provide.

The four introductory lessons about decimals and the two introductory lessons about percents build the foundation for developing understanding, and we suggest that you not skip these lessons. The other lessons are categorized to identify different aspects of learning about decimals and percents. Experiences in each of the categories are beneficial for students, but there is no particular sequence of categories that is best. However, the chapters within each category suggest a possible order. The section of additional activities offers further instructional ideas. And the section on assessments helps you think about making assessment an integral part of instruction.

You may choose to use these lessons as your primary source for helping children learn about decimals and percents, or use them along with other instructional materials or learning activities. It's important, however, to be consistent in your teaching so that all lessons encourage students to make sense of ideas, communicate about their reasoning both orally and in writing, and apply their learning to problem-solving situations.

CHAPTER ONE
REPRESENTING DECIMALS WITH BASE TEN BLOCKS

Overview

In this lesson, the students use base ten blocks to represent tenths, hundredths, and thousandths. Assigning the value of one whole to the flat, the students practice representing concretely various numbers. The focus in this lesson is on having students build numbers with the blocks and represent them using common fractions with which they are familiar.

Materials

▲ base ten blocks, at least 50 units, 25 rods, and 3 flats per pair of students
▲ place value mat, 1 per student (see Blackline Masters)
▲ optional: overhead base ten blocks
▲ optional: overhead transparency of place value mat

Time

▲ one class period

Teaching Directions

1. Distribute base ten blocks and place value mats. Review with the students what they already know about the base ten blocks. (If students aren't familiar with the blocks, allow them time to explore the blocks and look for relationships among them.)

2. Display on the overhead projector one of each of the three types of block—a unit, a rod, and a flat. (If you prefer, display one of each actual block, or ask students to place one of each block in the middle of their table.) Ask the following question: If the flat is worth one whole, what are the values of the rod and the unit?" Ask students to discuss at their tables and then verify with the class that the rod is one-tenth of the flat and the unit is one-hundredth of the flat.

3. Show the students the large cube. Ask the following question: "If the large cube is worth one whole, what are the values of the flat, the rod, and the unit?" After students identify their values, write on the board:

tenths

hundredths

thousandths

4. Again assign the flat the value of one whole and ask the students to state the values of the rod and the unit. As they do so, write on the board:

flat	*one whole*	1
rod	*one-tenth*	$\frac{1}{10}$
unit	*one-hundredth*	$\frac{1}{100}$

5. Direct the students: "With the flat representing one whole, use base ten blocks to show one-tenth on your place value mats." Check that students have placed a rod in the correct column on their place value mats.

6. Direct the students: "Show two-tenths on your mat." Ask a student to come up and show two-tenths on the overhead projector. Also ask the student to record $^2\!/_{10}$ on the board, or to tell you how to write two-tenths as a fraction.

7. Repeat for two-hundredths.

8. Repeat for thirteen-hundredths. Students will typically do this in one of two ways: with thirteen units or with one rod and three units. If students share only one way, show the other alternative. Write on the board two different ways to represent thirteen-hundredths with fractions and point out how each describes a different way of showing thirteen-hundredths with the blocks:

$\frac{13}{100}$

$\frac{1}{10} + \frac{3}{100}$

9. Repeat for twenty-hundredths and record several representations:

$\frac{20}{100}$

$\frac{2}{10}$

$\frac{1}{10} + \frac{10}{100}$

10. Ask the students: "Which is greater, one-tenth or one-hundredth?" Discuss their solutions and then record on the board:

$\frac{1}{10} > \frac{1}{100}$

$\frac{1}{100} < \frac{1}{10}$

11. Give the students other numbers to build, represent, and compare—three-tenths, three-hundredths, six-tenths, six-hundredths, eight-tenths, and eight-hundredths. Have students show each number with the blocks and then write inequalities to describe how they compare.

12. Next, ask the students to represent twenty-five–hundredths using the fewest number of blocks. Discuss the correct solution of using two rods and five units. Record on the board:

$$\frac{25}{100}$$

$$\frac{2}{10} + \frac{5}{100}$$

13. Conclude the lesson by asking the students to represent thirty-two–hundredths and forty-five–hundredths using the fewest number of blocks. As you did for twenty-five–hundredths, record fractional representations on the board. If there is time, continue with other numbers.

14. For homework, instruct the students to write a letter to a student who was absent that day or to a student in another class. Explain: "Write a letter explaining which is greater, one-tenth or one-hundredth, and why. Make sure you give details such as real-world examples or drawings."

Teaching Notes

Because this lesson uses base ten blocks to build students' understanding of decimals, it's necessary for students to have had experience with the blocks beforehand. If students have not had prior experience with the blocks, give them time to explore and look for relationships between them. It's important for students to know that a rod is equal to ten units, a flat is equal to ten rods or one hundred units, and a large cube is equal to ten flats, one hundred rods, or one thousand units. Also, it's convenient for communication for the students to use the same name for the different-size blocks. In this book, we consistently use *unit*, *rod*, *flat*, and *cube* to describe the pieces from smallest to largest.

In this lesson, no mention is made of the standard decimal symbolization. Rather, the focus is on concretely representing various tenths and hundredths and using the correct terminology to describe them. The standard symbolization is introduced on another day.

The Lesson

▲▲

Before class, I placed a bucket of base ten blocks at each table and a place value mat for each student. To begin the lesson, I held up a flat from the base ten block collection and asked the students what they knew about it. The students had had many expe- riences with base ten blocks and were accustomed to thinking that the flat was worth 100. They were also accustomed to the rod being worth 10 and the unit cube being worth 1.

I displayed one of each of the three

types of block on the overhead projector and said to the class, "We'll now be using the blocks differently and giving them different values. Let's suppose that a flat is now worth one instead of one hundred. Then what would be the value of a rod and a unit? Discuss this with your group members and make sure everyone in your group agrees."

After several minutes of discussing and manipulating the blocks, the students were eager to share their ideas. "So what did you notice?" I asked.

Chen said, "Well, it takes ten rods to make one flat and the flat is one whole, so the rod is one-tenth of the flat."

Jose said, "The rods are like dimes, since it takes ten dimes to make one dollar and it takes ten rods to make one flat."

"I knew they're tenths because that's what my brother uses in his high school homework," said Patrice.

I confirmed the students' ideas. "Yes, they're tenths. As Chen stated, if a flat is worth one whole, since ten rods equal one flat, a rod is worth one-tenth. What about the unit?"

"Well, it takes one hundred of them to make up a flat, so they're hundredths," replied Jason.

All of the students seemed to accept these values. I then showed the class a large cube from the set of base ten blocks. I said, "Suppose this large cube is worth one whole. Then what would be the values of a flat, a rod, and a unit cube?" Changing the values of blocks helps students focus on the relationship between and among the blocks. The students quickly began discussing in their groups. All of them figured out that since it takes ten flats to make one cube, the flats should be called tenths.

Jose reported, "Since it takes ten rods to make one flat, it would take one hundred rods to make the cube. So the rods are hundredths."

Even though no groups actually built the cube with unit blocks, they figured that since it takes one hundred units to make a flat, they needed to multiply 100 by 10 to get the answer of 1,000. To emphasize the correct names, and to point out the difference in these terms from *tens*, *hundreds*, and *thousands*, I wrote on the board:

tenths

hundredths

thousandths

I then asked, "Suppose the rod were equal to one whole. If this were true, what would be the values of the other blocks?" The students saw the pattern and swiftly concluded that the unit would be worth one-tenth, the flat would be ten wholes, and the cube would be one hundred.

Next I said, "Let's use the flat to represent one whole. Then what are the values of the rod and the unit cube?" I asked this to review what we had just discussed.

"Since it takes ten rods to make one flat, the rods are one-tenth of the flat, or tenths," Madison said.

"And the units are hundredths, or one-hundredth of the flat, because it takes one hundred of them to equal one whole," Jon added.

I wrote the values of the blocks on the board, both as words and as fractions:

flat	one whole	1
rod	one-tenth	$\frac{1}{10}$
unit	one-hundredth	$\frac{1}{100}$

I then gave the class practice using the base ten blocks to represent different numbers. I began, "Keep in mind that the flat is worth one whole and show one-tenth on your mat." Most students easily placed one rod on their mat in the correct column. I find that having students use place value mats makes it easy for me to look around the room and see who responds correctly

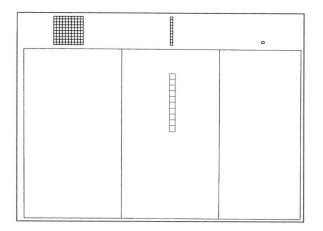

and who needs assistance. This makes assessment an ongoing and integral part of the lesson.

While students typically have the understanding that one-tenth represents one piece out of ten parts, and are familiar with the common fraction $\frac{1}{10}$, they haven't yet learned how to represent that fraction with a decimal numeral. However, in this introductory lesson, I prefer to keep the focus on building tenths and hundredths with the blocks and using the correct terminology to describe them. I introduce the standard symbolism for decimal numerals in another lesson. (See Chapter 2.)

"Now show two-tenths on your mat," I said. I gave the students a moment to do this.

"Who would like to come up to the overhead projector and place on the overhead mat what you placed on your own mat?" My students generally love to use the overhead for sharing solutions. Francesca came up and placed two rods on the overhead mat in the tenths column.

"Can you tell me how to write the fraction for two-tenths?" I asked.

"You write a two over a ten," Francesca responded. I wrote on the board:

$$\frac{2}{10}$$

I then gave the class another decimal to build. "Show two-hundredths on your mat."

Again, the students quickly did this, and Ken came up and put two units on the overhead place value mat.

"Before you sit down, can you write the fraction for what you built?" I asked Ken. He nodded and recorded on the board:

$$\frac{2}{100}$$

I then gave another instruction: "This time show thirteen-hundredths on your mat." As typically happens, some students used thirteen units and others used one rod and three units. I asked Tamara, who used all units, to come up and place the blocks on the overhead place value mat.

"Can you tell me how to write the fraction to show what you built?" I asked her. I recorded on the board what she reported:

$$\frac{13}{100}$$

"Raise a hand if you built thirteen-hundredths differently," I said. I had noticed that several students had done so, but if no one had, I would have presented what Rory was about to report.

"It was quicker to use one rod and three units," Rory said.

"Come up and show us on the overhead," I responded. Rory came up and replaced Tamara's blocks with one rod and three units.

"Does the fraction for Tamara's blocks also describe what Rory built?" I asked the class.

Misha responded, "He used different blocks but they're worth the same."

Madison said, "But Rory didn't really use all hundredths. He used some tenths, too, so I don't think it works."

"What would you write?" I asked Madison.

She shrugged. "I'm not sure," she said.

"Oh, I know," Jose said. "Rory built one-tenth and three-hundredths. You could write both of those. Can I come up?" I nodded. Jose came up and wrote on the board:

$$\frac{1}{10} \qquad \frac{3}{100}$$

He turned to look at me to see if what he wrote was correct. I looked at his classmates for their opinions. Several students said that what Jose wrote made sense.

"I agree," I confirmed. "I think that one-tenth and three-hundredths combined is the same as thirteen-hundredths. To complete what Jose wrote, we can write a plus sign to show that together they make thirteen-hundredths." I did this on the board:

$$\frac{1}{10} + \frac{3}{100}$$

I explained, "Both this and what Tamara wrote mean the same. They're just different ways to represent thirteen-hundredths, just as we can take a number like ten and break it apart to say that it's also five plus five, or six plus four."

"Let's try twenty-hundredths," I then said. After a moment, I asked Lena to place blocks on the overhead projector and her partner, Sheri, to record the fraction on the board. Lena counted out twenty units on the overhead place value mat and Sheri wrote $\frac{20}{100}$ on the board. Mark and Jeff began whispering at their table. When the girls finished, Mark commented that they had done it differently.

Jeff quickly came to the overhead and explained, "We started to count out twenty units, but the girls next to us were hogging them so we decided to use two tenths instead. Another way to look at this is one rod is ten-hundredths, so two rods would be twenty-hundredths."

"What fraction would you record?" I asked. Jeff wrote $\frac{2}{10}$ on the board. The class seemed satisfied that the two fractions were the same.

Misha, always looking for another solution, said, "You could have used just one rod and then ten units and it would be the same. Then you could write one-tenth and ten-

hundredths." I recorded this on the board under what Sheri and Jeff had written:

$$\frac{20}{100}$$
$$\frac{2}{10}$$
$$\frac{1}{10} + \frac{10}{100}$$

While these fractional representations may appear complicated, they make sense to students when they connect them to the base ten blocks. The concrete materials help bring meaning to numerical representations.

I then said, "Now clear your mat and show one-hundredth on it. Which is greater, one-tenth or one-hundredth?"

"One-tenth is bigger because it covers up more space on the flat," answered Marcus.

"One-tenth, because it takes ten hundredths to make one rod and you only have one of them, so one-hundredth is way less than one-tenth," Sheri said. I recorded on the board:

$$\frac{1}{10} > \frac{1}{100}$$
$$\frac{1}{100} < \frac{1}{10}$$

I continued asking the students to represent other numbers: three-tenths, three-hundredths, six-tenths, six-hundredths, eight-tenths, and eight-hundredths. The students showed each number with blocks on their mats and then volunteers came up to place blocks on the overhead projector and record the fractions.

I then instructed, "Using the fewest number of blocks possible, represent twenty-five–hundredths." I asked for the fewest number of blocks because building numbers in this way connects most easily to their decimal representations. (I planned to introduce how to write decimal numerals the next day.)

Kim placed on the overhead mat two rods in the tenths column and five units in the hundredths column. She picked up one rod at a time and counted aloud, "Ten hundredths, twenty hundredths." Then she picked up each unit at time and continued to count, "Twenty-one, twenty-two, twenty-three, twenty-four, twenty-five hundredths." Becky came up and recorded two ways:

$$\frac{25}{100}$$
$$\frac{2}{10} + \frac{5}{100} = \frac{25}{100}$$

I next asked the students to use the fewest number of blocks first to represent thirty-two–hundredths and then forty-five–hundredths. For each, one student built the number using the overhead blocks and another recorded the fraction.

HOMEWORK

Michael had been absent and I used him as an anchor for the assignment. "Write a letter to Michael or to another friend explaining which is greater, one-tenth or one-hundredth, and why. Make sure you give details such as real-world examples or drawings." If no student had been absent that day, I would have asked them to write a letter to an imaginary student in another class. Figures 1–1 through 1–5 show some students' letters.

> Dear Mike,
>
> A tenth is larger then a hundreth, simply because 10 hundreths equals 1 tenth. Here is a visual.
>
> tenths   hundreths
>   □ - ten of these
>   equals one
>   of those.
>
> Sincerly,

▲▲▲▲▲▲**Figure 1–1** *Misha explained which is larger and included a drawing of a rod and a unit to illustrate her idea.*

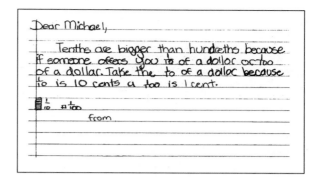

> Dear Michael,
>
> Tenths are bigger than hundreths because if someone offers you $\frac{1}{10}$ of a dollar or $\frac{1}{100}$ of a dollar. Take the $\frac{1}{10}$ of a dollar because $\frac{1}{10}$ is 10 cents a $\frac{1}{100}$ is 1 cent.
>
> $\frac{1}{10}$ $\frac{1}{100}$
>
> from

▲▲▲▲▲▲**Figure 1–2** *Sheri used the context of money and offered clear advice.*

> Dear Michael—
>
> 10ths are bigger than hundredths because if you think of money, and if I had 100 dollars, and I asked you, would you like $\frac{1}{10}$ of it or $\frac{1}{100}$. You would probably want to say $\frac{1}{10}$ because if you do division, and say $100 \div 10$, you would get 10 that is $\frac{1}{10}$ of 100. If you did $100 \div 100$ then you would get 1 and that is $\frac{1}{100}$ of 100. If you turn that into money, it is
>
> 10$ 10$
> 10$ 10$
> 10$ 10$ = 100$ ÷ 10 = 10$
> 10$
> 10$ = 100$ ÷ 100 = 1$
> 10$ You would want 10$
> 10$

▲▲▲▲▲▲**Figure 1–3** *Kim posed a problem to help her explain: Would you rather have $\frac{1}{10}$ or $\frac{1}{100}$ of \$100?*

Dear Kristi,

Did you know which one is bigger a tenth or a hundredth? If you didn't know a tenth is bigger. (One tenth is bigger because to is > too. If you don't get that one. it's like this, pretend you have two pizza. You cut out one hundred slices and then on the other one cut ten slices compare those two of course the ten slice one is bigger. one hundred one hundred is even smaller though. Now I think you should understand by now. So thats it and thats why a tenth is bigger than a hundredth.

your Friend,

▲▲▲▲▲▲**Figure 1–4** *Jeff used the context of slicing pizzas to explain tenths and hundredths to Cristi. His language is imprecise but his understanding seems clear.*

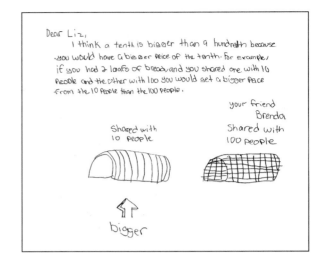

Dear Liz,
I think a tenth is bigger than a hundreth because you would have a bigger peice of the tenth. For example, if you had 2 loafs of bread, and you shared one with 10 people and the other with 100 you would get a bigger peice from the 10 people than the 100 people.

your friend
Brenda

Shared with 10 people   Shared with 100 people

⬆
bigger

▲▲▲▲▲▲**Figure 1–5** *In his letter to Liz, Jose used the example of a loaf of bread to clarify his idea.*

Questions and Discussion

▲▲

▲ *Why do you change the value of the blocks at the beginning of the lesson?*

Nothing inherent in the blocks determines specific values. Rather, it's the relationship among the blocks that models for students our place value system of numeration. For that reason, it's valuable to help students understand that they can assign any value they'd like to any block, but that once a block has a value assigned, the values of the others are determined.

▲ *Why did you decide to assign the value of 1 to the flat for most of the lesson?*

Doing so provides a way to address tenths and hundredths, an appropriate introduction for students' beginning experience with decimals and also for then helping them represent decimals symbolically. (See Chapter 2.)

CHAPTER TWO
INTRODUCING DECIMAL NOTATION

Overview

This lesson helps students extend their understanding of place value notation for whole numbers to include decimals. The students continue to use base ten blocks to show numbers with tenths and hundredths, and now connect the concrete representations to standard decimal notation.

Materials

▲ base ten blocks, at least 50 units, 25 rods, and 3 flats per pair of students
▲ place value mat, 1 per student (see Blackline Masters)
▲ *Donna's Decimals* worksheet, 1 per student (see Blackline Masters)
▲ optional: overhead base ten blocks
▲ optional: overhead transparency of place value mat

Time

▲ two class periods

Teaching Directions

1. Distribute base ten blocks and place value mats.

2. Write on the board:

flat	one whole	1	
rod	one- tenth	$\frac{1}{10}$	0.1
unit	one-hundredth	$\frac{1}{100}$	

Explain the decimal numeral: "This is another way to represent one-tenth, using what we call a decimal numeral. The zero is in the ones place, the one is in the tenths place, and the period is called the decimal point."

3. Instruct the students to use blocks to show one-tenth on their place value mats. Ask: "How many blocks are in the flat column?" Explain: "I wrote a zero before the decimal point to show that there are no ones or whole numbers." Ask: "How many tenths are in the tenths column?" Explain: "The one represents the tenth on your mat. The number just after the decimal point tells the number of tenths."

4. Instruct the students to show two-tenths with blocks on their mats and then ask: "How can we write two-tenths as a decimal numeral?" Record on the board and discuss.

5. Repeat for seven-tenths.

6. Next, ask the students to show one-hundredth and write on the board next to the fraction $\frac{1}{100}$ its decimal equivalent, *0.01*:

flat	one whole	1	
rod	one-tenth	$\frac{1}{10}$	*0.1*
unit	one-hundredth	$\frac{1}{100}$	*0.01*

Ask: "Who can explain why this decimal numeral represents one-hundredth?" Make sure students see that a zero is in the tenths column because there aren't any rods on their mats, and the 1 represents the unit.

7. Write on the board and review the values of the places:

| 2, | 3 | 4 | 6 |
| thousands | hundreds | tens | ones |

8. Add a decimal point and label three places after it:

| 2, | 3 | 4 | 6. | ___ | ___ | ___ |
| thousands | hundreds | tens | ones. | tenths | hundredths | thousandths |

Explain that the values of the places after the decimal point continue the pattern of whole number places, each becoming ten times smaller.

9. Refer to how in the first lesson, the students represented thirteen-hundredths: $\frac{13}{100}$ and $\frac{1}{10} + \frac{3}{100}$. Write *0.13* on the board and ask: "Who can explain why this decimal numeral is correct?" Discuss how 0.13 represents thirteen units as well as one rod and three units.

10. Write *0.10* on the board and ask: "What does this decimal numeral represent?" Instruct the students to talk with their partners, then ask for volunteers to explain.

11. Write *0.20* on the board and ask: "What does this decimal numeral represent?" Instruct the students to talk with their partners, then ask for volunteers to explain. Discuss with the class that twenty-hundredths and two-tenths are equivalent and, therefore, have the same numerical decimal representation.

12. On the board, write *0.10* next to 0.1.

one-tenth $\frac{1}{10}$ 0.1   0.10

Ask the students to think about why both of these decimal numerals represent one-tenth. Discuss.

13. For homework, list on the board for the students to copy:

six-hundredths

nine-tenths

fifteen-hundredths

thirty-five–hundredths

four-tenths

fifty-hundredths

Explain: "Find as many ways as you can to represent each of these numbers as fractions and as decimal numerals."

14. The next day, organize students into pairs. Explain: "You'll use one place value mat for the two of you and take turns being the banker and the mathematician. The banker takes the blocks from the bucket, and the mathematician places the blocks in the correct columns on the place value mat." Ask the students to decide who will play each role first.

15. Ask each banker to take blocks that represent the number seven-hundredths and each mathematician to place them on their mat. Ask a student to report the blocks and record on the board seven-hundredths in both fraction and decimal notation.

16. Instruct students to switch roles and represent seven-tenths on their mats. Most students will build seven tenths with seven rods. Ask if anyone modeled seven-tenths in a different way. If no one has a different solution, offer alternatives such as six rods and ten units or four rods and thirty units and ask the students to think about why each of these solutions also makes sense.

17. Ask for a volunteer to record on the board seven-tenths as a fraction and as a decimal numeral. Record on the board other possible notations, for example:

$\frac{4}{10} + \frac{30}{100} = \frac{7}{10}$

$\frac{6}{10} + \frac{10}{100} = \frac{7}{10}$

$0.4 + 0.30 = 0.7$

$.6 + .10 = .7$

Ask students to discuss with their partners why these representations are also correct and then have volunteers explain their reasoning to the class.

18. Instruct the students to switch roles and show thirty-two–hundredths on their mats. Have students share their different solutions and represent them symbolically.

19. Repeat Step 18 for thirty-four–hundredths, one and twenty-six–hundredths, and two and four-tenths.

20. Next, say: "Show forty-five–hundredths using the fewest number of blocks possible." Have students explain their solutions and write forty-five–hundredths in fraction and decimal notation.

21. Continue the lesson by listing on the board:

fifty-six–hundredths
four-tenths
one and twenty-four–hundredths
nine-hundredths
ninety-hundredths
one and nine-hundredths
one and ninety-hundredths

Ask the students to work in pairs. Explain: "Show each using the fewest number of blocks possible and write the number as a fraction and as a decimal. Also, sketch the blocks you use." As pairs finish, instruct them to compare their answers with another pair. Listen to their conversations and discuss with the class those numbers that caused disagreement or confusion.

22. For homework, distribute the *Donna's Decimals* assignment. Review with the class to be sure that students understand what to do.

Teaching Notes

While the symbolization for decimals calls for new learning from the students, the numerical concepts that the symbols represent aren't new for the students. Students are already familiar with fractions, and decimal notation is merely another way to represent fractions that have denominators of ten, one hundred, one thousand, and other powers of ten.

It's important for students to learn that the convention we use to represent decimal numerals is based in the logic of our place value system. Although they previously have studied about place value, their understanding may be shallow or fragile. For this reason, don't race through this lesson. Also, don't be surprised if students are confused. Keep in mind that the learning takes different amounts of time for different students and that confusion and partial understanding are natural aspects of the learning process. You most likely will have to revisit this lesson with your class.

During the lesson, it's beneficial to ask students for as many ways as possible to represent numbers. For example, twenty-hundredths can be represented as $\frac{20}{100}, \frac{2}{10}, \frac{1}{10} + \frac{10}{100}$, and, when using decimal notation, as 0.20, 0.2, .20, and .2. There are other ways as well. Asking students for multiple representations helps cement their understanding and builds their flexibility in thinking about and representing numbers.

The Lesson

▲▲▲

DAY 1

Learning the correct symbolism for decimal numerals best happens by connecting concrete representations and the students' knowledge of common fractions to decimal notation. To introduce the standard decimal notation, I wrote on the board what I had written previously. Then, next to the fraction $\frac{1}{10}$, I wrote its decimal equivalent, 0.1.

flat one whole	1	
rod one-tenth	$\frac{1}{10}$	0.1
unit one-hundredth	$\frac{1}{100}$	

I pointed to the decimal numeral and explained to the students, "What I've written is another way to represent one-tenth, as a decimal numeral. The zero is in the ones place, the one is in the tenths place, and the period is called the decimal point. Build one-tenth on your place value mat."

After all of the students had placed one rod on their mats, I asked, "How many blocks are in the flat column?"

"None," Elaine said.

"That's why I wrote a zero before the decimal point, to show that there are no ones, or whole numbers. How many tenths are in the tenths column?"

"Just one," Madison replied.

"That's what the one I wrote represents. The number just after the decimal point tells the number of tenths. Now show two-tenths on your mat." The students quickly put two rods on their mats.

"How do you think we could write this as a decimal numeral?" I asked. I waited to see how many students would raise a hand. More than half did, and I called on Maria.

"You write a zero, then a dot, and then a two," she directed. I wrote:

0.2

"That's right," I said. To reinforce the correct terminology, I added, "The dot is called the decimal point. Now show seven-tenths on your mat."

Again, the students did this easily. I asked, "Who would like to come up and write seven-tenths as a decimal?" Damon came up and wrote 0.7.

I then said, "Now clear your mat and show one-hundredth on it." The students immediately placed a unit cube on their place value mats. Others corrected the few at their tables who placed the unit in the rods column.

I continued, "Watch as I write one-hundredth as a decimal." On the board next to the fraction $\frac{1}{100}$, I wrote its decimal equivalent, 0.01.

flat	one whole	1	
rod	one-tenth	$\frac{1}{10}$	0.1
unit	one-hundredth	$\frac{1}{100}$	0.01

"Who can explain why this decimal numeral represents one-hundredth?" I asked. I waited to give the students time to think and then called on Jenny.

She said, "If you put the one after the decimal point, it would look like the rod. So you moved it over and put in a zero."

"You're right, Jenny," I said. "The two numbers have to look different or we wouldn't know which was which." I then gave an explanation for the standard convention of writing decimals. I said, "When you studied whole numbers, you learned that the value of each digit in a number depends on its place in the number." I wrote 2,346 on the board and labeled the places for each digit:

2,	3	4	6
thousands	hundreds	tens	ones

"Starting with the ones place, each place to the left is ten times larger. That's because our system of numbers is based on tens. To show numbers that are less than one using our place value system, we continue the pattern of the places." I added to what I had recorded (see below).

I continued, "For tenths, we write a number in the place after the decimal point. To show hundredths, we write a zero first after the decimal point in the tenths place and then the number of hundredths after it in the hundredths place. For thousandths, you write a number in the third place after the decimal point." I didn't expect students necessarily to understand or learn this immediately. Some would, I knew, but others would need many more experiences with decimals to internalize the rationale for this standard notation.

"Who remembers the two different ways you used the blocks yesterday to build thirteen-hundredths?" I asked.

Patrice reported, "Tamara did it with thirteen units and Rory did it with one rod and three units."

"Here's how we write thirteen-hundredths as a decimal," I said. I wrote:

0.13

"Who can explain why this decimal numeral makes sense for thirteen-hundredths?" I asked.

"You've got a number in the second place after the decimal point, and that tells that there are hundredths," said Bryant.

"What about the number in the tenths place?" I asked. The class was silent.

"Oh, I know," Kendra said. "If you cover up the three, then the one is in the tenths place, and that's the rod, like what Rory did, and the three is the units."

"What place is the three in?" I asked.

"The hundredths place. That's for the three units," Kim answered.

I then wrote on the board:

0.10

I asked, "What do you think this decimal is? Talk with your partner about this and raise your hand when you're ready to answer." Not all of the students were sure, but about half were willing to offer an idea. I called on Marcus.

"We think it's one-tenth," he said. "You have a one in the tenths place and zeroes in the wholes and hundredths, so it has to be only one-tenth." Others murmured their agreement.

"What about this decimal?" I asked. I wrote on the board:

0.20

More students were sure this time. Lena explained that it had to be two-tenths. "That's the only place that has a number in it," she said.

"Isn't zero a number?" I asked.

"Oh yeah," she said, "but it means that nothing is there."

"This time, with your partner, build twenty-hundredths, and decide how to

2,	3	4	6.	—	—	—
thousands	hundreds	tens	ones.	tenths	hundredths	thousandths

write it as a decimal numeral," I said. I repeated, "Twenty-hundredths." After a few moments, students were either ready to report or feeling confused.

"Who wants to explain?" I asked. I called on Kendra.

She said, "We were stuck first, but now we think we have it. We built it with twenty units and first we wrote it . . . can I come up and show?" I agreed and Kendra came to the board and wrote:

0.020

"First we decided to put a zero for the flats and a zero for the rods and twenty for the units. But then Madison thought that there was only two in the hundredths. And then we thought what to do if we exchanged the units for two rods, like Jeff did yesterday. Then we'd have to write this." Kendra wrote:

0.20

"Then we were mixed up, but I think the second one is right because the first one only has two in the hundredths place, and that's not enough."

Misha raised a hand. She said, "We agree with Kendra and Madison. You have no flats, so you put a zero in the ones column. Two-tenths is the same as twenty-hundredths, so you write a two in tenths column. And there aren't any hundredths left over, so that's why you put a zero in the hundredths column."

"Which is right?" Francesca asked, still not sure.

"What do you think?" I asked.

"I think it has to be the second one," she said. Conversation broke out in the room. I called the class back to attention and asked what the students thought. Most agreed with Francesca that Kendra and Madison's second way was correct.

I confirmed their decision. I said, "For their first idea, Kendra and Madison wrote a two in the hundredths place. That's two-hundredths or twenty-thousandths, not twenty-hundredths." I wrote on the board:

$0.02 = \frac{2}{100}$ *or* $\frac{20}{1000}$

From past experience, I knew that not all of the students would be totally clear about this. I returned to what I had recorded before and added another decimal representation next to the one I had previously written for one-tenth (see below).

I pointed to 0.10 and said, "This also makes sense for representing one-tenth. Who can explain why?"

Chen replied, "It says you have one-tenth, but no wholes and no hundredths."

Tamara asked, "Isn't it ten-hundredths?"

Misha responded, "That's the same. Ten hundredths is ten units, and that's the same as one-tenth." I wrote on the board:

$\frac{10}{100} = \frac{1}{10}$

Misha added, "You can add another zero, too, can't you?" I wrote on the board:

0.100

"Like this?" I asked.

"Yes," Misha said. Then it shows that you don't have any thousandths, either." I nodded my agreement but didn't discuss it further. I thought that the students had plenty to absorb already.

Homework

For homework, I listed on the board for the students to copy:

six-hundredths
nine-tenths
fifteen-hundredths
thirty-five–hundredths
four-tenths
fifty-hundredths

flat	one whole	1		
rod	one -tenth	$\frac{1}{10}$	0.1	0.10
unit	one-hundredth	$\frac{1}{100}$	0.01	

I explained, "Find as many ways as you can to represent each of these numbers as fractions and as decimal numerals." Figures 2–1 and 2–2 show two students' responses to this assignment.

DAY 2

I organized the students into pairs and gave each pair a place value mat. Also, I distributed base ten blocks so that all students had access to them. I said, "For this activity, you'll take turns being the banker and the mathematician. The banker takes from the bucket the necessary blocks, and the mathematician places the blocks correctly on the place value mat. You'll switch roles as you play." I gave the students a moment to decide who would play which role first.

I then said, "To begin, each banker should take out from the bucket the blocks that represent the number seven-hundredths. Then the mathematician should place them on your place value mat. Raise your hands when you're finished." It took only a moment for the students to do this. I called on Alex to report what he had built.

He said, "We have seven unit blocks, which represent hundredths. We need seven out of a hundred."

"Does anyone have another solution?" I asked. No one did.

"Who can come up and record seven-hundredths?" I asked. I called on Francesca.

"Should I write it like a fraction or a decimal?" she asked when she came to the board.

"How about both?" I replied. Francesca nodded and recorded:

$\frac{7}{100}$ .07

"Doesn't she need to write a zero first before the decimal point?" Madison asked.

"Do I?" Francesca asked.

"It's OK either way; both are worth the same," I responded. Francesca then added a third way to record to what she had written:

$\frac{7}{100}$ .07 0.07

Francesca returned to her seat and I gave the class another direction: "Now change roles so bankers become mathematicians and mathematicians become bankers. Show seven-tenths on your mat." After hands were raised, I called on Lena.

She said, "We used seven rods because each rod represents one-tenth and we need seven of them."

six hundredths $\frac{6}{100}$, .06, 0.06
nine tenths $\frac{9}{10}$, .9, 0.9
fifteen hundredths $\frac{15}{100}$, .15, 0.15
thirty-five hundredths $\frac{35}{100}$, .35, 0.35
four tenths .4, $\frac{4}{10}$, 0.4
fifty hundredths $\frac{50}{100}$, .5, 0.5, .50, $\frac{1}{2}$

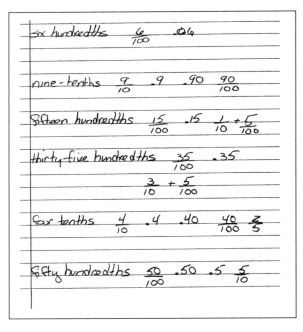

Figure 2–1 ***Tamara's representations are correct, but she didn't use hundredths to show either nine-tenths or four-tenths.***

six hundredths $\frac{6}{100}$ .06
nine-tenths $\frac{9}{10}$ .9 .90 $\frac{90}{100}$
fifteen hundredths $\frac{15}{100}$ .15 $\frac{1}{10} + \frac{5}{100}$
thirty-five hundredths $\frac{35}{100}$ .35
$\frac{3}{10} + \frac{5}{100}$
four tenths $\frac{4}{10}$ .4 .40 $\frac{40}{100}$ $\frac{2}{5}$
fifty hundredths $\frac{50}{100}$ .50 .5 $\frac{5}{10}$

Figure 2–2 ***Rory demonstrated his understanding of tenths and hundredths.***

"Did anyone show seven-tenths another way?" I asked.

Misha raised a hand. "I wanted to use seventy units but I didn't have enough, so I used six rods for six-tenths and ten units for ten-hundredths, and that's one more tenth."

"Any other solutions?" I asked.

"I used four rods and thirty units," Ken replied.

"Can you describe four rods and thirty units using tenths and hundredths?" I asked.

"It would be four-tenths and thirty-hundredths."

As I looked around the room, some students looked a bit confused, so I asked Ken to explain what he had done using the overhead base ten blocks. After Ken placed the four rods and thirty units on the overhead place value mat, he proceeded to pick up one rod at a time and count aloud, "Ten hundredths, twenty hundredths, thirty hundredths, forty hundredths, and with these thirty hundredths over here, I have a total of seventy-hundredths."

Some students still seemed confused. "I see how you have seventy-hundredths, but I asked for seven-tenths," I commented.

"They're the same," Ken said. "Look, ten-hundredths is the same as one rod, so ten-hundredths is the same as one-tenth." I find that using the base ten blocks helps students make this connection.

I then asked, "What about what Misha did? Do six rods and ten units represent seven-tenths?"

Misha raised her hand to come up and demonstrate, but I said, "How about someone else coming up to explain, and then, Misha, you can see if you agree." I did this because I was sure that Misha understood what she had done, and I wanted to give another student a chance to contribute.

Jenny came up and placed six rods and ten units on the overhead place value mat. She explained, "See, you could exchange the ten units for another rod, and then you'd have seven-tenths." Misha nodded her approval.

When I had asked the students to show seven-tenths, I had hoped that students would represent it with different blocks, and I was pleased that it occurred. With the blocks, it seems natural to understand that, for example, $\frac{6}{10}$ plus $\frac{10}{100}$ is equal to $\frac{7}{10}$. If no one had volunteered a different solution, I would have offered examples as Misha and Ken had done and asked the students to think about why they made sense.

"Who would like to come to the board and write seven-tenths?" I asked. Jose came and recorded:

$\frac{7}{10}$ 0.7

This seemed obvious to the students. I then said, "Watch as I record what Ken and Misha built." I wrote on the board:

Ken: $\frac{4}{10} + \frac{30}{100} = \frac{7}{10}$ $0.4 + 0.30 = 0.7$

Misha: $\frac{6}{10} + \frac{10}{100} = \frac{7}{10}$ $6 + .10 = .7$

I asked the class, "What do you think? Talk with your partner about these representations and raise your hand when you're ready to explain." There was a buzz in the room as the students talked. Then several students offered ideas.

For example, Chen said, "They make sense. For Misha's, ten-hundredths is the same as one-tenth, so six-tenths and one-tenth make seven-tenths."

Madison said, "Or you could go the other way. Six-tenths could be sixty-hundredths, and seventy-hundredths is the same as seven-tenths."

Misha added, "If I had used seventy-hundredths, then I could have written it with a zero at the end." She came up and wrote:

0.70

"That would be fine, too," I responded.

After all students who wanted had shared their ideas, I said, "Now switch roles again. This time show thirty-two–hundredths on your mat." As I scanned the room, some students used thirty-two separate unit blocks. Several used three rods and two units, and a few had other variations. For example, Melissa used two rods and twelve units. I had students share their different solutions on the overhead projector and represent them symbolically.

I continued in this manner, asking the students to represent different decimals and then having students share their solutions and represent them numerically. The decimals I chose were thirty-four–hundredths, one and twenty-six–hundredths, and two and four-tenths.

When I felt sure that all of the students could represent numbers and understand their classmates' different solutions, I changed my questioning. "Please show forty-five–hundredths using the fewest number of blocks possible." By changing my wording, I forced the bankers to make necessary exchanges before handing the blocks to their partners.

"We used four rods and five units, or four-tenths and five-hundredths," said Jenny.

"Can anyone explain it a different way?"

Kenny held up four rods, one by one, and said, "This is ten hundredths, this is twenty hundredths, this makes thirty hundredths, and this is forty hundredths because each rod is worth ten-hundredths each." Then he picked up each individual unit and counted on, "Forty-one, forty-two, forty-three, forty-four, forty-five hundredths."

"How do we write that number?" I asked. Paul came up and recorded:

$$\frac{45}{100} \qquad .45 \qquad 0.45$$

I pointed out, "When you build a number with the fewest blocks possible, you can represent it more easily with one decimal numeral."

I then gave the students an assignment to complete in pairs. I listed on the board:

fifty-six–hundredths

four-tenths

one and twenty-four–hundredths

nine-hundredths

ninety-hundredths

one and nine-hundredths

one and ninety-hundredths

I said, "For each, show it using the fewest number of blocks possible and write the number as a fraction and as a decimal. Also, sketch the blocks you use." (See Figures 2–3 and 2–4.) As pairs finished, I directed them to compare their answers with other pairs. I listened to their conversations and later discussed with the class those numbers that caused disagreement or discussion.

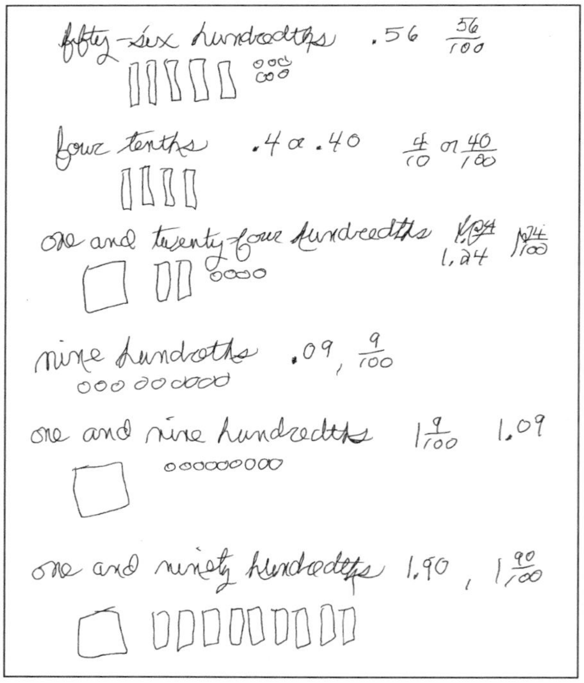

▲▲▲▲▲Figure 2–3 *Ken's paper showed his ability to represent decimal numerals pictorially and symbolically.*

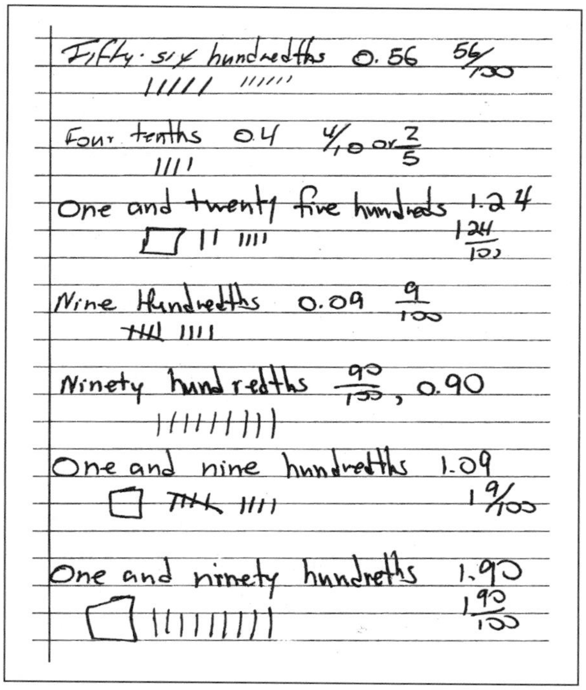

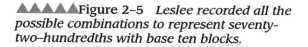

Fifty-six hundredths   0.56 $\frac{56}{100}$

Four tenths   0.4 $\frac{4}{10}$ or $\frac{2}{5}$

One and twenty five hundreds   1.24 $\frac{124}{100}$

Nine Hundredths   0.09 $\frac{9}{100}$

Ninety hundredths $\frac{90}{100}$, 0.90

One and nine hundredths   1.09 $1\frac{9}{100}$

One and ninety hundredths   1.90 $1\frac{90}{100}$

▲▲▲▲▲▲**Figure 2–4** *Michael correctly represented the decimal numbers with pictures, fractions, and decimal numerals.*

Homework

To introduce the homework assignment, I wrote on the board:

$$.6 + .12 = .72$$
$$\frac{6}{10} + \frac{12}{100} = \frac{72}{100}$$

I explained that in order to show seventy-two–hundredths, Donna had placed on her place value mat six rods and twelve units. Her classmate, Garrett, told her that she was wrong. Donna responded, "No, I'm right, and I could also build and write seventy-two–hundredths in other ways."

I said to the class, "Your homework assignment is to find as many other ways as you can to represent seventy-two–hundredths with the blocks. Draw each of your solutions and label them with fractions and decimals." I distributed a copy of the *Donna's Decimals* assignment to each student. Figures 2–5 and 2–6 show how two students worked on this assignment.

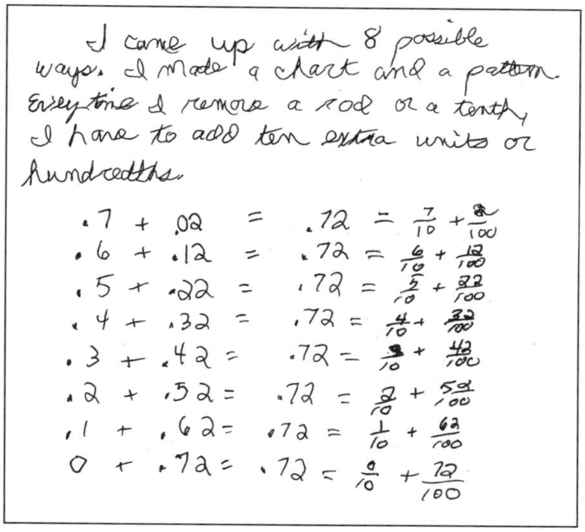

I came up with 8 possible ways. I made a chart and a pattern. Every time I remove a rod or a tenth, I have to add ten extra units or hundredths.

$$.7 + .02 = .72 = \frac{7}{10} + \frac{2}{100}$$
$$.6 + .12 = .72 = \frac{6}{10} + \frac{12}{100}$$
$$.5 + .22 = .72 = \frac{5}{10} + \frac{22}{100}$$
$$.4 + .32 = .72 = \frac{4}{10} + \frac{32}{100}$$
$$.3 + .42 = .72 = \frac{3}{10} + \frac{42}{100}$$
$$.2 + .52 = .72 = \frac{2}{10} + \frac{52}{100}$$
$$.1 + .62 = .72 = \frac{1}{10} + \frac{62}{100}$$
$$0 + .72 = .72 = \frac{0}{10} + \frac{72}{100}$$

▲▲▲▲▲▲**Figure 2–5** *Leslee recorded all the possible combinations to represent seventy-two–hundredths with base ten blocks.*

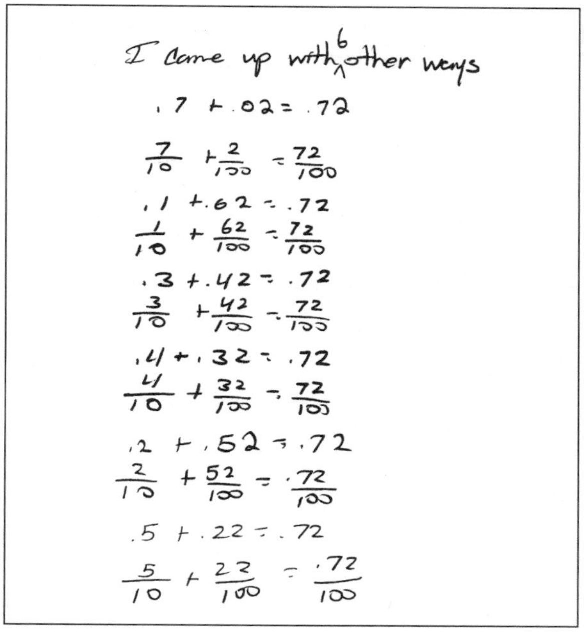

I came up with 6 other ways

$$.7 + .02 = .72$$
$$\frac{7}{10} + \frac{2}{100} = \frac{72}{100}$$
$$.1 + .62 = .72$$
$$\frac{1}{10} + \frac{62}{100} = \frac{72}{100}$$
$$.3 + .42 = .72$$
$$\frac{3}{10} + \frac{42}{100} = \frac{72}{100}$$
$$.4 + .32 = .72$$
$$\frac{4}{10} + \frac{32}{100} = \frac{72}{100}$$
$$.2 + .52 = .72$$
$$\frac{2}{10} + \frac{52}{100} = \frac{72}{100}$$
$$.5 + .22 = .72$$
$$\frac{5}{10} + \frac{22}{100} = \frac{72}{100}$$

▲▲▲▲▲▲**Figure 2–6** *Alex didn't list the representations in an orderly way that could help him see that his list isn't complete.*

Questions and Discussion

▲▲

▲ *Why do you sometimes write a zero before the decimal point and other times you don't?*

Exposing students to different ways to represent numbers symbolically is a good way to help build students' flexibility. A number like three-tenths can be represented correctly several ways: $\frac{3}{10}$, 0.3, and .3, to list a few. Because students will see these different representations from time to time, it's best to use them interchangeably. The concept they represent is the same; different mathematical conventions for representing them symbolically are appropriate.

▲ *What is the value of mixing the fractional and decimal representations when you introduce expanded notation?*

As for the previous question, one of my goals is to build students' flexibility with mathematical notations. When I write expanded notation for a number like twenty-seven–hundredths, it's beneficial to use both fractions and decimals. For example, $\frac{27}{100} = \frac{2}{10} + \frac{7}{100}$ and .27 = .2 + .07. While these abstractions may seem complicated, when students relate them to the base ten blocks, they have a concrete reference for making sense of them.

▲ *What if, after you teach these lessons, there are some students who still aren't understanding decimal notation? What do you do?*

All students learn in their own ways and on their own time schedules. The challenge of teaching is to provide learning experiences that help students make sense of new ideas and that are accessible to the slower learners while still of interest to those students who learn more quickly. The lessons that follow provide a variety of ways to help students get their minds around the concept of decimal representations, offering a variety that provides students with many ways to think and learn about decimals. At this point, be patient and see what the subsequent lessons accomplish. There will always be students who will benefit from extra help, ideally one on one. However, this is not the time to intervene. One exception: If a student doesn't have a basis of fractional understanding on which to build this instruction, then extra help would be essential.

CHAPTER THREE
DECIMAL RIDDLES

Overview

Decimal riddles provide an opportunity for students to think about and represent decimals. Students use base ten blocks to interpret clues and figure out the numbers they represent. After having experience solving riddles, students make up their own riddles for others to solve. The lesson reinforces for students the connection between concrete representations of decimals and reading and writing decimal numerals.

Materials

- ▲ base ten blocks, at least 50 units, 25 rods, and 3 flats per pair of students
- ▲ place value mats, 1 per student (see Blackline Masters)
- ▲ optional: *Decimal Riddles* worksheet (see Blackline Masters)
- ▲ optional: overhead transparency of place value mat
- ▲ optional: overhead base ten blocks

Time

- ▲ two class periods

Teaching Directions

1. Present a riddle to the class: *I have twenty-three-hundredths and four-tenths. What's the number?* Ask students to use base ten blocks to represent the clues. Then have a volunteer give the answer, explain his or her thinking, tell how to record the answer in decimal notation, and report how he or she showed the clues with base ten blocks.

2. Present a second riddle: *If you had two-tenths more, the number would be one whole. What's the number?* Again, ask a volunteer to give the answer, explain his or her thinking, and tell how to record the answer in decimal notation. Also, ask how he or she showed the clues with base ten blocks.

3. Give the students six other riddles to work on in pairs for the rest of the class. Either duplicate them (see Blackline Masters) or write them on the board:

    1. I have 2 ones, 12 tenths, and 6 hundredths. What's the number?

    2. I have 30 hundredths and 3 tenths. What's the number?

    3. The number is 45 hundredths. I have 25 hundredths. How much more do I need?

    4. I have 13 tenths, 2 ones, and 21 hundredths. What's the number?

    5. If you add 3 more tenths, the total would be worth 1 whole and 7 tenths. What's the number?

    6. I have 16 hundredths. I added some tenths and now I have more than 3 tenths and less than 4 tenths. What's the number?

4. At the end of class, instruct the students to copy the riddles they didn't have time to solve in class and solve them for homework. Also, for homework, instruct the students to make up and solve two riddles of their own.

5. The next day, begin class by discussing the first riddle from yesterday: *I have 2 ones, 12 tenths, and 6 hundredths. What's the number?* Ask the students to share their solutions, explaining their thinking, how they built the solutions on the place value mat, and how they recorded the answer in decimal notation. Record the answer and ask the class to read it aloud.

6. Repeat the same procedure for the rest of the riddles.

7. Next, ask the students to share the riddles they created for homework with partners and see if they agree with their partner's solutions. Circulate around the room listening to the different riddles being presented and pick several for a class discussion.

8. Ask students, one at a time, to present the riddles you chose. Have the students share their solutions, explain their thinking, and build the solutions on the place value mat. Then, as a class, decide how to record the answer in decimal notation and read it aloud.

9. Finally, assign several more student riddles for homework. Have each student author read aloud his or her riddle for the others to write down.

Teaching Notes

Children love riddles. Although the riddles presented in this lesson aren't the typical kinds of riddles that children hear, they still motivate children's interest and encourage them to think about decimals in nontraditional ways. The students' experience solving riddles helps them become flexible in their thinking about decimals.

You may find that some of your students don't need to use the base ten blocks in order to solve the riddles successfully. In this case, use your judgment about whether you'll require them to show the clues with blocks. However, don't be too hasty to abandon the materials; for other students they will be helpful and for some students they will be essential.

The Lesson

▲▲

DAY 1

To introduce the riddles, I said to the class, "I'm going to give you the clues you need to guess a number. Use the base ten blocks to build what I say, and then figure out what the number is. Raise your hand when you think you know."

I presented the first riddle: "I have twenty-three–hundredths and four-tenths. What's the number?" I repeated it twice more.

After a few moments most hands were raised. I called on Kim. She said, "I think your number is sixty-three–hundredths. Twenty-three–hundredths is the same as two-tenths and three-hundredths. You need to add the four extra tenths, which makes six-tenths and three-hundredths."

"How would you write that number as a decimal?" I asked.

Kim answered, "A decimal point and then sixty-three." On the board I recorded:

.63

"Do you agree?" I asked the class. Most nodded, but Misha raised a hand.

She said, "I think it's right, but I can explain it another way."

"What's your idea?" I asked.

"Well, you can take the twenty-three–hundredths and change it for two rods and three hundredths. Then you put the rods together and you have six rods, and that's six tenths. Plus you have the three hundredths. I used the fewest blocks."

I pointed first to the 6 in the decimal I had recorded and then to the 3. As I pointed, I said, "So you have six tenths and three hundredths."

I next presented another riddle for the class to try. I said, "Listen to the clue. If you had two-tenths more, the number would be one whole. What's the number?" As with the first riddle, students used blocks to figure out a solution. It didn't take them long.

Chen explained, "I think the number is eight-tenths. If you have eight rods and you add two more rods, you'll have ten, and that's the same as one whole."

I asked, "Can you explain using tenths and hundredths instead of rods?"

Chen said, "If we already have eight-tenths, I can count up by tenths until I get to one whole: nine tenths, ten tenths. I counted two extra tenths."

"How could we write that number as a decimal?" I asked.

Patrice answered, "A decimal point and then an eight." On the board I recorded .8.

"Do you agree?" I asked the class. Francesca raised a hand and said she figured it out a different way.

"What did you do?" I asked her.

"I started out with one whole, or flat. Then I exchanged the flat for ten rods and then took away the two tenths more I would get. I was left with eight tenths."

I then gave the students six other riddles to work on in pairs for the rest of the period.

"Even though you work with a partner, you should each do your own recording," I instructed them. In this way, the students would each have the experience of recording decimals. Also, their papers would give them a reference for the homework I planned to assign. I wrote the riddles on the board:

1. I have 2 ones, 12 tenths, and 6 hundredths. What's the number?

2. I have 30 hundredths and 3 tenths. What's the number?

3. The number is 45 hundredths. I have 25 hundredths. How much more do I need?

4. I have 13 tenths, 2 ones, and 21 hundredths. What's the number?

5. If you add 3 more tenths, the total would be worth 1 whole and 7 tenths. What's the number?

6. I have 16 hundredths. I added some tenths and now I have more than 3 tenths and less than 4 tenths. What's the number?

Homework

At the end of class, I explained the homework assignment. "Copy down the riddles you didn't have time to solve in class and solve them for homework. Also, make up and solve two riddles of your own." See Figures 3–1 through 3–4 for a few students' riddles.

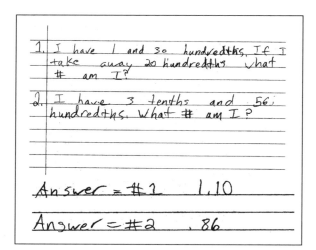

▲▲▲▲▲▲Figure 3–1 Jose's riddles are straightforward and his answers are correct.

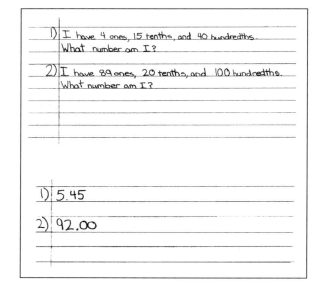

▲▲▲▲▲▲Figure 3–2 Kim solved her second riddle correctly but gave an incorrect answer for her first one.

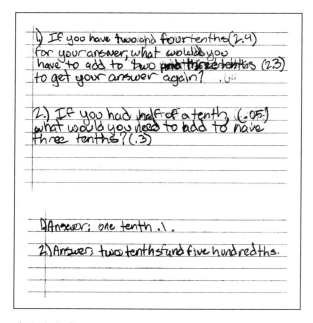

▲▲▲▲▲▲Figure 3–3 Shannon used both words and numbers to describe decimals. Her second riddle revealed that she knew that half of a tenth is equal to .05.

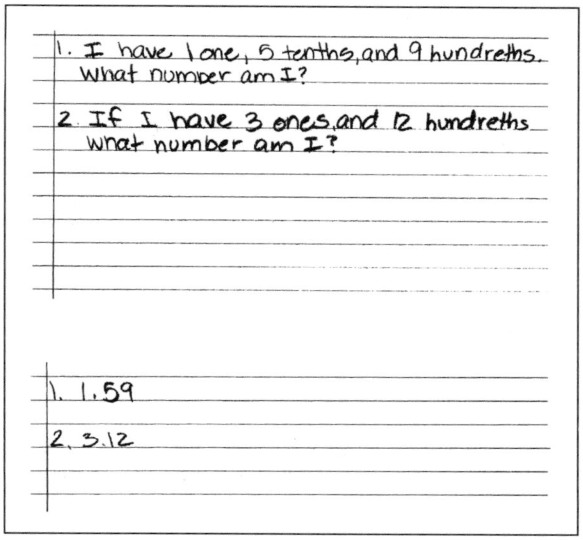

1. I have 1 one, 5 tenths, and 9 hundreths. What number am I?

2. If I have 3 ones, and 12 hundreths what number am I?

1. 1.59

2. 3.12

▲▲▲▲▲**Figure 3–4** *Madison wrote simple riddles, choosing ideas that she was sure about.*

DAY 2

To begin class I said, "Let's share our solutions to yesterday's riddles. Let's start with the first one: I have two ones, twelve-tenths, and six-hundredths. What's the number?"

Rebecca said, "I think it's two wholes and twenty-six–hundredths."

"I don't think that's right," Martin replied. "I got three wholes and twenty-six–hundredths. I think Becky forgot to add the extra one whole."

"Can you explain what you mean?" I asked.

Martin said, "Well, I already have two wholes, and twelve-tenths is really one whole and two-tenths. That's the same as one whole and two left over. Since I get a whole from that, I add it to the two wholes I already had. So I have three wholes and two-tenths left over. Then I need to add the six-hundredths, so I end up with three wholes, two-tenths, and six-hundredths, and that's three and twenty-six–hundredths."

I looked at Rebecca. "I get it; he's right," she said.

"How do we write the numeral for three and twenty-six–hundredths?" I asked.

Marcus said, "Three point two six."

I recorded on the board *3.26*, saying as I did so to reinforce the correct language, "Three and twenty-six–hundredths."

I then asked, "Who can explain how to show this number on a place value mat using the fewest possible number of blocks?"

Crystal said, "You need three flats, two rods, and three units." As Crystal explained, I placed the blocks on the overhead place value mat.

"Who can explain why the decimal numeral I wrote represents three and twenty-six–hundredths?" I asked.

Rory explained, "The three is the three flats; they're the wholes. Then the two is in the tenths column, and the six is in the hundredths place."

"Let's read the number together," I said. The class said aloud with me, "Three and twenty-six–hundredths."

We discussed the next four riddles in the same way. For each, we talked about the solutions, built the numbers with base ten blocks, wrote the numerals, and read them aloud. I think that it supports the students' learning to continue to make connections between the materials, the language, and the symbols being used.

"What do you think the number is for riddle number six?" I asked.

"I think the answer is two-tenths," Leslee said.

Shannon's hand shot up. She said, "I think she means she *added* two-tenths. You need to add two-tenths to sixteen-hundredths to get a decimal number between three-tenths and four-tenths. I think it's thirty-six–hundredths."

"Can you explain what you mean?" I asked.

Shannon continued, "I knew that sixteen-hundredths is the same as one-tenth and six-hundredths. And I knew the number had to be somewhere between three-tenths and four-tenths. I already had one-tenth and some left over. If I added one-tenth to it, I would only have two-tenths and six-hundredths, and if I added three-tenths, I would have four-tenths and six-hundredths. So I added two-tenths to the one-tenth and six-hundredths to get the number three-tenths and six-hundredths."

I then asked, "Who can explain how to show this number on the place value mat using the fewest number of blocks?"

Patrice explained, "You need three rods and six units."

As she explained, I placed the blocks on the overhead place value mat. I then wrote on the board .36 and asked, "Who can explain why the decimal numeral I wrote represents thirty-six–hundredths?"

Ian said, "The three is the three rods; they're the tenths. Then the six is in the hundredths column, which represents the six units."

"Let's read the number together," I said. The class said aloud with me, "Thirty-six–hundredths."

Using the Students' Riddles

One part of the previous night's homework assignment had been for students to make up two riddles of their own. After the class discussed the six riddles I had assigned, I asked the students to share their riddles with a partner and then to check their partner's solutions. I circulated around the room listening to the different riddles being discussed and picked several I wanted students to present in the class discussion. The whole-group discussion was similar to the discussion about the other riddles. Finally, I selected several more of the students' riddles and assigned them for homework. Each student author read aloud his or her riddle for the others to write down.

Questions and Discussion

▲▲

▲ *Do you have the students build with the base ten blocks even if they can figure out the riddles without the blocks?*

Yes, I do. I've learned that the blocks are of value. They verify the thinking of those who have figured without them, as well as give others a way to figure out solutions. Either way, I consider them to be supportive of students' learning.

▲ *What if students hadn't written their own riddles for homework? What would you do?*

This invariably happens, either because a student was absent or didn't do the assignment. Either have students who didn't write riddles join a pair and participate in their discussion, or ask them to write riddles as others are discussing. I prefer the first option as it gives the student a chance to get actively involved and benefit from a discussion with classmates.

CHAPTER FOUR
COMPARING DECIMALS

Overview

This lesson gives students experience with comparing decimals. The lesson begins with a class discussion in which students compare several sets of numbers presented in contexts. The students then consider numbers abstractly, using base ten blocks to represent and compare them concretely. They work in groups of four to compare and order sets with three decimals in each. Finally, they cement their understanding by playing *The Greatest Wins*, a game in which they try to make the largest decimals possible.

Materials

▲ base ten blocks, at least 50 units, 25 rods, and 3 flats per group of four students
▲ place value mats, 3 per group of four students (see Blackline Masters)
▲ dice, 1 per group of four students
▲ optional: rules for the game of *The Greatest Wins* (see Blackline Masters)

Time

▲ one to two class periods, plus additional time for playing *The Greatest Wins*

Teaching Directions

1. Distribute base ten blocks and three place value mats to each group of four students.

2. Write on the board:
$2.50 $2.05

Pose the following problem: *Susie has two dollars and fifty cents and I have two dollars and five cents. Who has more money?* After the students agree, insert on the board a "greater than" sign between the two numbers:

$2.50 > $2.05

3. Next write on the board:

98.5 lb   98.8 lb

Pose the following problem: *Tommy weighs ninety-eight and five-tenths pounds, and Marcus weighs ninety-eight and eight-tenths pounds. Who weighs more?* After the students agree, insert on the board a "less than" sign between the numbers:

98.5 lb < 98.8 lb

4. Write on the board:

6.9 min   6.09 min

Pose the following problem: *In a mile race, one runner finished in six and nine-tenths minutes and the other in six and nine-hundredths minutes. Which runner ran faster?* After the students agree, insert a "greater than" sign between the two numbers:

6.9 min > 6.09 min

5. Write another pair of decimals on the board but do not relate the numbers to a context:

.7   .29

Ask: "Which is larger?" Discuss. Then ask the question again, this time placing the numbers in the context of measuring time: "In a bicycle race, one rider shaved seven-tenths of a second off her best time and another shaved twenty-nine–hundredths off her best time. Who shaved off more time?" After the students share their ideas, direct them to build both decimals with base ten blocks to verify which is larger.

6. Lead a class discussion about why .7 is greater than .29 and why .7 is equal to .70.

7. Continue by writing on the board:

.3   .03

Ask the students: "Which decimal is larger?" Ask them to show the decimals with base ten blocks to verify their answers. After the students share their thinking, insert a "greater than" sign:

.3 > .03

8. Organize the class into groups of four. Instruct the students that for the next activity, one person in each group will be the banker in charge of the base ten blocks, and the other three will be builders and show numbers on a place value mat. Tell them that they'll switch roles for each problem so that each person has the opportunity to be the banker.

9. Tell the students that you'll give them three decimal numbers. Write on the board what they will do with the numbers:

Predict the order from least to greatest.

Build the numbers.

Compare and record.

10. Write on the board three decimals:

.4   .06   .12

Explain to the groups that the banker should take from the bucket the necessary blocks for each number and each builder should build one of the numbers on a place value mat. Then, as a group, they should compare the numbers, order them from least to greatest, and record the results using "less than" signs. After the groups have had the chance to do this, record on the board. Also model how to record using "greater than" signs.

.06 < .12 < .4

.4 > .12 > .06

11. Next write on the board five sets of numbers for the groups to build and compare. For each set, they should write an equality.

.7, .10, .07

.04, .14, .4

.19, .11, 0.2

0.03, 0.08, 0.1

.5, .50, .05

12. After students have finished the assignment, introduce the game *The Greatest Wins*. If no time remains in the period, introduce the game the next day. Model on the board how the students should set up their papers for this game.

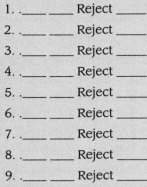

The Greatest Wins

   1. .____ ____ Reject ____
   2. .____ ____ Reject ____
   3. .____ ____ Reject ____
   4. .____ ____ Reject ____
   5. .____ ____ Reject ____
   6. .____ ____ Reject ____
   7. .____ ____ Reject ____
   8. .____ ____ Reject ____
   9. .____ ____ Reject ____
   10. .____ ____ Reject ____

Explain the rules for play. You may wish to reproduce and distribute the directions to each group, or post the rules for the students' reference (see Blackline Masters). Then have the students play the game in groups of four. Allow time for them to play at least ten rounds.

13. For homework ask the students to play ten rounds of *The Greatest Wins* with someone at home.

Teaching Notes

Students bring to their formal instruction about decimal numbers the understanding they have about whole numbers and fractions. For example, they know that for whole numbers, numbers that have more digits are larger than numbers with fewer digits. And they typically know that a fraction like seven-tenths is greater than seven-hundredths, while seven-tenths and seventy-hundredths are equal. However, when only given the symbolic notation for decimal representations of numbers—.7, .07, and .70, for example—many students get confused. The meaning of the numbers gets lost. Students who rely on their knowledge of whole numbers are confused when their knowledge doesn't transfer to numbers less than one.

The opportunity to think about numbers in contexts and to use base ten blocks to represent decimal numbers concretely helps students focus on the meaning of the numerical symbols. Their number sense with decimal numbers develops and they are less likely to use inappropriate rules or procedures for comparing and ordering decimals.

The Lesson

▲▲▲

For this lesson, each group of four had access to a supply of base ten blocks and three place value mats. To begin, I said, "I'm going to teach you a game today that requires making the largest possible decimal in order to win." I then wrote on the board:

$2.50 $2.05

I said, "Susie has two dollars and fifty cents, and I have two dollars and five cents. Who has more money?" Everyone agreed that Susie had more money. I knew that the answer would be obvious to the students, but I like to start with a real-world reference they can relate to. I inserted a "greater than" sign:

$2.50 > $2.05

I then wrote on the board:

98.5 lb   98.8 lb

I said, "Tommy weighs ninety-eight and five-tenths pounds, and Marcus weighs ninety-eight and eight-tenths pounds. Who weighs more?" The students were clear that

both boys weighed more than ninety-eight pounds and that Marcus weighed three-tenths of a pound more than Tommy. I added the "less than" sign to indicate the comparison:

98.5 lb < 98.8 lb

Next I wrote on the board:

6.9 min   6.09 min

I said, "In a mile race, one runner finished in six and nine-tenths minutes and the other in six and nine-hundredths minutes. Which runner ran faster?"

"I think the second runner is faster," Jack said. "Nine-hundredths of a second is less time than nine-tenths of a second."

"Does everyone agree?" I asked the class. Several students voiced objections so I asked each group to use base ten blocks to build nine-tenths on one mat and nine hundredths on another. I think that some of the students who disagreed knew that nine-hundredths was less time than nine-tenths, but were confused because in my two previous questions, I had asked which was the greater. In this example, the faster runner was the one who had the shorter time; identifying which time was greater didn't answer my question.

The students easily placed nine rods on one place value mat and nine units on the other. Discussing in their groups seemed to resolve the correct answer.

"Nine-hundredths is smaller because you only have nine little cubes," Justin said. "And nine-tenths is nine rods, and that's the same as ninety-hundredths. Ninety-hundredths is more than nine-hundredths."

"And the runner that ran it in six and nine-hundredths seconds was faster," Martin added. I entered an inequality sign:

$.9 \ min > .09 \ min$

I then wrote on the board another pair of decimals. This time I didn't relate the numbers to a context.

$.7 \qquad .29$

"Which is larger?" I asked. "Show thumbs up if you think seven-tenths is larger, and thumbs down if you think twenty-nine–hundredths is larger." The response was half and half, as it typically is when I introduce this activity. Many students revert to thinking about whole numbers, for which the more digits there are, the larger the number.

I asked the question again, this time placing the numbers in a context and again using them to describe measures of time. "In a bicycle race, one rider shaved seven-tenths of a second off her best time and another shaved twenty-nine–hundredths off her best time. Who shaved off more time? Once again, show thumbs up if you think seven-tenths is more and thumbs down for twenty-nine–hundredths." Several students changed their mind once the numbers were used in a real-world context, but some still weren't sure.

"Build both of these decimals with your blocks and then decide which is larger," I said.

"Seven-tenths is larger," Kerri said. "I have more than Ken." I recorded symbolically what Kerri said:

$.7 > .29$

"Seven-tenths is the same as seventy-hundredths and seventy-hundredths is much larger than twenty-nine–hundredths," Jose added. I wrote on the board:

$0.7 = 0.70$

"So according to Jose, these two numbers are the same. Who can explain why this makes sense?"

Tamara said, "They can't be the same. One is seven and the other is seventy."

Leslee responded, "But one is tenths and the other is hundredths. You either have seven rods or seventy unit cubes. I think they're the same."

"Oh yeah," Tamara conceded.

Rory said, "They're the same. They both say seven-tenths, but the second one also says zero hundredths, and that doesn't add anything."

I said, "So when I add a zero behind the seven, it doesn't increase the number. The numbers have the same value—they're equal." I then wrote on the board:

$.3 \qquad .03$

"Thumbs up if you think three-tenths is greater and thumbs down if you think three hundredths is greater." Most students agreed that three-tenths is larger. I had them build the numbers with blocks to verify that this was so.

"Who can explain?" I asked.

"I have three rods and Chen has three units, so three-tenths is more than three-hundredths," Isabella said.

"It's like money. If I add a zero at the end of the three-tenths, it reads thirty cents, and thirty cents is greater than three cents," Frank said.

"Anyone else?"

"If I compare the tenths column then I can easily see three-tenths is greater. One has three-tenths and the other number has zero tenths. I don't even have to look at the hundredths column," Kendra answered. I recorded:

.3 > .03

A GROUP ACTIVITY

I then introduced an activity for students to do in groups of four. I explained, "For this activity, one person in each group of four will be the banker and the other three will be builders. The builders each need a place value mat; the banker is in charge of the blocks. You'll switch roles for each problem so that you'll all have the chance to be a banker.

"To start, I'll give you three decimals to compare. As a group, first predict their order from least to greatest. Then the banker gets out all of the necessary blocks and each builder builds one of the numbers on a mat. Finally, as a group, compare the numbers you've built. Then each of you should record the results using 'greater than' or 'less than' signs." I wrote the directions on the board as I explained:

1. *Predict the order from least to greatest.*

2. *Build the numbers.*

3. *Compare and record.*

"Let's try one example as a class," I said. I wrote three decimals on the board:

.4   .06   .12

I said, "Without using the blocks, talk in your group for a moment about how you would order these numbers from least to greatest." I gave the groups a moment to talk and then called them back to attention.

"Now one of you in each group should take the role of the banker and give blocks to each of the builders to build a number on a mat. Once you've built the numbers, compare your blocks and agree how to order the numbers from least to greatest." I gave groups time to do this and again asked for their attention.

"Raise your hand if you'd like to report which number is the smallest and explain why," I said. I called on Madison.

"Mine was smallest," she said. "I only had six little blocks and everyone else had more."

"Which number did you build?" I asked.

"The middle one," Madison said, referring to how I had written them on the board.

"Can you read it?" I asked. I reinforce the correct reading of decimals as often as possible.

"It's six-hundredths," she said.

"Who built the largest number?" I asked. A hand went up from each group. I called on Martin.

"I had the most. I had four rods. It's four-tenths," he reported.

"Who can tell me how to rewrite the decimals in order from least to greatest?" I asked. I looked around the room waiting for hands to go up, then called on Bonnie.

"Erase the four-tenths and move it to the last position," she said. I did as Bonnie instructed and inserted "less than" signs:

.06 < .12 < .4

"Or I could order them from greatest to least, like this," I said, and recorded:

.4 > .12 > .06

I then wrote on the board five sets of numbers for the groups to build, compare, and order.

.7, .10, .07

.04, .14, .4

.19, .11, 0.2

0.03, 0.08, 0.1

.5, .50, .05

The groups got to work. (Figures 4–1 through 4–4 show how four students worked on this assignment.) I circulated and watched to see when groups would finish. By the time two groups finished, the others had compared at least three of the sets of numbers, and I interrupted the class.

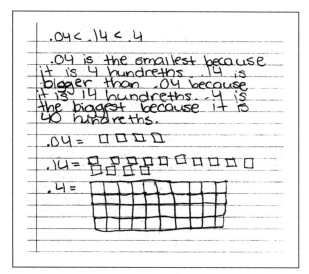

.04 < .14 < .4

.04 is the smallest because it is 4 hundreths. .14 is bigger than .04 because it is 14 hundreths. .4 is the biggest because it is 40 hundreths.

.04 = □ □ □ □

.14 = □□□□□□□□□□□ □□□□

.4 =

▲▲▲▲▲▲Figure 4–1   *Tamara thought about .04, .14, and .4 as hundredths in order to compare them.*

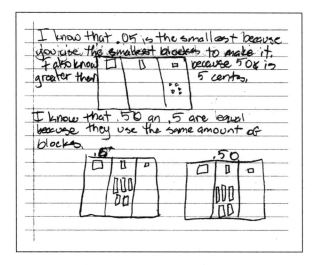

I know that .05 is the smallest because you use the smallest blocks to make it. I also know □ □ □ because .50 is greater then 5 cents.

I know that .50 an .5 are equal because they use the same amount of blocks.

.5   .50

▲▲▲▲▲▲Figure 4–2   *Ian referred to money and to base ten blocks to help explain his reasoning.*

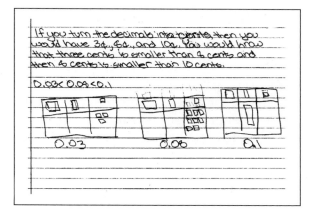

If you turn the decimals into cents, then you would have 3¢, 8¢, and 10¢. You would know that three cents is smaller than 8 cents and then 8 cents is smaller than 10 cents.

0.03 < 0.08 < 0.1

0.03   0.08   0.1

▲▲▲▲▲▲Figure 4–3   *Patrice compared 0.03, 0.08, and 0.1 by relating them to amounts of money.*

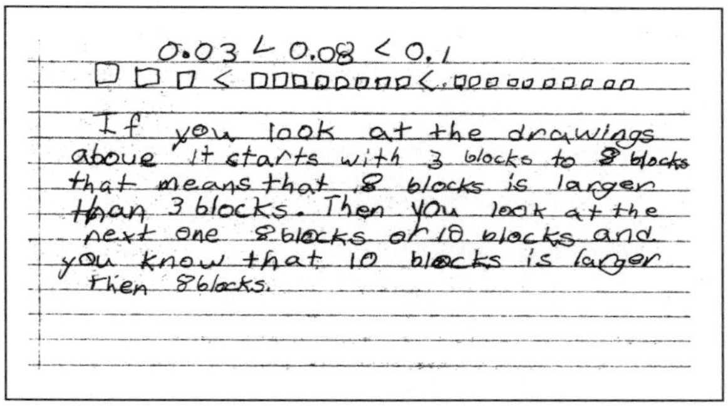

0.03 < 0.08 < 0.1

□ □ □ < □□□□□□□□ < □□□□□□□□□□

If you look at the drawings above it starts with 3 blocks to 8 blocks that means that .8 blocks is larger than 3 blocks. Then you look at the next one 8 blocks or 10 blocks and you know that 10 blocks is larger then 8 blocks.

▲▲▲▲▲▲Figure 4–4   *Marcus correctly ordered the decimals and his pictorial representations of them.*

THE GREATEST WINS

I said to the class, "I can see that you're able to compare the decimals, so I'd like to teach you a game in which you'll use this skill. Move the blocks aside and take out a clean sheet of paper." As the students did this, I wrote on the board how they were to set up their papers:

The Greatest Wins

```
 1. .___ ___ Reject ____
 2. .___ ___ Reject ____
 3. .___ ___ Reject ____
 4. .___ ___ Reject ____
 5. .___ ___ Reject ____
 6. .___ ___ Reject ____
 7. .___ ___ Reject ____
 8. .___ ___ Reject ____
 9. .___ ___ Reject ____
10. .___ ___ Reject ____
```

I distributed one die to each group and explained the rules. "The object of the game is to make the largest decimal. You'll play ten rounds and see who makes the largest decimal the most times. To play, the first player rolls the die and decides whether to use the number. If you don't want to use it, write it in the Reject column. If you use it, write it in one of the places. Once you record the number, you can't change its position. When you've recorded the number, pass the die to the next player. Each other person in the group rolls, records, and then passes on the die. When you've all filled in the first line on your score sheet, round one is complete. Each player must read aloud his or her number, and the group must agree on who has the largest number and, therefore, wins the round. Continue playing for nine more rounds. The overall winner is the player who wins the most rounds."

As I observed the students playing the game, one particular group caught my attention. Sophia had already placed the 5 that she rolled on her first turn in the hundredths place. She had just rolled a 3 for her second turn and was debating about where to place it. She noticed that Rory, who hadn't yet had his second turn, had also rolled a 5 on his first turn and had also placed it in the hundredths place. So both of them had the same result so far:

```
.___ 5 Reject ___
```

"Where do you think you should place the three?" I asked.

Sophia answered, "It isn't a very high number, so I should probably place it in the reject space, but then what if I roll a smaller number next time? But if I put it in the tenths column and then Rory rolls a larger number, I'm sure to lose."

Sophia paused to think and then said, "I think I'll leave the tenths column blank and write three in the reject space."

Rory then rolled a 4. "I'm going to reject it," he said. "I'll take my chances and try for a five or six next turn."

Play continued around the group. Sophia's last roll was a 5 and she placed it in the only space she had available, creating the number .55. She now had the greatest number in the group and only had Rory's roll to worry about. Rory rolled a 3! He knew he had lost.

"Does it matter now that you placed the four in the reject column?" I asked.

Rory responded, "Either way I would have lost. Fifty-five–hundredths is more than either forty-five–hundredths or thirty-five–hundredths. Let's play again!"

Homework

For homework, students were to teach someone at home how to play *The*

Greatest Wins and play ten rounds. If students don't have dice, either loan them one or show them how to cut out six slips of paper, number them from 1 to 6, put them in a bag, and draw without looking, replacing each time. Or suggest to students that they use playing cards, using the cards numbered from 1 to 6 or from 1 to 9.

EXTENSIONS

Students can extend the game *The Greatest Wins* by adding a third place for a thousandths place. Or they can play the game by the same rules except for changing the goal so that the smallest decimal each round. Your students may also come up with variations of their own.

Questions and Discussion

▲▲▲

▲ *How do you avoid students being confused and thinking, for example, that .06 is greater than .3 because 3 is less than 6?*

This confusion is common when students have no way to make sense of the numbers and are floundering for understanding. Often students erroneously assume that a number such as three-hundredths is greater than three-tenths either because they are confusing "hundreds" and "hundredths" or they think that more digits means a larger number. Or they assume that a number such as six-hundredths is greater than three-tenths because six is greater than three. Using the base ten blocks is enormously helpful. By having the students represent numbers with the blocks, they have a visual model of what the numbers mean and can compare them concretely. This helps them conceptualize tenths, hundredths, and the differences between them, and avoid misconceptions that come when they have no reference for the quantities.

▲ *Why do you switch back and forth between using contexts and just talking about the numbers themselves?*

Students benefit from as many references as possible when learning new ideas. Using both real-world contexts and concrete materials helps students make connections between things they know and new ideas that they are just beginning to understand.

▲ *Why do you have one student be the banker? Why don't you have all students take their own blocks?*

When students work together, they have the chance to talk about what they are doing and also to keep a check on each other's actions. Specifying jobs for each defines what each is to do and helps keep them focused. I've found this system to be helpful in keeping students on task.

CHAPTER FIVE
DECIMAL NIM

Overview

The value of teaching the game of *Decimal Nim* is both to give students experience with representing and adding decimals and also to encourage them to think strategically to figure out how to win. In this lesson, students learn several variations of the game. They play in pairs, using one calculator between them.

Materials

- ▲ calculators, 1 per pair of students
- ▲ optional: overhead calculator
- ▲ optional: rules for the games of *Decimal Nim*, *Target*, *Race to Zero*, and *Target II*, 1 of each per pair of students (see Blackline Masters)

Time

- ▲ one class period, plus additional time for playing

Teaching Directions

1. Introduce the game *Decimal Nim* by modeling with the class how to play. (See Blackline Masters for the rules.) Play against the class several times. It's extremely helpful to use an overhead calculator for introducing this and the other games in this lesson.

2. Once the students understand how to play, have them play several games in pairs. Observe the strategies students use.

3. Lead a class discussion about the students' strategies. You may want to ask a student who thinks that he or she has developed a winning strategy to come up to the overhead projector and play against you. Then allow time for the students to play several more rounds to redefine their strategies.

4. Next, introduce a different version of the game called *Target*, by modeling with the class how to play. (See Blackline Masters for the rules.) Once the students have had time to play at least one round of *Target*, interrupt them to introduce two other versions. List on the board the four games:

Decimal Nim

Target

Race to Zero

Target II

5. Explain the rules of the last two games and then give the students time to try each of them (see Blackline Masters for the rules).

6. Allow time at the end of the class for the students to write the rules for playing each game, or distribute copies of the rules.

7. For homework, ask the students to play each game at least one time with someone at home. Tell the students to bring back any ideas they may have about winning strategies.

Teaching Notes

Decimal Nim and the other versions of the game in this lesson have several aspects in common. The games do not involve any aspect of luck and are entirely games of strategy. When playing, there are no secret moves and all players know exactly what is happening. Also, the rules aren't difficult to learn and the games are easy to learn to play, therefore making the activities accessible to all students.

These features make the games excellent vehicles for providing students experience and practice with decimals. At the same time, the challenge of figuring out winning strategies gives students a problem-solving experience that promotes thinking and reasoning, thus embedding the lesson with richness beyond merely practicing with decimals.

Another feature of these games is that when both players know the winning strategies, the games are no longer interesting to play. For this reason, it's best not to reveal a winning strategy for any of the games. Telling strategies removes the challenge for students to think through the problem and is counterproductive to encouraging and building students' problem-solving skills. Instead, let students struggle with how they might win. Keep in mind that the goal of the lesson isn't for students to "master" the strategies of the games, but rather to motivate students to think strategically while they gain experience and practice working with decimals.

If you haven't thought about the strategies for nim-type games like these, try playing them with a colleague first. As happened in the lesson described, it's common for students to figure out, when playing the first version, that landing on .7 ensures that you can win. However, it's not common for students to think further and figure out how to be sure to be the player who lands on .7. Encourage students to make conjectures about possible strategies and then try them. It's helpful to have students play games, either against you or against another student, while the others watch.

When a student plays against me, I play to win. I have an unfair advantage, however, because I know the winning strategy. I know that I'd rather be the first player. If my opponent also knows the winning strategy, whoever goes first will win! I also know that to be sure to get to .7, I need to get to .4. That's because if I land on .4, no matter if my opponent adds .1 or .2, I'll then be able to add .2 or .1 and reach .7. Backing up further, if I start with .1, then I'll be sure to land on .4. (If my opponent adds .1, then I'll add .2 and land on .4; if my opponent adds .2, then I'll add .1 and land on .4.) So, by going first and entering .1, I can control the game. If a student who doesn't know the strategy makes the first move, I can sometimes still take control of the game by reaching .4.

Again, please don't reveal this strategy to your students. It's included here to offer you support in case the game is new to you, and to encourage you to figure out the winning strategies for the three other games. Most importantly, keep your students thinking and keep thinking yourself—that's what's most important about learning mathematics.

The Lesson

▲▲▲

To introduce the games, I used an overhead calculator. Students worked in pairs and used one calculator for the two of them.

I began with one of the several variations I planned to teach. "I'm going to teach you a game that you'll play with a partner. You'll use one calculator for the two of you. The winner of the game is the player who causes one whole to appear on the display. To play, first you start by clearing the display on your calculator so it reads zero. Then, taking turns, each of you adds either one-tenth or two-tenths. That means you'll press the plus sign, the decimal point, either one or two, and the equals sign." I wrote on the board:

+, .1, =

+, .2, =

I continued, "Let's play one game together, the class against me. I'll go first." I cleared the display on my overhead calcu-

lator, pressed plus, one-tenth, and equals. I asked the class, "What number is on the display?"

"One-tenth," they answered.

"Now what would you like to add, one-tenth or two-tenths?"

"Let's add two-tenths," Peter suggested.

"What should I press?" I asked.

Peter faltered a moment and then looked at the board and said, "Plus, point two, and equals."

"What number is on the display?" I asked.

"Three-tenths," responded the class.

"For my turn, I'll add one-tenth," I said, saying aloud as I did so, "Plus, decimal point, one, equals." Four-tenths was showing on the display.

"What would you like to add?" I asked.

"How about one-tenth this time?" Marisa proposed. As Marisa directed, on the overhead calculator I entered the addition sign, then one-tenth, and pressed the equals sign.

"What does the display read now?" I asked.

"Five-tenths," the students chorused.

"I'll think I'll add two-tenths this time," I said.

I did this and the class read the display, "Seven-tenths."

"Let's do two-tenths this time, too," shouted Matthew.

Maria disagreed, "No, let's add one-tenth. If we add two-tenths to seven-tenths, that will give Mrs. De nine-tenths and then she'll win."

"Yeah, if we put in one-tenth, then she'll have only eight-tenths," Laura said, and then added, "Wait, she could still win!"

Crystal chimed in, "No matter what we do, you'll win. If it's up to eight-tenths, you can add two-tenths and win, or if the display reads nine-tenths, you can add one-tenth and still win. No matter what we do, we've already lost."

"Does everyone agree? No matter what number you enter, can I win this game?" I asked. The students all seemed to understand their predicament.

"Let's play again and this time we go first," Peter said. I agreed and we played another game. Students weren't sure how to decide whether to add one-tenth or two-tenths, but they were beginning to think about possible winning strategies.

"Let's do whatever Mrs. De does," Leslee suggested.

"Don't let her get to seven-tenths again," Bryant said.

I again won the second game and then said, "Now you'll play this game with your partner. Play at least ten rounds and keep track of who won each time. As you play, think about strategies for winning this game. If you think you have a foolproof method for winning, test it to be sure it works every time." The students eagerly began playing.

As I walked around listening to conversations, I heard many students insisting on going first, convinced this was the winning secret. I approached Isaac and Jonathan playing. Isaac looked frustrated and Jonathan was calmly sitting back in his chair with a slight grin on his face.

"What's the matter, Isaac?" I asked.

"No matter what I do, he wins. Now I've got seven-tenths on the calculator and I know no matter what I press, he's going to win again."

I turned to Jonathan and asked, "Is there a method to your madness?"

He calmly responded, "Yep!"

I interrupted the class and called the students' attention to Isaac's dilemma. "Isaac is very frustrated. No matter what he does, Jonathan always seems to win. Is anyone else having this same problem?" Several hands went up.

I continued, "Jonathan seems to think he has a winning strategy. Is there anyone else who thinks he or she has developed a foolproof method for winning?" Several more hands went up.

"I think it's better to go first. Every time I go first, I win," Patrice said.

"I let Shannon go first every time and I still won," replied Crystal.

"I tried doing the same as my partner did, but it only worked sometimes," Leslee added.

"Jonathan, would you share your idea for a winning strategy?" I asked.

"Sure. I want to be the one who gets the calculator to seven-tenths. It doesn't matter what I punch in before that. Once I get to seven-tenths and pass the calculator to Isaac, I know I'm going to win." Jonathan's thinking was correct, and students often come to this same conclusion. If a player passes the calculator showing .7 on the display, that player can surely win. But that's only part of a winning strategy. It's important also to think about how to be sure to cause .7 to appear. I didn't tell any of this to the class, but instead invited Jonathan to play.

"Jonathan, why don't you come up to the overhead projector and play against me using your strategy. This will help your classmates understand what you mean." Jonathan and I played several rounds. Sometimes he got to seven-tenths and won, and sometimes I did, but whoever got to seven-tenths was the winner.

I then let the students return to playing with their partners to try Jonathan's method. Many were convinced this was indeed a winning strategy, but some were realizing that they also needed a strategy for being sure to be the player who gets to seven-tenths. I didn't resolve this with the students but decided to let them continue grappling with the issue.

When both players know the strategy for winning this game of *Decimal Nim*, the game isn't at all interesting to play. There's no luck involved and no further thinking required. However, even when students know how to win this first game, changing the specific parameters presents students with additional challenges. Students figure out the winning strategy in their own ways and on their own time schedules. I don't reveal winning strategies, but instead keep everyone's interest by suggesting variations.

INTRODUCING OTHER GAMES

"Now we are going to play a different version of this game. This one is called *Target*, and you still play with a partner and use one calculator. For this game, however, you first roll a die to determine the target number. Then you play just as you did in the first game, but the winner is the first person to reach exactly the target number. While playing, think about how the strategies you have for the first game apply to this version." Once again, the children eagerly began playing against each other.

After the students had enough time to try at least two games of *Target*, I interrupted them to introduce two other versions. I told them, "For *Race to Zero*, you take turns the same as for the other games, but you start with one on the display and try to be the player who reaches exactly zero. When it's your turn, instead of adding, you can subtract either one-tenth or two-tenths."

I listed on the board the three games and added one more that I planned to introduce:

Decimal Nim

Target

Race to Zero

Target II

I continued, "For *Target II*, as you did for *Target*, you roll the die for a target number. This time, on your turn you have four choices about what to add: one-tenth, two-tenths, one-hundredth, or two-hundredths. Again, you try to be the first person to reach the target number." I listed these possible numbers on the board:

.1

.2

.01

.02

After I introduced the games, I gave the students time to try each of them. Then, to end the class period, I asked students to write the rules for playing each game. I planned to use the games over the next several weeks as a choice activity when students finished classwork early and there was still time remaining in the period.

Homework
Students were to play each game at least one time with someone at home. "Bring back any ideas you have about winning strategies," I said. I planned to start the next day with a discussion of their experiences.

Questions and Discussion

▲▲

▲ *If I don't have an overhead calculator, what's a good way to introduce the games?*

If I didn't have an overhead calculator, I'd use a handheld one and have each pair of students follow along, doing all the actions on their own calculator. I'd be sure, however, to check after each move that everyone had the same number on the display. Also, I think it would be a good idea to record on the board the number on the display from each turn. Not only does this provide a way for students to check that they're on track, it's also another way to reinforce the connection between the spoken number—two-tenths, for example—and its symbolic representation—.2 or 0.2.

▲ *What do you do if students get frustrated because they can't figure out the winning strategy for even the first game?*

I've handled this situation in various ways. While I don't want frustration to result in students feeling discouraged and, therefore, not willing to persist, I still don't want to reveal the strategy too soon. Developing persistence is part of developing mathematical competence. My approach is to encourage students without doing all of the thinking for them. With the first version of the game, it's typical for students easily to realize the importance of reaching seven-tenths. If they remain stuck for a long while after that, I direct their thinking. For example, I say, "Other decisions to consider are whether it's important to go first or second, what your initial move should be, and how what your partner does should affect your next play." If some students are still stuck, I'll have others reveal the complete strategy. (See the "Teaching Notes" section above for a discussion of the strategy.) Then I'll let them grapple with finding winning strategies for the other versions of the game.

▲ *Aren't four different games too many to introduce in one lesson?*

When I taught this lesson, the students seemed fine with learning the four variations. But it would be fine to introduce just two games, have them play them at home for homework, and then introduce the other two the next day, or even several days or a week later.

▲ *Why did you have the students write the rules for the games instead of duplicating and distributing them?*

Having students write the rules themselves gives them practice organizing and expressing their thoughts. The assignment gives them practice with their writing skills while also requiring them to clarify their thinking. You may, however, prefer to distribute the rules. Or have the students write the rules themselves and then later post copies of the rules as a reference for the class.

CHAPTER SIX
THE LOBSTER PROBLEM

Overview

This lesson introduces students to thousandths by asking students to predict the possible weight of a lobster that weighed between 2.56 and 2.57 pounds. Using this context and the context of money, students learn about extending decimals beyond hundredths and identifying decimals that come in between other numbers.

Materials

▲ None

Time

▲ one class period

Teaching Directions

1. Pose this question: "According to a grocery's digital scale, a lobster weighs more than two and fifty-six–hundredths pounds but less than two and fifty-seven–hundredths pounds. How much do you think the lobster weighs?" Write on the board:

2.56 lb

2.57 lb

2. If the students can't answer the question or if some seem confused, simplify by discussing another question: "What if the scale said the lobster weighed between two pounds and three pounds? How much could the lobster weigh?" If the only solution students come up with is 2.5 pounds, rephrase the question again and ask: "What if the scale registered the lobster at a weight between two and a half pounds and three pounds? How much could the lobster weigh then?"

3. Now change the context of the question to money and ask: "Suppose that Matthew had more than two dollars and fifty cents but less than three dollars? How much money could Matthew have?" Have the students discuss all of the possible amounts of money between $2.50 and $3.00. It's important that students see that Matthew could have many different combinations of money between $2.50 and $3.00 by adding pennies or cents.

4. Present another version of the lobster question: "What if the digital scale registered the lobster at a weight between two and five-tenths pounds and three pounds? How much could the lobster weigh?" Write on the board:

   2.5 lbs

   3 lbs

Suggest to the students that they use the discussion about money to decide on weights between 2.5 and 3 pounds. Discuss the possible weights of the lobster.

5. Again present the original lobster question: "According to a grocery's digital scale, a lobster weighs more than two and fifty-six–hundredths pounds but less than two and fifty-seven–hundredths pounds. How much do you think the lobster weighs?" Ask the students to brainstorm with their partners the possible weights in between 2.56 pounds and 2.57 pounds and to discuss how to read aloud their solutions.

6. If the students are having difficulty reading aloud the possible weights, write on the board and draw their attention to the following numbers:

   2.5

   2.56

   2.562

Read the first number together while pointing to the decimal on the board. Repeat again with the second number. Ask for a volunteer to read the third number.

7. Ask: "What's the value of the base ten blocks if the large cube represents one whole?" Discuss thousandths and have the students together read 2.562 aloud as you point to the decimal on the board. To help students who find it easier to learn by reading than by listening, write the number on the board:

   two and five hundred sixty-two–thousandths

8. Continue having students give answers to possible weights between 2.56 pounds and 2.57 pounds. Record the weights on the board. Then ask the students: "What are the least amount and greatest amount the lobster can weigh?" Discuss that the least amount is 2.561 pounds and the greatest is 2.569 pounds.

9. If no student volunteers other weights between 2.561 pounds and 2.569 pounds, write the number 2.561 nine times in a column and then add the digits from one through nine to each of the numbers, creating possible weights with four decimal places, from 2.5611 to 2.5619. Writing the numbers this way can sometimes help students visually see that the possibilities can go on infinitely.

10. Write a question on the board for the students to answer for homework:

Are there an infinite number of possible weights between 2.56 lbs and 2.57 lbs? Explain your thinking and give examples.

Teaching Notes

The lesson begins by posing the following problem to the students: *According to a grocery's digital scale, a lobster weighs more than two and fifty-six–hundredths pounds but less than two and fifty-seven–hundredths pounds. How much do you think the lobster weighs?* The following vignette describes what happened when confusion existed for most of the class. It's typical for students not to be able to answer this question, or for at least some students to be confused by it. The problem was purposely created assuming this confusion, and the intent of the lesson is to build toward empowering the students to be able to answer it. The lesson does so by building on students' experience with money and base ten blocks, using their decimal representations as the foundation for new learning.

If, however, the problem doesn't pose any difficulty for your class, then you can use the experience as an indication that the students are comfortable extending hundredths into thousandths. Then, to be sure about the students' understanding, use the homework assignment presented in the last direction in the "Teaching Directions" section as an assessment. Also, be sure that students are comfortable reading aloud decimals that include thousandths and, if you'd like, ten thousandths.

The Lesson

▲▲▲

I began the class by asking the students, "According to a grocery's digital scale, a lobster weighs more than two and fifty-six–hundredths pounds but less than two and fifty-seven–hundredths pounds. How much do you think the lobster weighs?" On the board I wrote:

2.56 lb

2.57 lb

As I expected, I received several confused looks. Marcus replied, "There's nothing in between. Fifty-seven–hundredths comes right after fifty-six–hundredths." No one had a different idea.

"Let me ask a different question," I said. "What if the scale said the lobster weighed between two pounds and three pounds? How much could the lobster weigh?" Several hands now shot up.

Shannon answered, "The lobster could weigh two and a half pounds, couldn't it?"

"Yes, it could," I said. "Could it weigh anything else?" The room was quiet again.

I changed the question: "What if the scale registered the lobster at a weight between two and a half pounds and three pounds? How much could the lobster weigh then?" Still there was no response.

I changed the question again, this time

using a context that was more familiar to the students. "Suppose that Matthew had more than two dollars and fifty cents, but less than three dollars? How much money could Matthew have?"

Jonathan quickly responded, "He could have two dollars and fifty-one cents or two dollars and seventy-five cents or actually anything in between."

"What exactly do you mean by 'actually anything in between'?" I asked.

Jonathan continued, "Well, Matthew could have any amount more than two fifty but not more than three dollars, like two sixty, two seventy, two eighty, two ninety, all the way up to three dollars."

"Does anyone have another way to answer my question of the amount of money Matthew might have?" I asked. My students know that I'm often not satisfied with one answer or one explanation. I encourage students to push their thinking. I want students to see that there are many different ways to approach and solve problems and that it's possible for a problem to have more than one solution.

Elaine suggested, "He could also have different combinations of money between two sixty and two seventy. Matthew could have two sixty-one, two sixty-two, two sixty-three, and so on, all the way up to two seventy. And he could have even more combinations between two eighty and two ninety."

I proceeded by asking, "Is two dollars and ninety cents the most Matthew could have before exceeding three dollars?" Now the room was buzzing and more students were eager to answer.

"No, he can have two ninety-one, two ninety-two, two ninety-three, up to two ninety-nine," Laura answered. "So the most he could have is two ninety-nine."

"How do we know that?" I asked.

Luis explained, "You start with two-ninety and you keep adding cents or pennies until you get to the next dollar."

"Does everyone agree with Luis's thinking?" I inquired. There were nods. "Can anyone explain it another way?"

"It's like you have two dollar bills and nine dimes and if you add one more dime, you'll have three dollars, but you can't go over three dollars," Maria responded. "So you need to add pennies or nickels to your ninety cents until you get close to three bucks."

"So if we all agree that Matthew can't have more than two dollars and ninety-nine cents, what is the least amount of money he can have?" I asked.

Maria continued, "It's the same thing. You have to have more than two fifty, so you start adding pennies to your total. He can have two fifty-one, two fifty-two, two fifty-three, and so on."

"So what's the least amount of money he can have?" I reiterated.

Ian chimed in, "Two fifty-one." Others agreed.

I continued, "So Matthew could have many different combinations of money between two fifty and three dollars just by adding pennies or cents."

The students seemed clear about this, so I presented another version of the lobster question. "What if the digital scale registered the lobster at a weight between two and five-tenths pounds and three pounds? How much could the lobster weigh?" On the board I wrote:

2.5 lb

3 lb

I continued, "With your partner, think about our discussion about money. Decide if there could indeed be measurements between two and five-tenths pounds and three pounds and, if so, discuss the possible weights of the lobster." The students began to discuss in pairs, making connections between money and pounds and deciding on different possible weights. Many students felt that the lobster could weigh anywhere between 2.51 pounds and 2.99 pounds, much as Matthew could have had any amount of money between $2.51 and $2.99.

I then brought the students' attention back to the original question. "According to a grocery's digital scale, a lobster weighs more than two and fifty-sixth–hundredths pounds but less than two and fifty-seven–hundredths pounds. How much do you think the lobster weighs?" I pointed to the board where I had written 2.56 lb and 2.57 lb. "Brainstorm with your partner possible weights in between these. Make sure you and your partner agree on the numbers you come up with, know how to say them, and are able to explain your thinking to the class."

Several pairs of students tried to make a connection between money and weight but quickly realized that there isn't anything smaller than a penny in our money system. Many partners were able to make the assumption that they could add another decimal place behind the last number as they had done when the lobster weighed more than 2.5 pounds—2.561 or 2.562 pounds, for example. However, I noticed that they were having difficulty reading the possible solutions.

The ideal time for teaching is when a need arises for a particular skill or idea. To help students read the decimals they were coming up with, I took the opportunity to explain. I listed three decimals on the board:

   2.5

   2.56

   2.562

I asked for the students' attention and pointed to the decimal numerals on the board. "Let's read the first number aloud together," I said. The students did so easily. I repeated this for the second number, and again the students were able to do this.

"What about the last number?" I asked.

"I noticed that some of you weren't sure how to read numbers with three digits after the decimal point. Any ideas?"

Luis tried. "It's two and five hundred sixty-two something," he said.

"You're right. Now what about the 'something' part?" I asked.

"I remember," Jenny said. "When we had the big cube be one, then the little cube was one thousand." Jenny remembered our earlier exploration with base ten blocks.

"One-thousandth," I corrected, emphasizing the *th* at the end. I wrote on the board:

   one-thousandth

"So if you put together what Luis and Jenny said, the number is two and five hundred sixty-two–thousandths." I pointed to the digits as I read the number. I then had the class say it aloud with me. I also wrote the number on the board using words to help students who find it easier to learn by reading than by listening.

   two and five hundred sixty-two–thousandths

We read the number once more aloud, and then I asked the students for solutions to the question about the in-between weights. As students called out answers, I wrote them on the board. Most agreed that the least the lobster could weigh was 2.561 pounds and the most it could weigh was 2.569 pounds.

Then Blaire, one of my quiet students, timidly raised her hand and asked, "Couldn't the lobster have a lot more weights than that?"

"What do you mean, Blaire?" I asked.

"It's kind of hard to explain," she said.

"Can you come up and show what you think?" I asked. Blaire agreed. She came up and wrote *2.561* on the far left side of the board and *2.569* on the far right. Then, under the number *2.561*, she listed *2.561* nine times. At the end of the first 2.561 in her list, she added a *1* to make it 2.5611. At the end of the second 2.561, she added a *2*. Blaire continued down the list, creating a sequence of numbers each with four decimal places:

2.5611

2.5612

2.5613

2.5614

2.5615

2.5616

2.5617

2.5618

2.5619

Blaire turned around and quietly said, "I think this can go on and on." As she returned to her seat, a buzz broke out in the room. The others seemed impressed. Blaire's writing the numbers in a column and then adding the digits from 1 through 9 opened up for the others a new way of thinking about decimals. She introduced the class to the idea that it was possible to go on infinitely creating numbers between 2.56 and 2.57.

"We haven't yet talked about numbers with four digits after the decimal point," I said. "Does anyone have an idea about how to read the first number in Blaire's list? Talk with your partner."

After a moment, I called on Jose. With a grin, he said, "Two point five six one one." The others laughed. While this is a common way to hear decimals read, the students know that I'm interested in hearing the number read in a way that describes its meaning.

Madison had an idea. "If you follow the pattern, then you do ten times thousandths, but I don't know what it is."

Misha piped up, "Oh! I bet it's ten thousandths."

"How would you read the number?" I asked.

She replied, "Oh, boy, that's hard."

I said, "Listen as I read the first number." I pointed at each digit in 2.5611 as I

said, "It's two and five thousand six hundred eleven–ten thousandths. When you have four digits after the decimal point, the number refers to ten thousandths." I didn't dwell on this any more.

Isaac blurted out, "So what's the answer? What can the lobster weigh?"

"What do you think, Isaac?" I replied.

"I don't think there's one correct answer," he said. "I think there are tons of answers."

Homework

To end the class period, I gave a writing assignment to be completed for homework. I said, "Think about what we discussed today and decide if you agree with Isaac and Blaire. Answer this question." I wrote on the board:

Are there an infinite number of possible weights between 2.56 lbs and 2.57 lbs? Explain your thinking and give examples.

Figures 6–1 through 6–3 show how three students answered this question.

▲▲▲▲▲▲Figure 6–1 *Justin agreed with Blaire and was clear about the infinite number of weights between 2.56 lbs. and 2.57 lbs.*

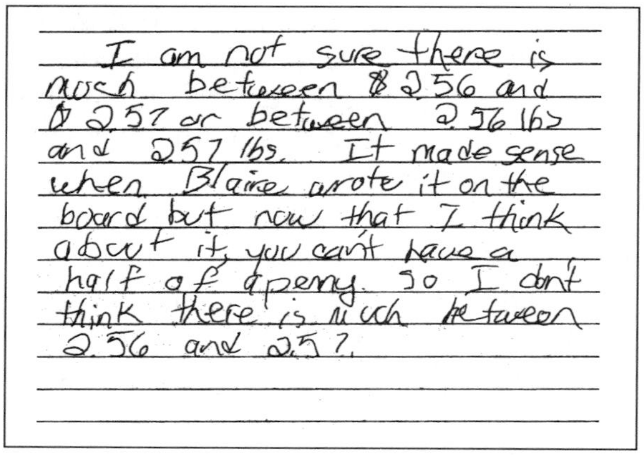

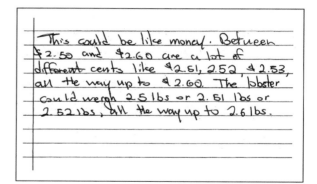

> I am not sure there is much between $2.56 and $2.57 or between 2.56 lbs and 2.57 lbs. It made sense when Blaire wrote it on the board but now that I think about it you can't have a half of a penny. So I don't think there is much between 2.56 and 2.57.

▲▲▲▲▲▲Figure 6–2 *When asked to write, Luis showed that he didn't understand Blaire's explanation.*

> This could be like money. Between $2.50 and $2.60 are a lot of different cents like $2.51, 2.52, $2.53, all the way up to $2.60. The lobster could weigh 2.5 lbs or 2.51 lbs or 2.52 lbs, all the way up to 2.6 lbs.

▲▲▲▲▲▲Figure 6–3 *Matthew wrote that there are weights between 2.56 lbs and 2.57 lbs, but his examples show his lack of understanding.*

Questions and Discussion

▲▲

▲ **Do you think it would be better to teach students about thousandths before giving them the problem of the lobster's weight? Wouldn't that have saved some confusion?**

This is an interesting pedagogical question. It is possible to offer students an explanation before presenting the problem, but the problem itself presents a reason for learning that helps students make sense of new ideas. Students' learning is supported when they can connect new ideas to a context or a purpose.

▲ **How do you respond to students' writing for this homework assignment?**

I think that it's important to respond to assignments, but for one like this where students are clarifying and justifying their thinking, I think the best way is to use their assignments for a class discussion at the beginning of the next period. However, I think some small-group discussion is good preparation first before a whole-class conversation. Sometimes I ask students to exchange papers, read them, and then talk about each other's ideas. Sometimes I ask students to exchange papers in groups of four and then have a small-group discussion. Either way, I'll then initiate a class discussion to find out what agreements they found from reading other papers and what differences they noted. The class discussion is useful for helping me assess the success of my lesson. Also, listening to the conversations they have prior to the class discussion gives me insights into how individual students are thinking.

CHAPTER SEVEN
CONSTANT CALCULATING

Overview

Along with providing students practice reading and representing decimals, this lesson uses the calculator as a learning tool for students to make and test conjectures and investigate patterns when adding decimals. Students use calculators to perform repeated additions, predicting results before they read answers on the display. The lesson helps students think about extending decimals into the thousandths.

Materials

▲ T130 calculators or any other kind with constant function, 1 per student

Time

▲ one class period

Teaching Directions

1. Ask the students to clear their calculators and press the following keys: the plus key, the decimal point, the number 1, and the equals sign. Instruct the students to read aloud the number on the display. Then ask the students to press the equals sign and again read aloud the number on the display. Continue until the number on the display reads 0.9.

2. Ask the students not to press the equals sign yet, but first to predict what number will appear next on the calculator. After discussing their predictions, direct them to press the equals key. Discuss the correct prediction.

3. Next ask the class to press the equals key again and read aloud the number on the display. Continue until the display reads 1.9. Again, ask the students to predict what number will come next before pressing the equals key. Continue adding one-tenth, predicting the outcome, and explaining the results until the display shows 5.

4. Follow the same procedure for adding hundredths on the calculator. Ask the students to clear their calculators and press the following keys: plus, decimal point, 0, 1, and equals. Instruct the students to read aloud each time the number on the display. Stop at .09 and ask students to predict the number that will appear next. Then have them press the equals sign and explain the outcome. Write on the board *.1 = .10* and discuss why the two numbers are equal.

5. Continue adding one-hundredth, reading aloud the number on the display, predicting the next number, and explaining the results. Continue until the display shows .5.

6. Pose the following three questions: "How many more times do you need to press the equals sign so the display shows fifty-six–hundredths? How many more times to reach six-tenths? And then how many more to reach one whole?" Write the numbers on the board:

.56

.6

1

Ask the students first to predict the answer to each and then to test their predictions with their calculators. Allow time for the students to discuss the questions.

7. Pose and discuss another question: "When you add one-hundredth to a number with a nine in the hundredths place, why does the digit in the tenths place increase by one?"

8. Write on the board *2.56* and *2.561*. Ask the students: "What number do we need to add to two and fifty-six–hundredths so that the display shows this number [point to 2.561]?" As students predict, write their suggestions on the board and have the others use their calculators to test them. Record and read aloud an equation for each; for example, *2.56 + .1 = 2.66*. When students figure out that the correct answer is .001, write on the board: *2.56 + .001 = 2.561*. Explain how to read .001 correctly.

9. Continue adding one-thousandth until the display number reads 2.569. Ask students to predict what the next number will be and then press the equals sign. Write *2.58* on the board and ask: "How many more times will you have to press the equals sign so that the display reads two and fifty-eight–hundredths?" After students test their predictions, do the same for the number 2.59.

10. Introduce an assignment for homework or an assessment. Explain: "If you clear your calculator, then press the plus sign, one-thousandth, and the equals sign, you'll see one-thousandth on the display." Write on the board:

Teaching Notes

This activity is appropriate after students have explored decimals to the hundredths with base ten blocks and hundred grids. Working with the base ten blocks, the students were introduced to the value of decimal fractions and were given plenty of opportunities to read and write decimal numbers. The activities posed in this lesson allow the students to further reinforce their understanding of decimal place value and to practice reading, writing, and adding decimal numbers.

The calculator is a useful and effective teaching tool for this lesson. It gives students a way to verify their thinking and encourages them to think about patterns. It helps foster students' thinking as they make predictions and test their ideas. In this way the calculator serves to support children's learning and extend their understanding.

The Lesson

▲▲▲

I began the lesson by asking the students to clear their calculators. I then said, "Press the following keys as I call them out: the plus key, the decimal point, the number one, the equals sign. Let's say together the number on the display."

The students said along with me, "One-tenth."

"Now press the equals sign again," I instructed. "Now what number is on your display?"

The class responded, "Two-tenths."

"Press the equals sign again. What number is on your display?"

"Three-tenths," they said.

I continued having the students press the equals sign and say the decimal number aloud. When their calculators displayed .9, I said, "Don't press the equals sign just yet. What number do you think will come up when we press it again?" Students offered a variety of answers.

"Point ten."

"Ten-tenths."

"One."

"OK, press the equals sign again and see what the display reads."

"Mine has one whole," Crystal answered. The others concurred.

"Why do you think that is?" I asked.

"I'm not sure, but isn't ten-tenths the same thing as one whole?" Crystal asked. "We pressed the equals sign ten times."

Ian explained, "It's like if you have ten dimes, you have one dollar."

I then instructed, "Press the equals sign again and see what number comes up." The students pressed the key and said aloud with me, "One and one-tenth."

We continued in this way, pressing the equals sign and saying the number displayed, until the display showed 1.9. I then asked the students once again not to press the equals sign yet but to predict what they thought would be the next number. This time, most of the students agreed the number would be 2.

I continued having the students press the equals sign and read aloud the numbers as they appeared until the display showed 5.

I then asked, "Can someone explain why a number with a nine in the tenths place changes the whole number when you add another tenth?"

"It's just like the base ten blocks we worked with," Martin said. "It takes ten rods or tenths to make one whole. So on the calculator, if you add one-tenth ten times, you'll also get one whole."

Laura added, "It's like what Michael said. It takes ten dimes to make one dollar so if you have one dollar and ninety cents and you add another dime, you now have two dollars."

ADDING HUNDREDTHS

I asked the students to clear their calculators and then I said, "This time press the following keys as I call them out: the plus key, the decimal point, zero, one, and finally the equals sign. Let's say together the number on the display."

"One-hundredth," they said.

I instructed, "Now press the equals sign again and read aloud the number on the display."

"Two-hundredths," the students responded.

We continued pressing the equals sign and reading the numbers until the display read .09. As I had done when we had reached .9 earlier, I asked the students not to press the equals key yet but to predict what number would come up next.

"Ten-hundredths," several answered in unison. Others weren't sure.

"Press the equal key," I said. Most seemed surprised that the display showed .1.

"How would you build ten-hundredths with base ten blocks when the flat is worth one whole?" I asked.

"You'd use ten of the little unit cubes," Madison answered.

"Hey," Jose said, "you could exchange those for a rod, so it's a tenth. I get it."

"What do you get?" I asked.

"Ten-hundredths is the same as one-tenth, so you can just write 'point one' like the calculator did."

"It's the same with money," Leslee added. "You can have ten pennies or one dime. They're both ten-hundredths of a dollar."

I added, "The only difference is that when we write money, we always show both the dimes and the pennies. Whether I have ten pennies or one dime, I write it the same way." I wrote on the board:

$.10

I continued, "But if I'm not talking about money, I don't have to include the zero in the hundredths place. It's OK to write it either way." I wrote on the board:

.1

.10

Rory asked, "But doesn't the first one mean one-tenth and the second one mean ten-hundredths?"

I responded, "If you were talking about the blocks you used to build the number, you would be right. Mathematically, however, both numbers are worth the same amount. One-tenth and ten-hundredths are equal." I wrote on the board using both decimals and fractions:

$$.1 = .10$$

$$\frac{1}{10} = \frac{10}{100}$$

I then said, "Before you press the equals sign again, predict what number will appear next."

"I think after ten-hundredths comes eleven-hundredths," Patrice said.

"Let's try it," I said.

They pressed the equals sign and read aloud, "Eleven-hundredths."

I asked, "How many more times do you think I will need to press the equals sign so that the display will read two-tenths?" I wrote on the board:

.2

Students made predictions. Some were able to think of two-tenths as the same as twenty-hundredths. Others still were making this connection and weren't sure how to think about my question. When they tried it, they found out that .2 appeared on the display after they pressed the equals sign nine more times.

I said, "I know that some of you were thinking that after nineteen-hundredths, twenty-hundredths should come. But the display on your calculator shows two-tenths. Who can explain this?"

Misha said, "They're the same. If you make twenty-hundredths with blocks, you have twenty cubes. And then you can exchange them for two rods. So they're the same."

I continued the activity with the class, pressing the equals sign and reading the numbers until the display showed .5.

I then posed some questions for the students to work on in groups. "How many more times do you need to press the equals sign so the display goes from five-tenths to fifty-six–hundredths? How many more times to reach six-tenths? And then how many more to reach one whole?" I wrote on the board:

.56

.6

1

I added, "Share your ideas with your group and then test them with your calculators."

After the groups had a chance to discuss these questions, I called them back to attention and asked, "When you add one-hundredth to a number with a nine in the hundredths place, why does the digit in the tenths place increase by one?"

"This is like pennies and dimes. It takes ten pennies to make one dime and if I have nine cents and add one more penny, I now have ten cents or one dime," Crystal proudly responded.

"Does anyone have another way to explain this?"

Rory said, "It takes ten-hundredths to make one-tenth, and one hundred–hundredths to make one whole."

ADDING THOUSANDTHS

I then wrote on the board:

2.56

This was the weight I had used for the *Lobster* problem (see Chapter 6), but any number with hundredths would do as well. "Clear your calculator and enter two and fifty-six–hundredths." I gave them a moment to do so.

I then asked, "What number do we need to add on to two and fifty-six–hundredths so that the display shows this number?" I wrote on the board:

2.561

"I think one," Martin offered.

I said, "Let's try it. Press plus, then one, then the equals sign." As the students did this, I recorded on the board, entering the answer the students got:

2.56 + 1 = 3.56

"Let's read aloud the math sentence I wrote," I said. We read aloud, "Two and fifty-six–hundredths plus one equals three and fifty-six–hundredths."

"Who has another suggestion?" I asked.

"Point one," Kendra said.

I said, "Let's try it. First clear your calculator and again enter two and fifty-six–hundredths. Then press plus, decimal point, one, and equals." Again I recorded on the board and had the class read the sentence aloud with me:

2.56 + .1 = 2.66

"Try plus one-hundredth," Damon said. The students did this, I recorded, and we read aloud:

2.56 + .01 = 2.57

"It has to be plus point zero zero one," Chen said. A cheer went up in the room after the class tested Chen's suggestion. I recorded:

2.56 + .001 = 2.561

I said, "So Chen's suggestion gave the correct answer." We read the number Chen suggested to add as "one-thousandth." I wrote this on the board:

one-thousandth

"The one is in the thousandths place. Who would like to try reading the answer?" I pointed to 2.561. Kim read it correctly, and then I had the class read the entire mathematical sentence aloud with me.

"If we press the equals sign again, what number will be on the display? Let's say it together aloud," I asked the class.

"Two and five hundred sixty-two–thousandths," they responded.

The students continued pressing the equals sign and reading the numbers aloud. When the display read 2.569, I asked the students to predict the next number and then to press the equals sign. A few students were surprised that the display went from 2.569 to 2.57 instead of going to 3.

"How many more times will you have to press the equals sign to make the display read two and fifty-eight–hundredths?" I asked. I wrote on the board:

2.58

The students made predictions and then they tried it. They repeated this for 2.59.

Homework

To introduce the homework assignment, I explained, "If you clear your calculator, then press the plus sign, one-thousandth, and the equals sign, you'll see one-thousandth on the display." I wrote on the board:

+

.001

=

I then said, "If you continue to press the equals sign, the calculator will add one-thousandth each time. Predict what the next three numbers will be, then try it. Record the numbers that come up each time and then, next to each, write the number in words." I modeled for the students by writing out *one-thousandth* on the board:

+

.001   one-thousandth

=

I continued, "Figure out how many times altogether you'd have to press the equals sign, including the three times you already pressed it, so that one-tenth would appear on the display. Then figure out the total number of times it would take to show one whole. Explain how you figured." I wrote on the board:

How many times in all do you need to press the = sign to reach 0.1?

How many times in all do you need to press the = sign to reach 1?

See Figure 7–1 for one student's response to this problem.

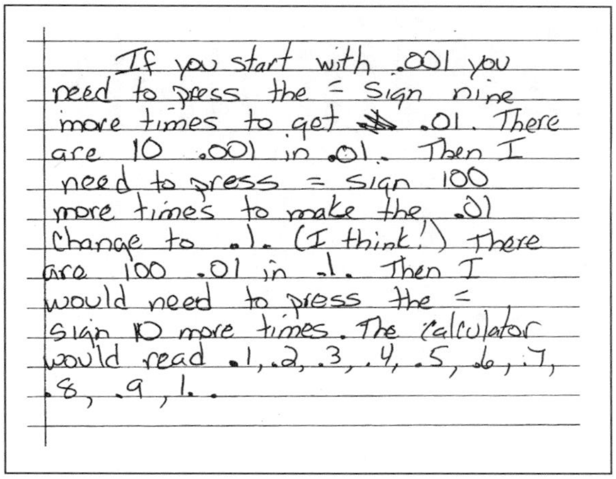
If you start with .001 you need to press the = sign nine more times to get .01. There are 10 .001 in .01. Then I need to press = sign 100 more times to make the .01 change to .1. (I think!) There are 100 .01 in .1. Then I would need to press the = sign 10 more times. The calculator would read .1, .2, .3, .4, .5, .6, .7, .8, .9, 1.

Figure 7–1 ***While Blaire was correct about how many times she needed to press the equals sign to reach 0.1, her other solutions aren't correct.***

Questions and Discussion

▲ *Do you supply calculators for students or do they bring their own?*

I have a class set of calculators and an overhead calculator as part of my regular instructional supplies for teaching math. Calculators are another tool that students use to learn mathematics, just as they use pencils, paper, rulers, books, manipulative materials, and other supplies. However, some students bring to school their own calculators and I think it's fine for them to use their own.

▲ *If students use their own calculators, how do you deal with the differences among them?*

Calculators do differ, and it's good experience for students to become comfortable working with a variety of calculators. Students benefit from the experience of using different calculators as tools for thinking and learning.

▲ *I notice that you often write decimals on the board when you say them out loud. Is this necessary?*

There are always students who have difficulty interpreting decimals symbolically, and especially so when a number is just given verbally. I try to remember to record decimals on the board when I give them orally. This is useful both for those students who have difficulty with oral instructions and for those students who are still shaky in general about how to represent decimals.

CHAPTER EIGHT
THE SUM AND DIFFERENCE GAME

Overview

Students need practice adding, subtracting, and comparing decimals, and this game provides repeated experiences doing so. Students use a die and a place value spinner to generate two numbers. They find the sum and the difference of the two numbers, compare them with an opponent's sum and difference, and then use the flip of the coin to determine whether the greater or the smaller results score points.

Materials

▲ place value spinner divided into thirds for "tenths," "hundredths," and "thousandths," 1 per pair of student (see Place Value Spinner Directions, Blackline Masters)

▲ dice, 1 per pair of students

▲ coins, 1 per pair of students

▲ *Sam and Sally* worksheet, 1 per student (see Blackline Masters)

▲ optional: rules for the *Sum and Difference* game (see Blackline Masters)

▲ optional: directions for making a place value spinner (see Blackline Masters)

Time

▲ one class period, plus additional time for playing

Teaching Directions

1. Introduce the rules for the *Sum and Difference* game by playing a practice round with the class. (See Blackline Masters for the rules.) Model for students how to line up decimal points when writing numbers in a column.

2. Allow the remaining class time for students to play the game in pairs.

3. For homework, distribute the *Sam and Sally* worksheet. Be sure that the students understand the sums and differences that Sam and Sally computed and the problem they are to solve.

Teaching Notes

When introducing this game, it's helpful to focus on eliciting students' strategies for adding and subtracting, rather than on teaching specific computation procedures. This encourages students to make sense of the numbers to be added and subtracted. If, after modeling a round with the class, you think that the students need further help doing computations on their own, play several more rounds and continue to have students present their methods for class discussion.

The game is a game of luck and doesn't give students a chance to think strategically. However, the homework assignment extends the context of the game into a problem-solving challenge in which students search for pairs of numbers that, when added and subtracted, can produce a winning sum yet a losing difference. Searching for these numbers not only gives students additional practice computing with decimals but also gives them a chance to think about numerical relationships.

About the place value spinners: It's easy for students to construct them, especially if you model making one for the class. Having students make the spinners not only saves you the work of creating all of the spinners you need but also fosters the students' participation with the activity.

The Lesson

▲▲

I introduced the rules for playing the *Sum and Difference* game by first telling the class, "This is a game for two players. You need a place value spinner, a die, a coin, and pencil and paper for each player. We'll play a few rounds together, the class against me, and then you'll break into pairs and play the game against your opponent. The first thing you do is roll a die." I rolled a die and a 3 came up.

I held up the spinner. "Then you spin the spinner. The place value you spin—tenths, hundredths, or thousandths—determines the value of the number you

rolled." I gave the spinner to Chen and asked him to spin it for me. It landed on hundredths.

I said, "So my first number is three-hundredths." I wrote *.03* on the board. "Now I repeat this to create a second number." I rolled the die and reported that a 5 came up. Chen spun the spinner and said, "It came up tenths."

"So what's my second number?" I asked.

"Five-tenths," responded the class. I wrote *.5* on the board.

I explained, "Now I write two problems using my numbers, an addition problem and a subtraction problem." On the board, I wrote an addition problem, lining up the decimal points:

.03
+ .5

Before writing the subtraction problem, I said, "For the subtraction problem, make sure you record the larger number on top and the smaller number underneath. Which number is larger, three-hundredths or five-tenths?"

"Five-tenths," the students chorused. If the answer had been tentative, or if only a few students had responded, I would have taken time to talk about this. But since the students were confident, I recorded on the board:

.5
– .03

I pointed to the addition problem. "What's the sum?" I asked.

"Fifty-three–hundredths," Jose responded.

"How did you figure out the answer?" I asked.

Jose explained, "Five-tenths is the same as fifty-hundredths. Fifty-hundredths plus three-hundredths makes fifty-three–hundredths." I recorded the answer:

.03
+ .5
.53

I then said, "Can anyone picture in your head how you could add these numbers with base ten blocks?" I called on Isabella.

She said, "You'd have three units and five rods, and that's the same as what Jose got. The five stands for the rods and the three for the units."

Kendra added, "You could exchange the five rods for units and you'd have fifty of them, plus the three extras makes fifty-three units, and that's fifty-three–hundredths."

I then pointed to the subtraction problem. "And what's the answer when we subtract? What's the difference between the two numbers?" I asked.

"It would be forty-seven–hundredths," Crystal said.

"How do you know this?"

"It's like what Jose said, five-tenths is the same as fifty-hundredths. So I subtracted three-hundredths from fifty-hundredths," Crystal responded.

"It's the same with the base ten blocks," Damon said. "If you make the rods into units, you'll have fifty. Take away three and you have forty-seven."

Misha had another idea. "You wouldn't have to exchange all of the rods. Just change one into ten units, then take away three. You'll have four rods and seven units, and that's four-tenths and seven-hundredths." I wrote on the board:

.5 = .4 + .10

"So you're saying that five-tenths is the same as four-tenths plus ten-hundredths?" I asked Misha.

She answered, "Yes, so you take away the three-hundredths and then you have seven-hundredths. Plus the four-tenths." I knew that not all of the other students understood Misha's reasoning, so I recorded to help students follow her thinking:

.4 + .10 - .03 = .4 + .07 = .47

"That's it," Misha said.

"Did anyone do it a different way?" I asked.

Ian said, "I turned five-tenths into five dimes, and that's fifty cents. Then I subtracted three cents to get forty-seven cents. That's forty-seven–hundredths." I recorded the answer to the subtraction problem:

.5
– .03
.47

"So I have a sum of fifty-three–hundredths and a difference of forty-seven–hundredths. Now you have to roll, spin, and figure out your sum and difference. Let's see what you get."

I asked Blaire to roll the die and Leslee to spin the spinner. The two numbers they generated were four-thousandths and six-tenths. The two girls came up and Blaire recorded the two problems, carefully lining up the decimal points:

$$.004$$
$$+.6$$

$$.6$$
$$-.004$$

I said, "Let's get some help from the class for finding the answers. Talk at your tables and then we'll share ideas." As the tables worked, I talked with Blaire and Leslee about their ideas. Then I called the class to attention.

"What's the sum of these two numbers?" I asked.

"I think it's point six zero four," Luis said. I wrote .604 on the board.

"Can you read that number?" I asked.

Luis looked down at his paper and said, "Six hundred four–thousandths."

"I got point zero one zero," Kim said. I wrote .010 on the board.

"Hmm, so we have two different answers. Luis, can you explain what you did?"

Luis came to the front of the room and said, "I know I have six-tenths, and that's the same as sixty-hundredths or six hundred–thousandths. So I wrote this." He recorded on the board:

$$.600$$
$$+.004$$

Luis continued, "Six hundred–thousandths plus four-thousandths is six hundred four–thousandths."

Kim said, "Oh, I see what I did. I put the six under the four and added. It looked right, but if you think about it, why would I add thousandths to tenths? I want to change my answer; I think Luis is right." Blaire nodded and wrote the sum on the board:

$$.004$$
$$+.6$$
$$.604$$

"What's the difference between the two numbers?" I asked.

"We got five hundred ninety-six–thousandths," Rory said. "We put the larger number on top, which is six-tenths, and the four-thousandths on the bottom. But it looked funny. So we added two zeros behind the six and then subtracted." I wrote on the board:

$$.600$$
$$-.004$$
$$.596$$

"Why did you add zeros?" I probed.

"Like Luis said, six-tenths is the same thing as six hundred–thousandths," Rory responded.

Misha had thought about subtracting in a different way. She explained, "I left five of the six-tenths alone. Then I took the other and changed it into ten-hundredths, but I still couldn't take away four-thousandths. So I left nine of the hundredths and changed the last one into ten-thousandths. Then it was easy to take away the four-thousandths. So I had six-thousandths, nine-hundredths, and five-tenths."

"What answer did you get?" I asked.

"The same as Rory," she answered. Again, not all of the students could follow Misha's reasoning, but I didn't take time to dwell on how she had figured. I felt it was better to keep moving with the directions for playing the game. Then I could deal with computation issues with the students individually as they played.

I explained, "Once you and your opponent have your sums and differences, then you compare them to decide who scores. First we'll do the sums. I had fifty-three–hundredths, and you had six hundred four–thousandths." I pointed to .53 and .604 on the board and then continued, "To decide who scores a point, we need to flip a coin. Heads up means the larger number wins, and tails up means the smaller number wins."

Leslee flipped the penny I gave her. "Tails!" she exclaimed with a grin, but then she added, "Uh oh, that's not good news. We lose."

"What were you thinking when you seemed pleased?" I asked her.

Leslee said, "I was thinking that tenths are bigger than thousandths and since we had thousandths, our number was smaller. But then I realized that we have six-tenths and four-thousands, and you only have five-tenths. So you get a point."

"Do you agree?" I asked the class. The students nodded.

"Who scores a point for the difference?" I asked. I pointed to the differences, .47 and .596.

"You do again," Chen said.

"So you get two points?" Francesca asked.

"Yes, that round would be over and I would have two points," I answered. "Does anyone have any questions?"

"What if your opponent adds or subtracts wrong?" Misha asked.

"When you play, you both have to agree that the answers are correct. If you can't agree, ask someone else to help you or let me know. If you catch someone else's error, you get two extra points." If Misha hadn't raised the ques-

tion, I would have explained the rule about the extra points for finding a computation error.

I gave a few last directions. "You'll each play against one opponent, not in pairs as we did. Also, we just played one round. A complete game has ten rounds. Then both players count up points to see who is the winner."

For the remainder of the class period, students played the game. The students were fully engaged. By the end of the week, the students had a firm understanding of why the decimal points must be aligned and made fewer computation errors with decimal numbers that were of different values.

Homework

I presented a game scenario to the class. I said, "Sam and Sally were playing. Sam's two numbers were three-tenths and one-tenth. Sally's were three-tenths and two-tenths." I wrote on the board .3 and .1, and then .3 and .2.

I continued, "Sam flipped the coin and it came up heads, so the larger sum and difference would score. Sally's sum won, but Sam's difference won." I stopped to write Sam and Sally's numbers on the board and do the calculations with the class.

I then presented the homework assignment, "Figure out other numbers that would split the score. Do this for three other rounds." I distributed the *Sam and Sally* worksheet. Figures 8–1 and 8–2 show two students' responses to this assignment.

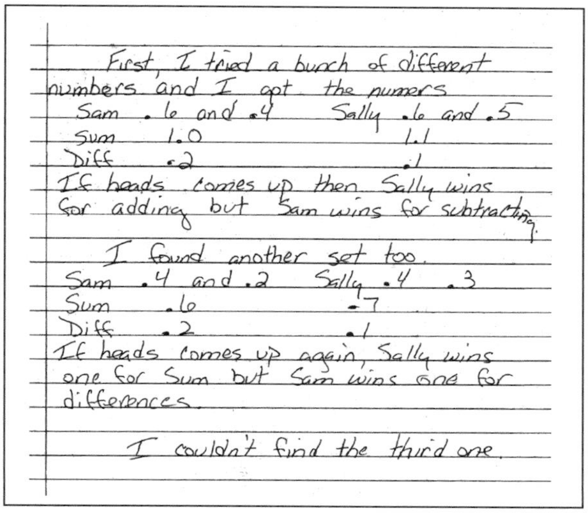

First, I tried a bunch of different numbers and I got the numbers
Sam .6 and .4   Sally .6 and .5
Sum   1.0   1.1
Diff   .2   .1
If heads comes up then Sally wins for adding but Sam wins for subtracting.

I found another set too.
Sam .4 and .2   Sally .4   .3
Sum   .6   .7
Diff   .2   .1
If heads comes up again, Sally wins one for Sum but Sam wins one for differences.

I couldn't find the third one.

▲▲▲▲▲▲**Figure 8–1** *Justin reported that he was able to find two possible combinations of numbers that split the score.*

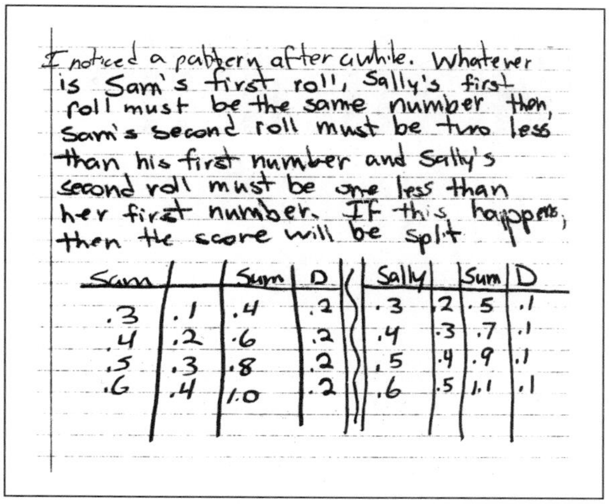

I noticed a pattern after awhile. Whatever is Sam's first roll, Sally's first roll must be the same number then, Sam's second roll must be two less than his first number and Sally's second roll must be one less than her first number. If this happens, then the score will be split.

Sam		Sum	D	Sally		Sum	D
.3	.1	.4	.2	.3	.2	.5	.1
.4	.2	.6	.2	.4	.3	.7	.1
.5	.3	.8	.2	.5	.4	.9	.1
.6	.4	1.0	.2	.6	.5	1.1	.1

▲▲▲▲▲▲**Figure 8–2** *Chen organized his data and looked for patterns to solve the problem.*

Questions and Discussion

▲▲

▲ ***My students understand that the sum is the answer to an addition problem, but they don't seem to know that the difference is the answer to a subtraction problem. How do you teach this?***

I've had the same situation. I think that students typically think about subtraction as taking away, and the word *difference* doesn't seem to relate to what's left. Also, in common usage, they understand what *difference* means, and this doesn't connect to subtraction. Probably *left-over* would be easier for them to remember than *difference*. However, *difference* is the correct word, so I'm sure to use it as often as possible. Repeated experiences will help students become familiar and comfortable with the terminology. It may help, as I did, to explain the word *difference* as you use it. For example, in the first problem in the lesson, I asked, "And what's the answer when we subtract? What's the difference between the two numbers?"

▲ ***How do you handle the situation where students continue to make errors?***

From time to time as students play the game, it's helpful to have a class discussion about computing the sum and the difference, much as I did when I introduced the game. Discussions that focus on making sense of the numbers and the procedures for adding and subtracting are essential for building students' understanding. If students continue to have problems, I find time to work with them individually.

CHAPTER NINE
INTRODUCING PERCENTS

Overview

This lesson builds on what students already know about percents and helps them think about how fractions, decimals, and percents connect. After discussing what they already know about percents, students shade in different numbers of squares on 10-by-10 grids. For each grid, they represent the amount shaded with fractions, decimals, and percents.

Materials

▲ *10-by-10 Grids* worksheets, 2 per student (see Blackline Masters)

Time

▲ one class period

Teaching Directions

1. Initiate a discussion about the meaning of percents by asking the following questions and having students discuss each: "Can someone tell me what you think one hundred percent means?" "What does a coach mean when he says he wants you to give one hundred and ten percent?" "If I have a two percent chance of winning the raffle at our school fair, what do you think about my chances?" "Can anyone explain in his or her own words what the word *percent* means?" Inform the students that the word *percent* is derived from the Latin *per centum*, which means "per hundred" or "out of one hundred."

2. Continue the discussion by posing several problems: *(1) If there were one hundred problems on a test, what would a score of one hundred percent mean? (2) If there* were only twenty problems on a test, not one hundred, how many would you have to answer correctly to get a score of one hundred percent? (3) If you only answered ten problems out of twenty correctly, what would your score be?

3. Discuss that twenty out of twenty questions is the same as one hundred out of one hundred, and that ten out of twenty is the same as fifty out of one hundred. Write on the board:

> 100 out of 100 = 100%
>
> 20 out of 20 = 100%
>
> 50 out of 100 = 50%
>
> 10 out of 20 = 50%

4. Discuss the relationship between percents and decimals by asking: "How do you think percents are related to decimals? What percent of the whole is one-tenth? What percent of the whole is twenty-five–hundredths?" Write on the board:

> 0.1 is 10% of one whole
>
> 0.25 is 25% of one whole

5. Distribute to each student the worksheet of 10-by-10 grids. Ask the students to shade in three small squares on the first grid. Then ask the students how to represent the shaded part of the grid as a fraction, a decimal, and a percent of the grid. As students respond, record on the board and then instruct the students to write each representation underneath the grids they shaded on their worksheets:

> $\frac{3}{100}$
>
> .03
>
> 3%

6. Next ask students to shade in three columns on the second grid. Then ask the students how to represent the shaded part of the grid as a fraction, a decimal, and a percent of the grid. As students respond, record on the board and then instruct the students to write each representation on their worksheets:

> $\frac{30}{100}$
>
> $\frac{3}{10}$
>
> .30
>
> .3
>
> 30%

7. Present a third problem: *In the next grid, shade in two complete columns and then seven more squares.* Again ask the students how to represent this part of the grid as a fraction, a decimal, and a percent of the grid. As the students respond, record on the board and then instruct students to record on their worksheets.

$\frac{27}{100}$

.27

27%

$\frac{2}{10} + \frac{7}{100}$

.2 + .07

0.2 + 0.07

8. Present a fourth problem: *In the next grid, shade in three complete columns plus two more squares.* Again ask the students how to represent this part of the grid as a fraction, a decimal, and a percent of the grid. As the students respond, record on the board and then instruct students to record on their worksheets.

$\frac{32}{100}$

.32

32%

$\frac{3}{10} + \frac{2}{100}$

.3 + .02

0.3 + 0.02

9. Give a new direction: "Shade in one whole grid and fifty-six–hundredths on the next grid. Once you've done this, discuss at your table as many ways as you can to represent this numerically." After several minutes have the students share their solutions and write them on the board. For example:

1.56

156%

$1 \frac{56}{100}$

1.56

$1 + \frac{5}{10} + \frac{6}{100}$

1 + .5 + .06

100% + 56%

10. Give a final direction for the worksheet: "Shade in two wholes and forty–hundredths. Then discuss at your table as many ways as you can to represent this numerically." After several minutes have the students share their solutions and write them on the board. For example:

2.40

2.4

240%

$\frac{240}{100}$

$\frac{24}{10}$

$2 + \frac{4}{10}$

$2 + \frac{40}{100}$

11. For homework, distribute to each student a blank worksheet. Instruct the students: "Color in a part of each grid. Then in as many ways as you can, use fractions, decimals, and percents to represent the amounts you shaded."

Teaching Notes

Percents are both similar to and different from decimals. They are similar in that .75 lb is the same as 75% of a pound. However, while decimal numerals can also represent particular quantities, percents are ratios that always represent a portion of a given amount. If we're talking about all of something, then we're talking about 100 percent of it; half of it is 50 percent. But while we can locate a number like 0.75 on a number line, we don't do so with percents. It's important to talk with students both about how percents and decimals are different and how they relate.

A tip for teaching this lesson: To keep from getting confused, I find it helpful to make the distinction between "grids" and "squares." I reserve using "squares" for the one hundred small squares that make up each grid.

The Lesson

▲▲

Can someone tell me what you think one hundred percent means?" I asked to begin the lesson.

Madison answered, "It means you got all of the questions correct on a test."

"Anyone else?"

"It means you did as best as you could," Kendra said.

Jonathan added, "You can't do better than one hundred percent. If you eat all the pizza, you ate one hundred percent of it. Or if you made all of the free throws, you made one hundred percent of them." While Jonathan's comment was correct in relation to the examples he gave, it implied that you couldn't have more than 100 percent of anything. To deal with this possible misconception, I posed another question.

"What does a coach mean when he says, 'I want you to give a hundred and ten percent?'" I asked.

"He's trying to tell the team he wants them to do their best and to try really, really hard throughout the whole game," Shannon replied.

"It's like he wants you to try to do even better than you thought you could," Ian added.

"If I have a two percent chance of winning the raffle at our school fair, what do you think about my chances?" I asked.

"Not so good!" Martin said. "You only have two out of a hundred chances to win."

"You have a ninety-eight percent chance of losing," added Chen.

"Can anyone explain in his or her own words what the word *percent* means?"

"I think it's something out of a hundred," Patrice said.

"Why do you think that?" I probed.

"Well, the best you can do is get one hundred percent, so it must be out of a hundred. It's like if there are a hundred questions on a test and I get all of them right, I get one hundred percent," Patrice answered.

"I agree with what you said, Patrice. Percent is actually derived from the Latin *per centum*, which means 'per hundred' or 'out of one hundred.'"

I then asked another question to push the students' thinking further. "Suppose there were only twenty problems on a test, not one hundred. How many would you have to answer correctly to get a score of one hundred percent?"

"All twenty," Ian said.

"So if we think of percent as being 'out of one hundred' as Jose said, how can twenty problems be one hundred percent?" I asked.

"Because it's all of them," Leslee said.

Elaine added, "It's twenty out of twenty, and that's the same as a hundred out of a hundred."

"And if you answered only ten out of twenty problems correctly, what would your score be?" I asked.

"It would be fifty percent," Maria replied.

"So ten out of twenty problems would give the same grade as fifty out of one hundred problems?" I asked. This seemed clear to the students. I wrote on the board:

100 out of 100 = 100%

20 out of 20 = 100%

50 out of 100 = 50%

10 out of 20 = 50%

"How do you think percents are related to decimals?" I asked.

"The unit block from the base ten blocks is worth one-hundredth because it takes a hundred of them to make a whole,

and one percent is one-hundredth, too," answered Matthew.

"Does anyone else have another idea about how to explain the relationship between percents and decimals?"

Blaire said, "I'm not sure how it's connected to the tenths, but it's the same as the hundredths. It takes one hundred units to make one whole, and it takes a hundred of one percents to make one hundred percent."

"What percent of a whole is one-tenth?" I asked.

"It has to be ten percent," Jonathan said. "It takes ten ten percents to make one hundred percent." I wrote on the board:

0.1 is 10% of one whole

"What percent of the whole is twenty-five–hundredths?" I asked.

Crystal answered, "It has to be twenty-five." I wrote on the board:

0.25 is 25% of one whole

SHADING GRIDS

I then distributed to each student a worksheet that contained nine 10-by-10 grids on it. I said, "I'm going to ask you to shade in parts of these grids and then think about how to represent what you've shaded with fractions, decimals, and percents. But first, how many small squares are there on each grid?" I asked. The students quickly verified that each was a 10-by-10 grid with one hundred squares.

I then said, "On the first grid on your worksheet, shade in three small squares." I gave the students a moment to do so. Most shaded in three squares at the top of the grid, but a few shaded in three squares scattered on the grid.

"What fractional part of the grid did you shade?" I asked.

"Three out of a hundred," Rory said. I wrote on the board:

$$\frac{3}{100}$$

"How could we write this as a decimal?" I asked.

"You can write decimal point, zero, three, because each square represents one-hundredth and we colored in three of them," Susan answered. I wrote on the board:

.03

"Why do we need the zero?" I asked.

"A column is a tenth. We didn't shade in a whole column, so we don't have any tenths," Chen said.

"That's why you have to put a zero in the tenths place," Blaire added.

"What percent of the grid is shaded in?" I asked.

"Three percent," several students replied in unison. I wrote on the board:

3%

"Why?"

"Because percent means out of one hundred and we shaded in three out of a hundred," Frank said.

"Write underneath your first grid what three small squares represent with a fraction, a decimal numeral, and a percent," I said. I pointed to the $\frac{3}{100}$, .03, and 3% I had recorded on the board.

After the students had recorded on their worksheets, I gave a new direction. I said, "On the second grid, shade in three complete columns." I gave the students time to do this.

"What fractional part of the grid did you shade?" I asked.

"Thirty squares out of a hundred," Jose said.

Shannon added, "A column is a tenth, so three-tenths is shaded in if we look only at the columns." I wrote on the board:

$\frac{30}{100}$

$\frac{3}{10}$

If Shannon hadn't suggested this alternative, I would have written $\frac{3}{10}$ on the board along with $\frac{30}{100}$ and asked who could explain why three-tenths was another rep-

resentation for what they had shaded. Or, if the students had suggested only three-tenths, I would have written $\frac{30}{100}$ on the board for them to explain.

"How can we write what you shaded as a decimal?" I asked.

"Since it's thirty out of a hundred, we can put decimal point and then thirty," Jonathan answered.

"Or we can just put decimal point and three," Misha said.

"Why?"

"Because each column represents one-tenth and we have three columns shaded in," Misha explained. As with the fractional representation, if no students had suggested the alternative, I would have recorded it and asked the class why it made sense. I wrote on the board:

.30

.3

"What percent of the grid did you shade?" I asked.

"Thirty percent," Crystal said. I wrote on the board:

30%

"Underneath your second grid, write these fraction, decimal, and percent notations," I instructed. The class quickly recorded.

"Let's do another one together. In the next grid, shade in two complete columns and then seven more squares."

When the students had done this, I asked, "What part of the grid did you shade?"

"Twenty-seven–hundredths," Peter said.

"Can we name it anything else?"

"Twenty-seven out of a hundred," Maria said.

"Twenty-seven percent," Kim said.

"We could say two-tenths and seven-hundredths," Francesca answered.

"How could we write each of these?"

Each student who gave a suggestion came up and recorded:

$\frac{27}{100}$

.27

27%

$\frac{2}{10} + \frac{7}{100}$

Damon had another suggestion for recording Francesca's idea. He came up and wrote:

.2 + .07

Then Susan raised a hand to show another way. She came up and wrote:

0.2 + 0.07

Mark raised a hand to show his idea. He came up and wrote:

$\frac{2}{10} + .07$

I thought for a moment and then said, "Both of these make sense mathematically. We often see decimal numerals written with a zero in the ones place. And Mark, what you did is mix together a fraction and a decimal numeral." Mark grinned and nodded.

I continued, "Even though what you wrote makes sense, it's not something that's done. There's nothing wrong with what you wrote, but it is unusual, and it doesn't follow the convention that mathematicians use. It's a good idea to keep fractions with fractions and decimals with decimals."

I asked the students to write these representations under the grids on their worksheets. Then I gave a new direction: "Shade in one whole grid and fifty-six–hundredths on the next grid. Once you've done this, discuss at your table as many ways as you can to represent what you shaded numerically." After several minutes the students were ready to report and I called on Madison and Adam.

Madison reported, "We came up with

three different ways—one and fifty-six–hundredths, one hundred fifty-six percent, and one hundred fifty-six out of one hundred." As Madison reported, Adam wrote on the board:

1.56

156%

$\frac{156}{100}$

"Can you explain what you mean by the last one, one hundred fifty-six out of one hundred?" I asked.

Madison replied, "Since one whole grid was shaded in, we had one hundred squares colored, plus the fifty-six squares colored in the second grid makes one hundred fifty-six. Since it's out of hundredths, we put one hundred as the denominator."

"Did anyone else come up with another way to name or represent this number?"

"We came up with two more ways," Kendra said. She came up and wrote:

$1 + \frac{56}{100}$

$1\frac{56}{100}$

"Any other ways?" I asked.

Jose raised a hand. "I just thought of one more. It's like Kendra's but different." He came up and recorded:

1 + .56

"So you used Kendra's ideas but used decimal notation," I said. Jose nodded.

"Any other ways?" I asked again.

Damon raised a hand. "I don't have another way, but I don't get the one hundred fifty-six percent."

"Can you tell me more about what confuses you?" I asked.

"It's more than a hundred percent, and I thought that was the most," Damon answered. This common misconception comes up often when students are studying decimals and percents.

I turned the question to the class. "Can

anyone explain why one hundred fifty-six percent makes sense?" I asked.

Crystal tried first. She turned to Damon and asked, "Do you get why one whole grid is one hundred percent?" Damon nodded. Crystal continued, "So if you have fifty-six percent of another grid, just add them up." She recorded as she talked:

100% + 56% = 156%

"But you couldn't get one hundred fifty-six percent as a grade on a test," Damon said, still not convinced.

Misha piped up, "You could if there were extra credit problems and you got them all right."

Damon considered Misha's idea for a minute and then said, "Yeah, you could."

I then said, "It's important to remember that one percent is a part of a whole, one-hundredth of the whole. Each small square is worth one percent of a grid. OK so far, Damon?" He nodded.

"For this example, you shaded in one hundred fifty-six small squares, or one hundred fifty-six–hundredths." Damon nodded again. I wasn't sure that Damon was totally sure about percents greater than 100 percent, but I knew that he would have many other opportunities to confront this same idea. I then gave time for the students to record all of the different representations on their worksheets.

For a final direction for the worksheet, I said, "Shade in two wholes and forty hundredths. Then discuss at your table how to represent numerically what you shaded."

After students had reported and recorded on the board several ways, I asked, "Can we also say twenty-four–tenths?" I wrote on the board:

$$\frac{24}{10}$$

There were many blank expressions, so I probed a little further. "How many tenths make up one grid or one whole?"

"Ten."

"And how many tenths are colored in the first grid?"

"Ten."

"How many are colored in the second grid?"

"Ten."

"And how many tenths are colored in the third grid?

"Four."

"So how many total tenths or columns are shaded?" Finally, several faces lit up.

Elaine explained, "We have twenty-four columns or tenths colored. That's why you can also write twenty-four over ten." Figures 9–1 through 9–3 (see pages 70–72) show three students' claswork.

Homework

For homework, I distributed to each student a blank worksheet. I said, "Color in a part of each grid and then represent the amount you shaded in as many ways as you can, using fractions, decimals, and percents." (See Figures 9–4 and 9–5 on pages 73 and 74.)

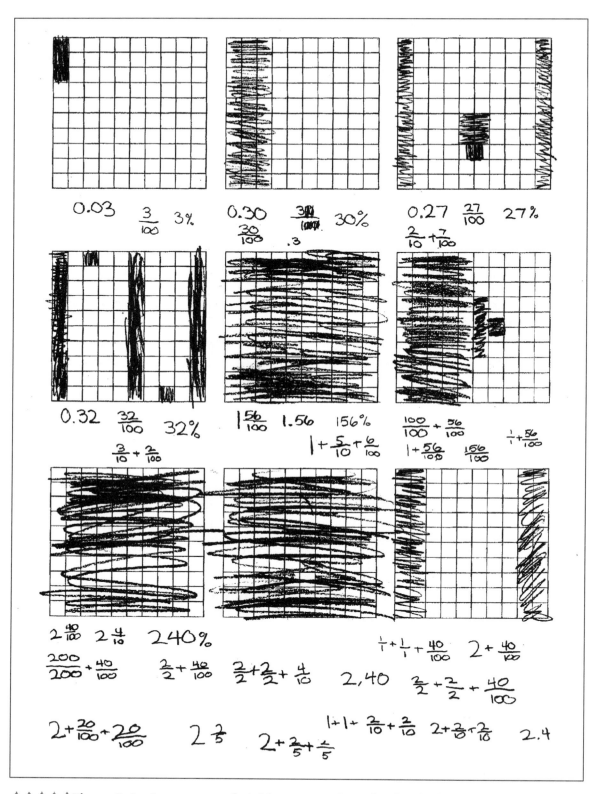

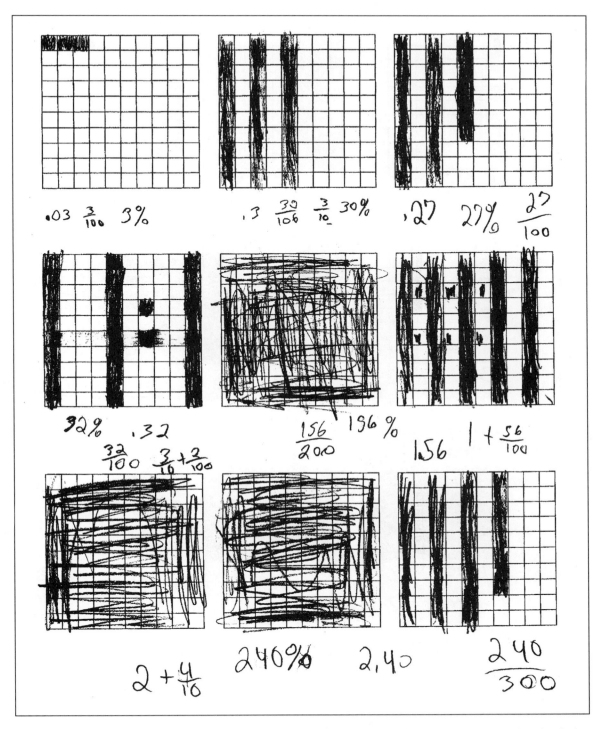

Figure 9–2 *Kendra's paper showed her confusion with fractions when she shaded more than one grid.*

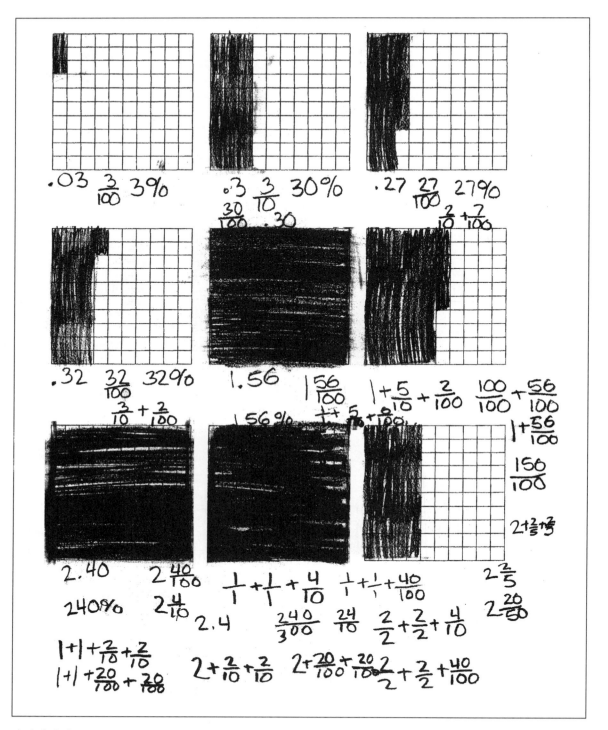

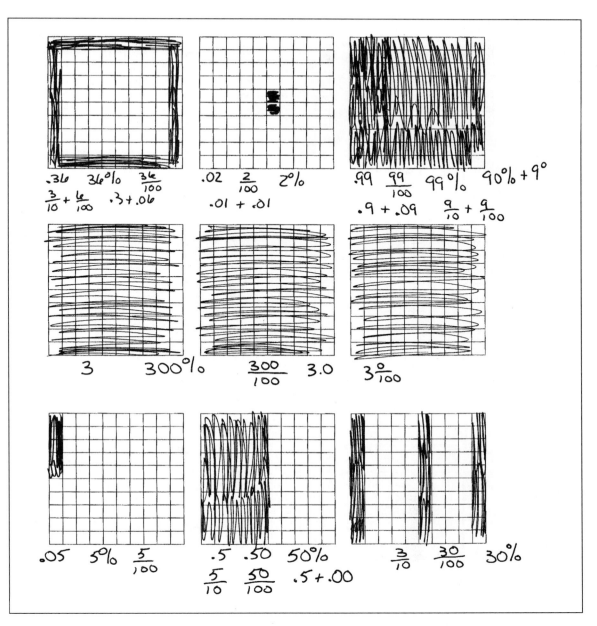

▲▲▲▲▲▲Figure 9–4 *As with his classwork, Jose's homework showed full understanding.*

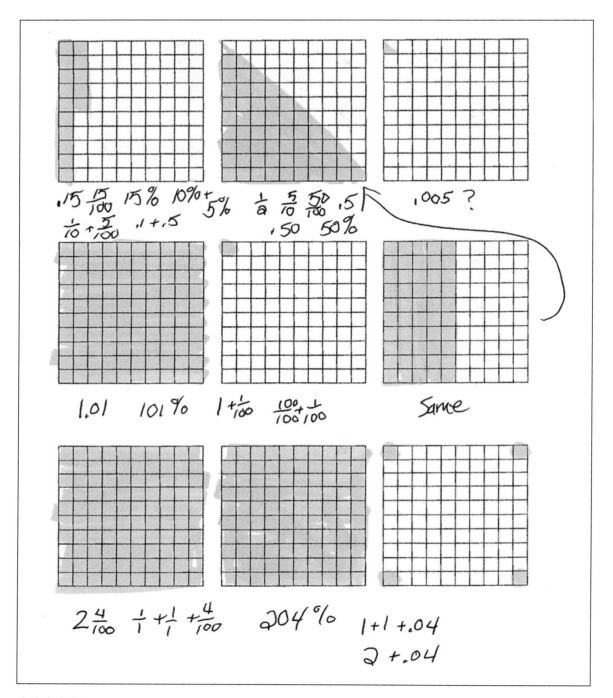

.15 $\frac{15}{100}$ 15% 10%+ 5% $\frac{1}{2}$ $\frac{5}{10}$ $\frac{50}{100}$ .5 .005 ?
$\frac{1}{10}$ + $\frac{5}{100}$ .1+.5 .50 50%

1.01 101% 1+$\frac{1}{100}$ $\frac{100}{100}$+$\frac{1}{100}$ Same

2$\frac{4}{100}$ $\frac{1}{1}$+$\frac{1}{1}$+$\frac{4}{100}$ 204% 1+1+.04
2+.04

▲▲▲▲▲▲Figure 9–5 *Kendra's confusion about how to represent .005 on a hundred grid was useful for a follow-up class discussion.*

Questions and Discussion

▲▲

▲ *When I ask the first question in the lesson, what if my students don't know anything about percents?*

This has never happened to me. Percents are commonly used and children are exposed to them before they begin to study them formally in school. However, while students have typically heard about percents, their understanding of percents is typically limited and shaky. Still, it's good to begin teaching any new concept with the students' prior understanding, no matter how incomplete or fragile.

CHAPTER TEN
PERCENT DESIGNS

Overview

In this lesson, the students create designs on blank squares and color them using two colors. They then estimate the percent of each design that is each color. Finally, they check their estimates using transparent squares of the same size ruled into 10-by-10 grids. Students repeat the experience by exchanging designs with one another.

Materials

▲ *Percent Designs* worksheet, 2 per student (see Blackline Masters)
▲ *Percent Grids* worksheet, 1 per student; copy worksheet onto transparencies and cut apart (see Blackline Masters)
▲ *T Design* sheet, 1 to post; color the T red and the rest of the square blue (see Blackline Masters)
▲ large 10-by-10 grid, 1 for demonstration; copy worksheet onto transparency (see Blackline Masters)

Time

▲ two class periods

Teaching Directions

1. Post on the board a design in a square colored red and blue (or any other two colors). (**Note:** Use the T design provided or a design of your own.) Ask the students: "About what percent of my design do you think is colored red and what percent is colored blue?" Record the students' estimates on the board and ask them to explain their reasonings.

2. Distribute to each student a copy of the *Percent Designs* worksheet and explain: "Create a different design in each of the six squares. First pencil in your design, then color it using red and blue markers. Don't leave any space uncolored. When you're done, on another sheet of paper, write an estimate of what percent of each square is red and blue."

3. When several students finish their designs, interrupt the class and explain what they are to do when they complete their designs: "Find someone else who is also finished and exchange your designs. However, don't exchange your estimates. Look at each other's designs and estimate about what percent of each square is colored red and what percent is colored blue. On a separate sheet of paper, record your estimates for each design. When you've both made estimates, meet again and compare your estimates for each other's designs. If you have time, exchange with someone else."

4. At the end of class, collect all of the students' designs and estimates.

5. To begin the second day, distribute to each student a transparent 10-by-10 grid that is the same size as one of the squares on the worksheet. Ask: "How many squares are on the transparent grid? Why do you think I made these grids with one hundred squares?"

6. Using a large transparent grid and the design you posted the first day, model for the students how to use the grid to estimate the percent of the design that's red and the percent that's blue.

7. Hand back the designs from the previous lesson. Instruct the students to use the transparent grids to check the estimates they made the day before. When the students are finished, have them exchange papers and figure the percentages for each other's designs.

8. For homework, distribute another *Percent Designs* worksheet to each student and ask them to make designs again. Instruct the students: "This time, color your designs with either three or four colors, and then make your estimates. Tomorrow you will use the transparent grids to test your predictions."

Teaching Notes

It's a good idea to precede this lesson with an introduction to percents. (See Chapter 9.) The initial preparation of working with 10-by-10 grids helps prepare students to think about the percents of the red and blue regions on their designs.

A nice aspect of this lesson is that students create their own designs and can make them as simple or intricate as they like. Not only is this good for students who are particularly artistic, but it also allows students to give themselves challenges that they decide are appropriate. Some students will make designs that allow them to make estimates more easily and precisely, and others will enjoy estimating about more complex designs.

The Lesson

▲▲

DAY 1

I posted on the board a T design I had made in a square and had colored red and blue. I had colored the T shape red and the rest of the square blue.

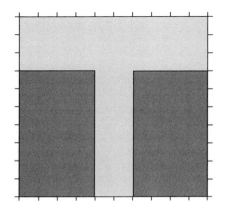

I asked, "About what percent of my design do you think is colored red and what percent is colored blue?" I recorded students' estimates on the board and asked them to explain their reasoning.

Martin replied, "I think they're about half and half. They're different-shaped pieces, but I think it's fifty percent for each."

Blaire added, "I think a little more is colored red than blue."

"What percent do you think is red?" I asked.

"I think it more like fifty-five or sixty percent," answered Blaire.

"Explain your thinking, please," I said.

She continued, "The design looks like a capital T. It looks like almost half of the top half is shaded red and then the vertical line coming down looks a little thinner than the top horizontal line. I think the horizontal line

is almost fifty percent already and then you have the vertical line to consider as well."

I asked the class, "Blaire estimates that my design might be fifty-five percent red. If it were, then what percent of my design would be blue? Talk with your neighbor about this question." In a moment many hands were up. I called on Frank.

"It would have to be forty-five percent blue because it's one hundred altogether," he answered.

Chen added, "The whole design is one hundred percent, so if you use up fifty-five for red, then you have forty-five left for blue."

"Does anyone have any other ideas about my design?" I asked.

"I agree more with Blaire than with Martin, but I think it is closer to sixty-forty," Kim said.

"What do you mean?" I asked.

Kim clarified, "I think it's sixty percent red and forty percent blue." I recorded the students' predictions on the board:

50% red, 50% blue

55% red, 45% blue

60% red, 40% blue

I then distributed to each student a *Percent Designs* worksheet with six squares on it and explained, "Create a different design in each of the six squares. First pencil in your design, then color it using red and blue markers. Don't leave any space uncolored. When you're done, on another sheet of paper, write an estimate of what percent of each square is red and what percent is blue. Write your estimates as I did for the estimates Martin, Blaire, and Kim made for my design." I pointed to their predictions on the board.

"Can we use curvy lines?" Patrice asked.

"You can make your designs anyway you'd like," I said.

"Can we use more than two colors?" Martin asked.

"No, just use red and blue, and be sure not to leave any areas uncolored," I answered. I restricted them to two colors for this class assignment, but I had plans for them to make three-color designs on a later homework assignment.

There were no more questions and the students quickly began the task. I circulated, encouraging students who were being too detailed to hurry a bit and prompting those who had completed their designs to begin writing predictions on another sheet of paper.

When a few students had completed the assignment, I interrupted the entire class. "For those of you who haven't finished yet, you can get back to work in just a minute. But first I want to explain what you're to do when you've completed your designs and estimates. Find someone else who is also done and exchange your designs. Don't exchange your estimates, however. Look at your neighbor's designs and, as you did for yours, estimate about what percent of each square is colored red and what percent is colored blue. On a separate sheet of paper, record your estimates for each design. When you've each finished making estimates, meet again and compare what you thought. If you have time, then exchange with someone else." This extension allowed time for those who were working more slowly while also giving those who worked more quickly more to think about.

It was interesting to notice the various strategies that students used to make estimates. Many used a benchmark of 50 percent, noticing that a region looked "close to a half" or "a little more than a half" and then making an estimate. Those who had complex designs had more difficulty and had to think about combining estimates for each

portion; this gave them practice adding mentally. At times, I'd notice a student had made predictions and the total of the red and blue regions didn't equal 100 percent. In those situations, I'd have a conversation.

For example, I said to Frank, "If you used just a red marker and colored in the entire square, what percent of the square would be red?"

"It would be one hundred percent," Frank answered.

"And suppose I made a simple design by splitting the square in half." I sketched a square, divided it in half on the diagonal, and shaded one half red and the other blue.

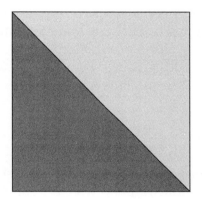

"It's fifty percent red and fifty percent blue," Frank said.

"What about this?" I said. I divided a square into four smaller congruent squares and shaded diagonally opposite squares the same color.

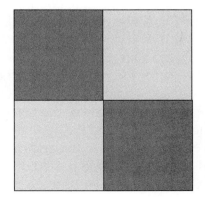

Frank said, "It's still fifty-fifty."

"How do you know?" I asked.

"Each part is a quarter, so it's twenty-five four times, and that's a hundred."

"So altogether I've shaded in one hundred percent, part red and part blue?" I asked. Frank nodded. I pointed to his paper where he had estimated the blue region was 70 percent and the red region was 25 percent.

"Oops," Frank said.

"Why oops?" I asked.

He answered, "I've got to have a hundred altogether. I'll fix it."

At the end of the class, I collected all of the students' designs and predictions. They had all finished their own designs and predictions and had made predictions for at least one other student's designs. See Figures 10–1 and 10–2 for two students' designs and predictions.

DAY 2

To begin class, I distributed to each student a transparent 10-by-10 grid, the same size as one of the squares on the worksheet on which they had drawn designs.

"How many small squares are on the transparent grid I just gave you?" I asked. Students quickly verified that it had one hundred squares.

"Why do you think I made these grids with one hundred squares?" I asked.

"Because we're learning about percents, and they have to do with hundreds," Crystal said.

I then used a large 10-by-10 transparent grid to model for the students what they were to do next. I said, "I can use the grid to make a better estimate of the percent of my design that's red and the percent that's blue," I explained. I taped the grid over the red-and-blue design I had posted the day before and showed how I counted the

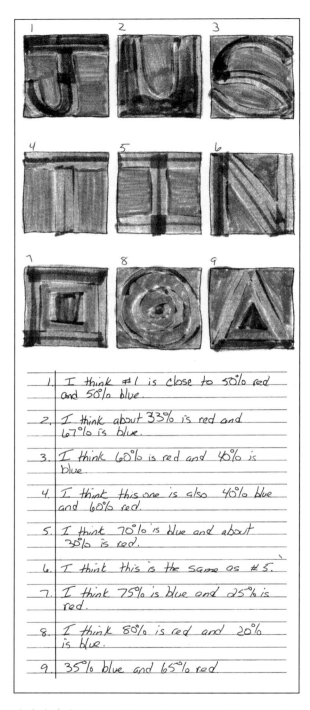

1. I think #1 is close to 50% red and 50% blue.

2. I think about 33% is red and 67% is blue.

3. I think 60% is red and 40% is blue.

4. I think this one is also 40% blue and 60% red.

5. I think 70% is blue and about 30% is red.

6. I think this is the same as #5.

7. I think 75% is blue and 25% is red.

8. I think 80% is red and 20% is blue.

9. 35% blue and 65% red

▲▲▲▲▲▲Figure 10–1 *Justin used letters of his name for his designs.*

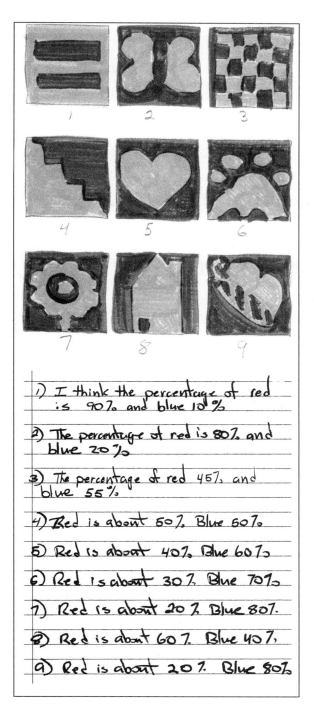

1) I think the percentage of red is 90% and blue 10%

2) The percentage of red is 80% and blue 20%

3) The percentage of red 45% and blue 55%

4) Red is about 50% Blue 50%

5) Red is about 40% Blue 60%

6) Red is about 30% Blue 70%

7) Red is about 20% Blue 80%

8) Red is about 60% Blue 40%

9) Red is about 20% Blue 80%

▲▲▲▲▲▲**Figure 10–2** *Misha made approximate predictions for her fanciful designs.*

squares in the T that covered the red region. There were forty-four.

I said, "Since forty-four of the squares are red, what percent of my design is red?"

"It has to be forty-four percent," Jose said.

"It's forty-four out of a hundred, so he's right," Shannon said. The others concurred.

"What about the blue region? What shall I do?" I asked.

"Count the squares," Matthew said.

"You don't have to. Forty-four and fifty-six makes one hundred, so it has to be fifty-six percent blue," Misha said. I wrote an addition problem on the board and verified Misha's thinking:

$$\begin{array}{r} 44 \\ + 56 \\ \hline 100 \end{array}$$

I then said, "I'll hand back the designs you made yesterday. Use your transparent grid to check the estimates you made for the percent of each color in your designs. See how close you were."

"What do you do if you used curves?" Matthew asked.

"What do you think you might do?" I asked.

"You'd have parts of squares. It will be tricky," Matthew answered. But he was delighted by the thought of the challenge.

The students got to work using the transparent grids to check their estimates. Then, as before, they exchanged papers and figured the percentages for each other's designs.

Homework

I distributed another *Percent Designs* worksheet to each student and asked them to make designs again. "This time, color your designs with either three or four colors, and then make your estimates. Tomorrow you'll use the transparent grids to test them."

Questions and Discussion

▲▲

▲ *Wouldn't it be easier if the students didn't use curved lines in their designs?*

I don't see the need to simplify the activity in that way. I prefer to let the students have their free rein of creativity in making designs and then deal with the problems that occur. Sometimes a student will feel too challenged by a complex design. In that case, he or she can simply get another worksheet and make designs that are more within his or her ability to estimate.

▲ *Is it OK to point out to the students first that they should be sure to account for 100 percent of the square?*

This is one of those pedagogical choices for which there isn't a right or best way. It would be fine to introduce this idea at the outset and then ask students to check their estimates by adding to be sure they have accounted for a total of 100 percent. It's also fine to deal with the situation as it arises and connect the idea to students' firsthand experience.

CHAPTER ELEVEN
BENCHMARKS

Overview

Students investigate benchmarks for equivalent fractions, decimals, and percents that are useful for estimating and calculating mentally. They use money as an introductory reference to figure out the benchmark equivalents, linking their new learning to a real-world context that they can represent concretely.

Materials

▲ coins: 4 quarters, 10 dimes, and 10 pennies per group of four students

Time

▲ one class period

Teaching Directions

1. Begin by asking the class: "Does anyone have an idea about what a benchmark is? What do you think might be some numbers that we could consider benchmark numbers?" Discuss.

2. Place a bag of coins at each table. Then rule six columns on the board and label them as shown. Write *one-tenth* under the first column.

Word	Fraction	Decimal	%	Money	Diagram
one-tenth					

3. With the class, fill in the first line of the chart. Record on the board:

Word	Fraction	Decimal	%	Money	Diagram
one-tenth	$\frac{1}{10}$	.1, 0.1	10%	$.10	

Ask students to make a diagram on their charts for one-tenth, and lead a class discussion about representing one-tenth in different ways and why each representation is equivalent.

4. Repeat the same procedure for one-hundredth.

5. Now have someone at each table take four quarters from the bag of money and place them in a line on the table. Make sure that they agree that the four quarters are worth one dollar. Then ask: "How would I record one quarter in the money column using a dollar sign?" Record on the board. Discuss with the class how to complete the row for one quarter. Record on the board:

Word	Fraction	Decimal	%	Money	Diagram
one-tenth	$\frac{1}{10}$	.1, 0.1	10%	$.10	
one-hundredth	$\frac{1}{100}$	.01	1%	$.01	
one-fourth	$\frac{1}{4}, \frac{25}{100}$	.25	25%	$.25	

6. Instruct the students to work on their own and fill in three more lines on the chart, writing the representations for two, three, and four quarters. Write on the board:

    2 quarters

    3 quarters

    4 quarters

7. Discuss with the class the various representations that students found for fourths. Record on the board and direct students to add to their own charts any representations that they hadn't found:

one-fourth	$\frac{1}{4}, \frac{25}{100}$	.25	25%	$.25
one-half, two-fourths	$\frac{1}{2}, \frac{50}{100}$	.50	50%	$.50
three-fourths	$\frac{3}{4}, \frac{75}{100}$	.75	75%	$.75
four-fourths	$\frac{1}{1}, \frac{4}{4}$	1.00	100%	$1.00

8. Ask the students to replace the quarters and take out enough dimes to make one dollar. Ask them to arrange their dimes into groups of two. Ask: "How many groups do you have? How many dimes are in each of the groups? Why does it make sense to call the first group of dimes one-fifth?"

9. Instruct the students to write *one-fifth* on the next line of the chart. Discuss with the class how to fill in the row for one-fifth:

one-fifth	$\frac{1}{5}, \frac{20}{100}, \frac{2}{10}$	.2, .20	20%	$.20

10. Direct the students to work on their own and fill in four more lines on the chart by writing representations for four, six, eight, and ten dimes. Write on the board:

    two-fifths (4 dimes)

    three-fifths (6 dimes)

four-fifths (8 dimes)

five-fifths (10 dimes)

11. Lead a class discussion about the various representations students found for fifths. Record on the board and direct students to add to their own charts representations that they hadn't found:

one-fifth	$\frac{1}{5}, \frac{20}{100}, \frac{2}{10}$	.2, .20	20%	$.20
two-fifths	$\frac{2}{5}, \frac{4}{10}$	.4, .40	40%	$.40
three-fifths	$\frac{3}{5}, \frac{6}{10}$	.6, .60	60%	$.60
four-fifths	$\frac{4}{5}, \frac{8}{10}$	.8, .80	80%	$.80
five-fifths	$\frac{5}{5}, \frac{10}{10}$	1.00	100%	$1.00

12. Pose a problem to provide students experience with percents greater than 100 percent: *Suppose you had two more dimes so that you had six groups with two dimes in each. How much money would you have? How would we fill in the other columns for this line?* As the students respond, write their solutions on the board:

| six-fifths | $1\frac{1}{5}, \frac{6}{5}$ | 1.2, 1.20 | 120% | $1.20 |

13. Introduce the homework assignment by first asking the class: "How can we record the amount of money for five quarters?" Write on the board *$1.25* in the money column. Then explain: "For homework, there are two parts to the assignment. One is to figure out what to record in the other columns of the row we just started for five quarters. The other part is to complete your chart by drawing diagrams and pictures."

Teaching Notes

Benchmarks are common or familiar numbers that as consumers and mathematicians we need to be able to work with on a daily basis. Benchmarks appear commonly in advertisements, on sale prices, in newspaper articles, on signs in stores, and so on. They are generally friendly numbers that are easy to use. It's useful for students to become familiar with common fraction, decimal, and percent equivalents and learn how to convert back and forth between them. Using money as the vehicle for helping children think about benchmarks is a way for them to connect new learning to ideas with which they're already familiar.

Another way for students to connect their new learning to prior knowledge is to ask the students to create and sketch their own mental and visual pictures of decimals that make sense to each of them. Some students will draw pictures of the base ten blocks, some will draw circular representations, while others will draw coins. Each sketch is to help students create a pictorial cue to help them later to remember the abstract notation.

This lesson also suggests how to introduce students to the idea of percents larger than 100 percent, an idea that is surprising to many students first learning about percents. Also, the first extension to the lesson suggests how to incorporate thirds into the lesson, giving students experience with one way to handle decimal and percent equivalents for one-third and two-thirds.

The Lesson

▲▲▲

I began the lesson by asking the class, "Does anyone have an idea about what a benchmark is?"

"Something important?" Madison answered tentatively.

"An important marker," Ian added.

"Something to remember," Jonathan said.

"What do you think might be some numbers that we could consider benchmark numbers?" I asked.

"I think one hundred," Elaine offered.

"Or a million," Crystal added.

I said, "I think of the numbers that are important to our place value system of numbers as benchmarks—ten, one hundred, one thousand, and so on. I also think of some fractions as benchmarks, fractions that we use often or use to compare other amounts to, like one-half. Benchmarks are useful for when we estimate and when we calculate in our heads. Today we're going to look at benchmark numbers that connect fractions, decimals, money, and percents."

I placed a bag of coins at each table. Then I drew six columns on the board and labeled them *Word, Fraction, Decimal, %, Money,* and *Diagram.* Also, I wrote *one-tenth* in the first column. I directed the students to do the same on a sheet of paper (see below, first box).

"Who can tell me how to record a decimal that represents one-tenth?" I asked.

Luis answered, "Decimal point and a one, or first a zero and then decimal point, one," Luis said. I recorded both of Luis's suggestions and directed the students to do the same on their charts (see below, second box).

"How should I write one-tenth as a fraction, in the Fraction column?" I asked.

"One over ten," Blaire told me. I recorded and again asked the students to do the same (see below, third box).

"Now take out the fewest coins possible to show one-tenth of a dollar," I said. The students quickly removed a dime from their money bags.

"One-tenth of a dollar is ten cents, so you write point one zero," Matthew explained.

"You need a dollar sign, too," Rebecca added. We all recorded (see below, fourth box).

"What about as a percent? What percent of a whole is one-tenth?" I asked.

Word	Fraction	Decimal	%	Money	Diagram
one-tenth					

Word	Fraction	Decimal	%	Money	Diagram
one-tenth		*.1, 0.1*			

Word	Fraction	Decimal	%	Money	Diagram
one-tenth	$\frac{1}{10}$	*.1, 0.1*			

Word	Fraction	Decimal	%	Money	Diagram
one-tenth	$\frac{1}{10}$	*.1, 0.1*		*$.10*	

"That's easy, it's ten percent," Ian said. We recorded 10% in the Percent column (see below, first box).

"And what could I draw in the last column that would represent one-tenth?" I asked.

"You could draw a rod," Patrice said, referring to base ten blocks.

"You could draw a pizza with ten slices and one slice shaded," Martin suggested. I told the students to make a sketch for one-tenth that made sense to them.

I then explained, "What we've done is represent one-tenth in different ways—as a decimal, a fraction, money, and a percent of a whole. All of these representations are equivalent to one-tenth. Who knows what I mean by *equivalent*?"

"I think it means equal," Misha answered.

"That's right. We've written the same amount in different ways; they're all equivalent or equal." I then repeated the same experience for one-hundredth, helping the students fill in the second line on their charts. The students all agreed that a penny was one-hundredth of a dollar, and that one-hundredth was 1 percent of the whole. Together we recorded in each column (see below, second box).

REPRESENTING QUARTERS

I then said, "Would someone at each table please take four quarters from the bag of money and place them in a line on the table?" I gave the students a moment to do this.

"How much money are the four quarters worth?" I asked.

"One dollar," Francesca answered.

I then said, "Let's think about one of the quarters in the line. How would I record one quarter in the money column using a dollar sign?" Madison came up to the board and recorded, starting a third line on the chart (see below, third box).

"I can write it as a decimal, too," she said. "You just don't use the dollar sign." Madison did this.

"Four quarters equals one dollar, so the fraction should be one-fourth," said Chen. He came up and recorded this.

"You could also write twenty-five over a hundred because it takes twenty-five out of a hundred pennies to make one quarter," Kendra added. She came up and recorded.

"And what about the percent column?"

"That would be twenty-five percent because like Kendra said, it's twenty-five

Word	Fraction	Decimal	%	Money	Diagram
one-tenth	$\frac{1}{10}$	.1, 0.1	10%	$.10	

Word	Fraction	Decimal	%	Money	Diagram
one-tenth	$\frac{1}{10}$	.1, 0.1	10%	$.10	
one-hundredth	$\frac{1}{100}$	.01	1%	$.01	

Word	Fraction	Decimal	%	Money	Diagram
one-tenth	$\frac{1}{10}$	.1, 0.1	10%	$.10	
one-hundredth	$\frac{1}{100}$	.01	1%	$.01	
				$.25	

percent of a dollar," Justin said. After Justin recorded, the third line was almost complete.

I wrote *one-fourth* in the first column and said, "You have four quarters and everything on this line is referring to just one of them, so we've represented one-fourth of a whole" (see below, first box).

I then asked the students to work on their own and fill in three more lines on the chart. "Write the representations for two, three, and four quarters," I said. I listed on the board:

> *2 quarters*
>
> *3 quarters*
>
> *4 quarters*

Some students worked on this independently while others got help from their neighbors. I circulated to make sure all of the students understood the task. When most had completed it, I led a class discussion, having students come up and fill in the amounts on the chart on the board (see below, second box).

REPRESENTING DIMES

I then said, "Please put the quarters back into the bag. This time, someone from each table remove enough dimes to make one dollar." The students quickly removed ten dimes.

"Now arrange your dimes into groups of two," I said. I looked around to make sure that someone at each table did this.

"How many groups do you have?" I asked.

"Five," said the class.

"How many dimes are in each of the five groups?"

"Two. It's twenty cents," Kim said.

"Or it's two-tenths because we have ten dimes altogether," Damon added.

I concurred, "Two dimes are worth twenty cents, or two dimes are two-tenths of a dollar." I then said, "Let's look at just the first group of dimes, the first twenty-cent pile. I think we could call this group 'one-fifth.' Why do you think that makes sense?"

Jenny answered, "We have five groups and so one group is one out of five and that's one-fifth."

Misha added, "And Damon said it was two-tenths, and one-fifth is the same as two-tenths." I recorded *one-fifth* on the next line and directed the students to do the same.

Word	Fraction	Decimal	%	Money	Diagram
one-tenth	$\frac{1}{10}$	.1, 0.1	10%	$.10	
one-hundredth	$\frac{1}{100}$	.01	1%	$.01	
one-fourth	$\frac{1}{4}$, $\frac{25}{100}$	.25	25%	$.25	

Word	Fraction	Decimal	%	Money	Diagram
one-tenth	$\frac{1}{10}$	.1, 0.1	10%	$.10	
one-hundredth	$\frac{1}{100}$	.01	1%	$.01	
one-fourth	$\frac{1}{4}$, $\frac{25}{100}$	.25	25%	$.25	
one-half, two-fourths	$\frac{1}{2}$, $\frac{50}{100}$	.50	50%	$.50	
three-fourths	$\frac{3}{4}$, $\frac{75}{100}$	.75	75%	$.75	
four-fourths	$\frac{1}{1}$, $\frac{4}{4}$	1.00	100%	$1.00	

I said, "Let's fill in the rest of this line of the chart. How could we write one-fifth as a decimal?"

"We could write point two zero because it's twenty cents out of one hundred," Bryant said.

"Or we could just write point two," Francesca said.

"Can you explain?"

"If I look at this as dimes, I only have two dimes out of ten dimes, so that would be two-tenths. Besides, point two is the same thing as point twenty. It takes twenty hundredths to make two-tenths," Francesca replied.

"What about a fraction for one-fifth?"

"I think we can write one over five because two dimes is one pile out of five piles, or twenty over a hundred because it's twenty cents out of a hundred cents in a dollar," Ian said.

"Or two over ten because that's two dimes out of the ten dimes," Elaine added.

The students easily filled in the Money and Percent columns. I didn't have them draw pictorial representations of one-fifth at this time. I decided to save that task for their homework assignment. This would give them a chance to review what they had written in order to decide how to represent it pictorially.

I then said, "Continue once again on your own by filling in the next four lines on the chart for four, six, eight, and ten dimes. For the next line, for example, you should think about two piles of dimes. That's two-fifths. Then you can do three-fifths, four-fifths, and five-fifths." I wrote on the board:

two-fifths (4 dimes)

three-fifths (6 dimes)

four-fifths (8 dimes)

five-fifths (10 dimes)

I had to help a few students get started, but soon all of them were busy and completed their charts correctly. As we did with the quarters, we recorded on the board and discussed the various representations (see box below).

There were a few minutes remaining in the period and I took the time to extend the activity a bit further. I said, "Suppose you had two more dimes so that you had six groups with two dimes in each. How much money would you have?"

"A dollar twenty," Chen answered. I wrote $1.20 underneath $1.00 to start another line on the chart.

Word	Fraction	Decimal	%	Money	Diagram
one-tenth	$\frac{1}{10}$	.1, 0.1	10%	$.10	
one-hundredth	$\frac{1}{100}$	.01	1%	$.01	
one-fourth	$\frac{1}{4}$, $\frac{25}{100}$	.25	25%	$.25	
one-half, two-fourths	$\frac{1}{2}$, $\frac{50}{100}$	.50	50%	$.50	
three-fourths	$\frac{3}{4}$, $\frac{75}{100}$	.75	75%	$.75	
four-fourths	$\frac{1}{1}$, $\frac{4}{4}$	1.00	100%	$1.00	
one-fifth	$\frac{1}{5}$, $\frac{20}{100}$, $\frac{2}{10}$	.2, .20	20%	$.20	
two-fifths	$\frac{2}{5}$, $\frac{4}{10}$	.4, .40	40%	$.40	
three-fifths	$\frac{3}{5}$, $\frac{6}{10}$	.6, .60	60%	$.60	
four-fifths	$\frac{4}{5}$, $\frac{8}{10}$	.8, .80	80%	$.80	
five-fifths	$\frac{5}{5}$, $\frac{10}{10}$	1.00	100%	$1.00	

"Does anyone have any ideas about how to fill in the other columns for this line?" I asked. A few hands went up, but I could tell that some students weren't sure what to do. I asked them to talk about this at their tables for a moment. After giving them a few minutes to do so, I called the class back to attention.

"We're pretty sure about the Decimal column," Jose said. "It's the same without the dollar sign."

"Can you read this decimal number?" I asked after recording *1.20* in the correct column.

"One and twenty-hundredths," Jose answered.

"Or one and two-tenths," Matthew added.

Francesca said, "We had an argument about what to write in the fraction column but we think both are right."

"What are your ideas?" I asked.

"One and a fifth, or six-fifths," she said. I recorded $1\frac{1}{5}$ and $\frac{6}{5}$ in the fraction column.

"Can someone at Francesca's table explain how you figured this out?" I asked.

Rory said, "Each pile of two dimes was one-fifth, so with six piles you have six-fifths."

Hunter added, "If you took away the first five piles and put a dollar bill there instead, you have a dollar and twenty cents. And you can see on the chart that twenty cents was one-fifth. So you have one whole and one more fifth."

"Did anyone have a different fraction?" I asked. No one raised a hand.

I pointed to the first column and said, "I agree with both answers, and in this column, I could write either in words. But to follow the pattern, I think I'll write six-fifths." I did so.

Now only the Percent and Diagram columns were empty.

"Who has an idea about the Percent column?" I asked.

Shannon answered, "We don't think you can fill in that column because percents only go up to one hundred." This is a common misconception that students have when first studying percents. Their prior experience has been with percents less than 100 percent.

Patrice said, "We thought that it had to be more than one hundred percent because you have two more dimes. We thought it would be one hundred percent plus twenty more percent."

"What would you write?" I asked. Patrice came up and wrote:

100% + 20%

I turned to Shannon's table. "What do you think?" I asked.

"It makes sense," Damon said. "Can you do that?"

"If something makes sense, then you usually can do it," I said. "Also, you can write Patrice's idea like this." I wrote on the board in the correct column:

120%

I explained, "One hundred twenty percent of a whole means the whole plus twenty percent more. Percents can be more than one hundred, as long as you know what the whole is. It's the same as thinking about the decimal as one whole and twenty-hundredths more. Or with money as one dollar and twenty cents more." I then directed the students to copy this last line onto their charts (see box below).

HOMEWORK

I asked the class how to record the amount of money for five quarters. Brian came up to the board and wrote *$1.25*. I asked the students to write this amount in the Money column on the next line. I then said, "For

Word	Fraction	Decimal	%	Money	Diagram
six-fifths	$1\frac{1}{5}$, $\frac{6}{5}$	*1.2, 1.20*	*120%*	*$1.20*	

homework, there are two parts to the assignment. One is to figure out what to record in the other columns of the row you just started for five quarters. And the other part is to complete your chart by drawing diagrams or pictures." (See Figures 11–1 through 11–3.)

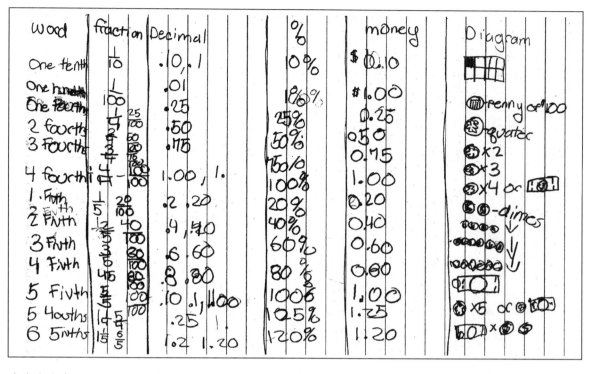

▲▲▲▲▲▲Figure 11–1 *Crystal used drawings of money to represent the fraction and decimal benchmarks.*

Word	fraction	Decimal	%	Money	Diagram
one-tenth	$\frac{1}{10}$	.10, .1	10%	$0.10	
one-hundreth	$\frac{1}{100}$	.01	100%	$0.01	×5
one-fourth	$\frac{1}{4}, \frac{25}{100}$	.25	25%	$0.25	$\frac{1}{4}$= 25%
two-fourths	$\frac{2}{4}, \frac{1}{2}$	.50	50%	$0.50	$\frac{1}{2}$=50%
three-fourths	$\frac{3}{4}$	.75	75%	$0.75	$\frac{3}{4}$= 75%
four-fourths	$\frac{4}{4}, 1$	1.	100%	$1.00	=1 100%
one-fifth	$\frac{1}{5} \frac{20}{100}$	.20, .2	20%	$0.20	$\frac{1}{5}$= 20%
two-fifths	$\frac{2}{5} \frac{40}{100}$	.40, .4	40%	$0.40	$\frac{2}{5}$= 40%
three-fifths	$\frac{3}{5} \frac{60}{100}$	.60, .6	60%	$0.60	$\frac{3}{5}$= 60%
four-fifths	$\frac{4}{5} \frac{80}{100}$	.80, .8	80%	$0.80	$\frac{4}{5}$= 80%
five-fifths	$\frac{5}{5}$ 1	1.00, 1.	100%	$1.00	1= 100%
five-fourths	$1\frac{1}{4}$	1.25	125%	$1.25	
six-fifths	$1\frac{1}{5}$	1.20	120%	$1.20	

▲▲▲▲▲▲Figure 11–2 *Rebecca divided up circles to illustrate the common benchmarks.*

Word	fraction	decimal	%	money	Diagram
1 tenth	$\frac{1}{10}$	0.1, 0.10	10%	$0.10	(diagram)
1 hundredth	$\frac{1}{100}$	0.01	1%	$0.01	(diagram)
1 fourth	$\frac{1}{4}$	0.25	25%	$0.25	(diagram)
2 fourths	$\frac{2}{4}, \frac{1}{2}$	0.50	50%	$0.50	(diagram)
3 fourths	$\frac{3}{4}$	0.75	75%	$0.75	(diagram)
4 fourths	$\frac{4}{4}, 1$	1.00	100%	$1.00	(diagram)
1 fifth	$\frac{1}{5}, \frac{20}{100}$	0.20	20%	$0.20	(diagram)
2 fifths	$\frac{2}{5}, \frac{40}{100}$	0.40	40%	$0.40	(diagram)
3 fifths	$\frac{3}{5}, \frac{60}{100}$	0.60	60%	$0.60	(diagram)
4 fifths	$\frac{4}{5}, \frac{80}{100}$	0.80	80%	$0.80	(diagram)
5 fifths	$\frac{5}{5}, 1$	1.00	100%	$1.00	(diagram)
5 fourths	$1\frac{1}{4} \ \frac{5}{4}$	1.25	125%	$1.25	(diagram)
6 fifths	$1\frac{1}{5} \ \frac{6}{5}$	1.20	120%	$1.20	(diagram)

▲▲▲▲▲**Figure 11–3** *Luis's work is correct, but his last entry shows his difficulty dividing a circle into fifths, a common problem for students in these grades.*

EXTENSIONS

1. To extend the lesson, write *one-third* in the first column of another row on the chart. Ask students how to write this as a fraction, and then record $\frac{1}{3}$ in the appropriate column. Then ask students to organize one dollar's worth of coins into three groups, each with the same amount of money. Students typically figure out fairly quickly that each group has $.33 and there is a penny left over. Show students how to write the decimal equivalent of $\frac{1}{3}$ as $.33\frac{1}{3}$ and the percent equivalent as $33\frac{1}{3}\%$. Discuss with them what to do in the Money column. They could write $.33\frac{1}{3}$, or they could decide to write something else, such as *Not Possible*. Then repeat for two-thirds and help students see the decimal and percent equivalents as $.66\frac{2}{3}$ and $66\frac{2}{3}\%$.

2. Ask each student to make a set of forty-four cards by transferring one representation for each line from the Decimal, Fraction, Money, and Percent columns onto separate index cards. For example, for one-fourth, they might label four cards with *.25*, $\frac{1}{4}$, *$.25*, and *25%*. They then use their cards to play a version of Concentration. The students pair up and use one set of the cards they made. They shuffle them and place them facedown in a rectangular array. The students take turns flipping over four cards. If all four cards represent the same decimal number, the player collects the four cards and takes another turn. If all four cards are not equivalent, then the player flips the cards facedown again and the other player tries. The winner is whoever has collected the most cards at the end of the game. For homework, each student takes the set of cards home and plays the game with a family member.

Questions and Discussion

▲▲

▲ *Would you extend this activity further and ask the students to think about the equivalents for sixths or other fractions that don't convert so easily?*

This is eventually important, but I keep in mind that students will have many more experiences in later grades converting fractions to decimals and percents. My goal for fifth and sixth graders is to introduce them to important ideas and help create a foundation of understanding on which their later experiences can build. Also, I was building the lesson on the reference of money, and sixths aren't benchmarks when we think about monetary values. However, if you feel you want to extend the lesson, try it. And, as with all lessons, follow the students' leads to judge the appropriateness of what you offer.

▲ *Wouldn't it be easier to teach students to convert fractions to decimals by dividing numerators by denominators?*

The computational method of dividing the numerator of a fraction by its denominator is helpful and important for students to learn. But this sort of procedural learning is best built on a conceptual foundation. This lesson seeks to build students' number sense about fraction, decimal, and percent equivalents using numbers with which they are familiar. They shouldn't have to use the standard computational method for any of these benchmarks. For suggestions about how to introduce a computational method, see Chapter 12.

CHAPTER TWELVE
RELATING FRACTIONS AND DECIMALS

Overview

One aspect of learning about how fractions and decimals relate is understanding that dividing the numerator of a fraction by its denominator produces a decimal equivalent. While students can learn to do this mechanically, it's important that they also learn to make sense of this procedure. This lesson uses calculators to help build students' understanding about converting fractions to decimals.

Materials

▲ calculators, 1 per student

Time

▲ one class period

Teaching Directions

1. Ask the class to tell you some decimal numbers to record on the board. As the students suggest decimal numbers, record them on the board both as common fractions and decimal numerals.

2. Point out to the class: "All of the decimal numerals have something in common—a decimal point with numbers after it." Then ask: "What do all of the common fractions have in common?" Students typically notice that the denominators are 10, 100, 1,000, or 10,000. You may choose to tell the class that these numbers are powers of ten.

3. Write on the board the fraction $\frac{1}{2}$ and ask: "Can you think of a way to write one-half as a decimal number?" Ask students to talk with a neighbor and then ask for volunteers to report. If students don't know, represent $\frac{1}{2}$ as $\frac{5}{10}$, then as a decimal, and then as other equivalent common fractions; e.g., $\frac{1}{2} = \frac{5}{10} = 0.5 = \frac{3}{6} = \frac{4}{8} = \frac{10}{20}$.

4. Instruct the students to clear their calculators and do the following: press five, the divide key, ten, and the equals key. Ask: "What's on your display?" Record on the board:

$\frac{5}{10} = 0.5$

5. Add to what you had recorded:

$\frac{5}{10} = 0.5$

$\frac{10}{10} = 1$

$\frac{15}{10} = 1\frac{5}{10} = 1.5$

$\frac{20}{10} = 2$

Talk with the students about the fraction and decimal equivalents. Ask them to use their calculators and divide the numerator by the denominator of each to check the results.

6. Explain to the class: "Fractions are related to division. If you have ten apples and divide them among ten people, each person gets one apple. If you have fifteen apples and divide them among ten people, each gets one apple and half of another. If you have twenty apples and divide them among ten people, each gets two apples. Fractions are another way to represent a division." Point to $\frac{5}{10}$ and ask: "If you have five apples and divide them among ten people, how much does each person get?" Once the students agree that each person gets half of an apple, ask them to divide one by two on their calculators to see that the display reads 0.5.

7. Point to $\frac{1}{2} = \frac{5}{10} = 0.5 = \frac{3}{6} = \frac{4}{8} = \frac{10}{20}$, which you previously wrote on the board. Give the students time to use their calculators to divide the numerator by the denominator of each fraction to verify that each produces the same answer of 0.5.

8. Next, write on the board $\frac{1}{4}$ and ask: "Without dividing the one by the four, think about how you could represent this fraction on the calculator." Give a hint: "It may help to think about money." Then allow time for students to talk with a neighbor and then test their predictions with their calculators. Record on the board:

$\frac{1}{4} = 0.25$

Ask for other fractions equal to one-fourth and have students divide their numerators by their denominators to verify that they are all equivalent to 0.25.

9. Repeat Step 8 for the fraction $\frac{3}{4}$.

10. Repeat Step 8 for the fraction $\frac{6}{20}$. (Note: The hint about money won't be useful.)

11. Repeat Step 8 for the fraction $\frac{7}{2}$. (Note: The hint about money won't be useful.) Establish that $\frac{7}{2} = 3\frac{1}{2} = 3.5$.

12. Repeat Step 8 for $4\frac{1}{2}$. Record the mathematical sentence on the board along with a written explanation. The written explanation prepares students for their homework assignment.

$4\frac{1}{2} = 4.5 = \frac{9}{2}$

$4\frac{1}{2} = 4.5$ because 4.5 is the same as $4\frac{5}{10}$ and $\frac{1}{2}$ and $\frac{5}{10}$ are equal.

13. Focus the students' attention to the original list of fractions and decimals that were recorded in the beginning of the class. Instruct: "Use your calculator to verify that these fractions and decimals are equivalent."

14. Give the homework assignment: "Choose any ten fractions. For each, before using your calculator, predict what decimal you'll get by dividing its numerator by its denominator. Then use your calculator to divide. Finally, write a sentence or two that explains why it makes sense for the fraction and decimal to relate. If you find one you can't explain, or that surprised or confused you, mark it for the class to discuss."

Teaching Notes

When studying decimals, students have traditionally learned to divide the numerators by the denominators of fractions to convert fractions to decimals. However, this procedure has often been taught as a rule to learn and practice. While students can learn to do the computations and get correct results, it's important to keep in mind that being able to compute correctly doesn't necessarily guarantee students' understanding about why the procedure makes sense. This lesson aims at building student understanding about how fractions and decimals relate. It uses calculators as a tool for building student understanding.

For this lesson, keep in mind that this is an introductory experience and that children will revisit converting fractions to decimals many times in the next few grades. I don't expect this lesson to provide all of the instruction that students need, but rather to give students initial experience thinking about fraction and decimal equivalents. In fifth and sixth grades, some students need additional experience reasoning numerically with whole numbers and fractions, skills that are important for them to learn to reason with decimals.

The Lesson

▲▲

"Tell me some decimal numbers to record on the board," I said to begin the lesson.

"Three-tenths," Patrice said.

"Seven-tenths," Tamara said.

"Seventeen-hundredths," Blaire offered.

"Two hundred forty-eight–thousandths," Rory said.

"Two hundred forty-eight–*ten* thousandths," Misha said.

"One-thousandth," Justin said.

"One-ten thousandth," Maria said.

I recorded on the board as students dictated, writing each number both as a common fraction and as a decimal numeral:

$\frac{3}{10}$	0.3
$\frac{7}{10}$	0.7
$\frac{17}{100}$	0.17
$\frac{248}{1,000}$	.248
$\frac{248}{10,000}$	.0248
$\frac{1}{1,000}$	0.001
$\frac{1}{10,000}$	.0001

I then said, "All of the decimal numerals have something in common—they all have a decimal point with numbers after it. What do all of the common fractions have in common?"

Blaire said, "They have a one in the denominator."

Jose added, "And they have zeros in the denominator, too."

Misha said, "The denominators are either ten, one hundred, one thousand, or ten thousand. They're ten times numbers."

"Tell me more about that," I said.

"Well, it's ten, or ten times ten, or ten times ten times ten, like that," Misha said.

"I agree," I said, and restated what Misha reported using different terminology. "The denominators are all powers of ten. They're either ten or ten times itself one,

two, three, or four times. Another way of thinking about decimal numerals is that they are a way to write certain fractions, those whose denominators are a power of ten." I then wrote $\frac{1}{2}$ on the board and asked, "Can you think of a way to write one-half as a decimal numeral? Talk with your neighbor about this."

For a moment, most students just gazed at the $\frac{1}{2}$ I had written on the board. Then heads began to move together as students began to share ideas. After a moment, a few hands went up. I waited a bit more and then called the class to attention. I called on Crystal.

"First we thought it couldn't be done," she said. "But then Patrice thought about money. If you have half a dollar, you can write that with a decimal point. We think that's one-half."

"What should I write?" I asked.

Patrice answered, "A dollar sign, then a decimal point, then fifty." I wrote:

$.50

"If I didn't have the dollar sign, would it still be worth one-half?" I asked. Some students thought yes, some thought no, others weren't sure.

Ian said, "If you didn't have the dollar sign, then it would be like five rods and no units. And five rods is half of a flat. I think it's still a half." Ian's explanation convinced most of the others.

"Or it could be fifty-hundredths, and that would be fifty units," Madison added.

"Is that one-half?" I asked.

"Yes," Madison said, nodding.

"I know another way to explain," Chen said. "One-half is the same as five-tenths in fractions."

"What do you mean 'in fractions'?" I asked.

Relating Fractions and Decimals 97

"Can I come up and show?" Chen asked. I agreed. He came up and wrote on the board:

$$\frac{1}{2} = \frac{5}{10}$$

"How do you know they're equal?" I asked Chen.

"Easy, one is half of two, and five is half of ten," he answered.

"Can you think of another fraction that is also equal to one-half or five-tenths?" I asked.

"There are lots of them," Chen said. "Can I write some?" I agreed. Chen added to what he had written:

$$\frac{1}{2} = \frac{5}{10} = \frac{3}{6} = \frac{4}{8} = \frac{10}{20}$$

I stopped Chen and laughed, saying, "I bet you can go on forever doing that."

"Yup," he said.

"So any fraction that's worth one-half can be written as the decimal five-tenths," I said. "I'd like each of you to try something with your calculator. Please take it and clear the display." I waited until all of the students had done this.

"I want you each to have five-tenths appear on your display, but I don't want you just to press the decimal point and then five. I want to show you another way. Follow along with me. Start by pressing five." I waited a moment for everyone to do this, and I also pressed five on the overhead calculator.

"Now press the divide button," I said. Again I waited.

"Now press ten," I said. "And, finally, press the equals sign. What's on your display?"

"Five-tenths," most of the students replied. A few had incorrectly pressed keys and needed to do it again. I went through the procedure once more so that everyone had success. I wrote on the board:

$$\frac{5}{10} = 0.5 = \frac{1}{2}$$

"That's cool," Peter said.

"But why does it work?" Jenni asked. I added to what I had written on the board:

$$\frac{5}{10} = 0.5 = \frac{1}{2}$$
$$\frac{10}{10}$$
$$\frac{15}{10}$$
$$\frac{20}{10}$$

I pointed to $\frac{10}{10}$ and said, "Do you agree that this is worth one whole?" The students agreed. They also agreed that $\frac{15}{10}$ was worth one whole and five-tenths, and that $\frac{20}{10}$ was worth two wholes. I added these values.

$$\frac{5}{10} = 0.5 = \frac{1}{2}$$
$$\frac{10}{10} = 1$$
$$\frac{15}{10} = 1\frac{5}{10} = 1.5 = 1\frac{1}{2}$$
$$\frac{20}{10} = 2$$

"Try dividing the numerator by the denominator for each of these and check that you get the results I recorded. Of course, the calculator will write the numbers in decimals."

"I don't get it," Rory said.

"For the first one, press ten divided by ten and then the equals sign," I said.

"Oh, I get it," Rory said.

I then explained, "Fractions are related to division. If you have ten apples and you divide them among ten people, each person gets one apple. If you have fifteen apples and divide them among ten people, each gets one apple and half of another. If you have twenty apples and divide them among ten people, each gets two apples. Fractions are another way to represent a division."

I pointed to $\frac{5}{10}$ on the board and continued, "If you have five apples and divide them among ten people, how much does each person get?"

"Half of an apple," Leslee answered.

"So five divided by ten is equal to one-half," I said. "And the calculator can only write one-half by showing five-tenths as a decimal."

I pointed to the $\frac{1}{2}$ on the board and said, "You can think of one-half as one apple divided between two people. Each person gets a half of the apple. On your calculator, try dividing one by two." I pointed to the numerator and denominator of the $\frac{1}{2}$ as I said this. Some students were surprised to see five-tenths on the display.

I pointed to the other fractions that Chen had written. "You can think of three-sixths as three apples divided among six people, and four-eighths as four apples divided among eight people, and so on. For each of these, see what result you get on your calculator if you divide the numerator by the denominator." I gave the students time to discover that each division produced the same answer of 0.5.

"But you never divided the apple into ten parts," Jeff objected.

"No," I agreed, "but when we're talking about what numbers mean, five out of ten parts, or five-tenths, means the same as four out of eight parts, or four-eighths. Both are half the apple, just cut up differently. And even though you can write one-half in many, many different ways, and cut apples into halves with different numbers of pieces, the calculator can only write one-half in one way, as the decimal five-tenths."

I then wrote on the board:

$$\frac{1}{4}$$

"How do you think you could represent this fraction on the calculator? You could find out by dividing the one by the four, but don't do that yet. First talk with your neighbor and see if you can think about this. It may help to think about money." Several students quickly figured out that a fourth was a quarter of a dollar or twenty-five cents. I had them divide one by four, and I recorded the result on the board:

$$\frac{1}{4} = 0.25$$

"That's twenty-five–hundredths, or two-tenths and five-hundredths," I said. "Can anyone explain why this makes sense to be the same as one-fourth?"

"Twenty-five cents is a fourth of a dollar," Matt said.

"If you have four quarters, you have one dollar. So one quarter is a fourth of a dollar," Marisa added.

"With the blocks, you need two rods and five units. If you had two more rods and five more units, you'd cover half of the flat. And then you would do that two more times. Two rods and five units is one-fourth of a flat," Misha said.

"Who knows another fraction that's worth the same as one-fourth?" I asked.

"Three-twelfths," Isabella offered. I wrote $\frac{3}{12}$ on the board.

"Divide three by twelve on your calculator and see what comes up," I said. Some expected to see .25 on the display, but others were still surprised.

I then said, "Let's try another fraction. Talk with your neighbor about what decimal numeral represents three-fourths. Don't use your calculator yet." I wrote on the board:

$$\frac{3}{4}$$

Conversation was more animated this time, and more students were sure that three-fourths would be seventy-five–hundredths. Again, the context of money helped. After they divided three by four on their calculators, I recorded:

$$\frac{3}{4} = 0.75$$

"Now, without using your calculator, think about how to write this fraction as a decimal," I said. I wrote on the board:

$$\frac{6}{20}$$

The students were stumped and the room got quiet. Then Misha said, excitedly, "Change it to three tenths and it's easy." I wrote on the board:

$$\frac{6}{20} = \frac{3}{10}$$

"Is this what you're saying?" I asked Misha. She nodded.

"That's right," Chen added. Others agreed.

"So what's the decimal numeral?" I asked.

"It's zero point three," Crystal said.

"Now try dividing six by twenty on your calculator," I said. I recorded:

$$\frac{6}{20} = \frac{3}{10} = 0.3$$

"You get the same thing if you divide three by ten," Chen said. Others tried this and concurred.

I then wrote on the board:

$$\frac{7}{2}$$

"What do you know about this fraction?" I asked.

"It's more than one," Jonathan said.

"It's three and a half," Patrice said. "Three twos are six, and there's still one-half left."

"How can we write this as a decimal?" I asked. "Talk among yourselves first, no calculator." About half of the class figured out that it had to be three and five-tenths, and they verified this with their calculators, dividing seven by two. I recorded:

$$\frac{7}{2} = 3\frac{1}{2} = 3.5$$

"How would you write four and a half as a decimal?" I asked.

It was easy for the class to answer this. I wrote on the board:

$$4\frac{1}{2} = 4.5$$

"What would you divide on your calculator to prove this?" I asked. "Experiment and see what you can figure out."

After a few moments, Blaire reported, "One divided by two is point five, so that's where the five-tenths comes from."

"What about the four? What would you divide so that you would see four and five-tenths on your calculator display?"

"I know," Shannon said. "Divide nine by two." Heads dove as others tried this.

"How did you figure that out?" I asked.

"Well I knew that if you divide eight by two you get four, and if you divide ten by two you get five, so it has to be nine," Shannon said. I recorded on the board:

$$4\frac{1}{2} = 4.5 = \frac{9}{2}$$

"Is this what you meant?" I asked.

Shannon faltered. She hadn't thought about nine halves, but after a moment she said, "Oh yeah, that's right. Nine halves is four and a half. I just didn't think of it that way." To model what I would assign for homework at the end of class, I wrote an explanation on the board:

$4\frac{1}{2} = 4.5$ because 4.5 is the same as $4\frac{5}{10}$ and $\frac{1}{2}$ and $\frac{5}{10}$ are equal.

I then focused the class's attention on the list of fractions and decimals I had recorded at the beginning of the period:

$\frac{3}{10}$	0.3
$\frac{7}{10}$	0.7
$\frac{17}{100}$	0.17
$\frac{248}{1,000}$	.248
$\frac{248}{10,000}$	.0248
$\frac{1}{1,000}$	0.001
$\frac{1}{10,000}$	.0001

I instructed, "Use your calculator to verify that these fractions and decimals are equivalent. For each fraction, divide the numerator by the denominator and check that you get the decimal on the board."

Homework

The assignment for homework was for students to investigate further writing numbers as both fractions and decimals. I said to the class, "Choose any ten fractions. For each, without your calculator, predict what decimal you'll get by dividing its numerator by its denominator. Then use your calculator to divide. Finally, write a sentence or two that explains why it makes sense for the fraction and decimal to relate. If you find one you can't explain, or that surprised or confused you, mark it for the class to discuss." Figures 12–1 through 12–4 show some of the numbers students picked to convert.

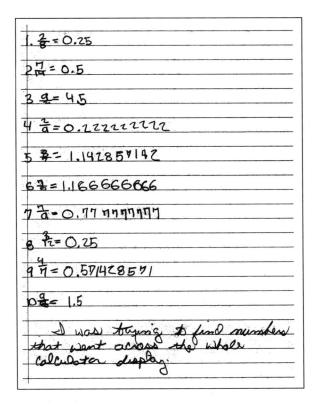

1. $\frac{2}{8} = 0.25$
2. $\frac{7}{14} = 0.5$
3. $\frac{9}{2} = 4.5$
4. $\frac{2}{9} = 0.222222222$
5. $\frac{8}{7} = 1.142857142$
6. $\frac{7}{6} = 1.16666666$
7. $\frac{7}{9} = 0.77777777$
8. $\frac{3}{12} = 0.25$
9. $\frac{4}{7} = 0.57142857$
10. $\frac{3}{2} = 1.5$

I was trying to find numbers that went across the whole calculator display.

▲▲▲▲▲▲**Figure 12–1** *Shannon deliberately tried to find fractions that converted to repeating decimals.*

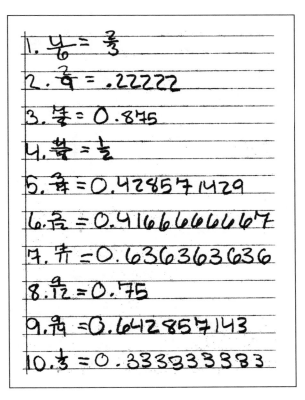

1. $\frac{4}{6} = \frac{2}{3}$
2. $\frac{2}{9} = .22222$
3. $\frac{7}{8} = 0.875$
4. $\frac{12}{24} = \frac{1}{2}$
5. $\frac{3}{7} = 0.428571429$
6. $\frac{5}{12} = 0.41666667$
7. $\frac{7}{11} = 0.636363636$
8. $\frac{9}{12} = 0.75$
9. $\frac{9}{14} = 0.642857143$
10. $\frac{3}{9} = 0.333333383$

▲▲▲▲▲▲**Figure 12–2** *Crystal reported that she was surprised by her answers.*

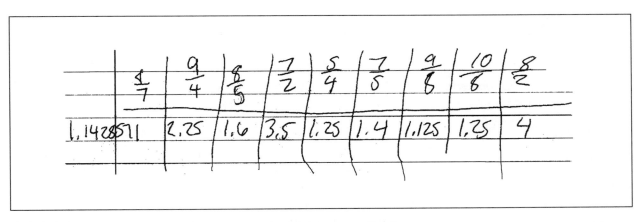

$\frac{4}{7}$	$\frac{9}{4}$	$\frac{8}{5}$	$\frac{7}{2}$	$\frac{5}{4}$	$\frac{7}{5}$	$\frac{9}{8}$	$\frac{10}{8}$	$\frac{8}{2}$
1.1428571	2.25	1.6	3.5	1.25	1.4	1.125	1.25	4

▲▲▲▲▲▲**Figure 12–3** *Rory experimented with improper fractions.*

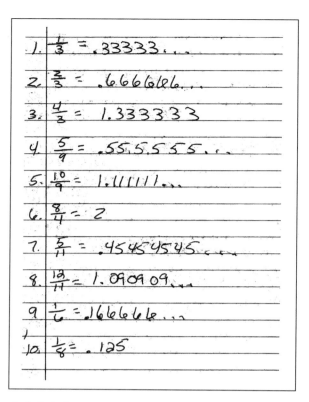

1. $\frac{1}{3} = .33333...$

2. $\frac{2}{3} = .666666...$

3. $\frac{4}{3} = 1.333333$

4. $\frac{5}{9} = .555555...$

5. $\frac{10}{9} = 1.111111...$

6. $\frac{8}{4} = 2$

7. $\frac{5}{11} = .45454545...$

8. $\frac{12}{11} = 1.090909...$

9. $\frac{1}{6} = .166666...$

10. $\frac{1}{8} = .125$

▲▲▲▲▲▲**Figure 12–4** *Blaire tried several fractions with the same denominators.*

Questions and Discussion

▲▲▲

▲ *Is this idea too abstract for fifth and sixth graders to grasp? Is it necessary to teach at these grades?*

Thinking about abstract ideas is difficult for students. They need many experiences to sort out ideas and make sense of them for themselves. Representing fractions as decimal numerals requires students to understand and connect the structure of our place value system to how fractions relate to division. Students will have more experience with this idea in later grades. Introducing the concept at these grades gives students a first chance to think about how fractions and decimals relate. The calculator is one useful tool for building their understanding, but it's important to remember that students still need to process the information for themselves, and they do so at their own pace.

CHAPTER THIRTEEN
INTRODUCING REPEATING DECIMALS

Overview

This lesson builds on Chapter 12, "Relating Fractions and Decimals," and engages students in thinking about repeating decimals. Students use calculators as tools for generating repeating decimals from fractions that are thirds, ninths, and elevenths. They also learn the standard mathematical notation for representing repeating decimal numerals.

Materials

▲ calculators, 1 per student

Time

▲ one class period

Teaching Directions

1. Begin class by having the students compare their results from the homework assignment from Chapter 12. (If students haven't done this homework assignment, then begin class by asking them to do the following: "Choose any ten fractions. For each, before using your calculator, predict what decimal you'll get by dividing its numerator by its denominator. Then use your calculator to divide.")

2. Initiate a class discussion by asking: "Who would like to share a result that surprised or confused you?" Ask students to record on the board and explain what they noticed.

3. In the discussion, if students don't bring up repeating decimals, introduce the idea by asking if anyone figured out decimal equivalents for fractions that are ninths. List on the board the fractions from one-nineth to eight-ninths with their decimal equivalents:

$\frac{1}{9} = 0.1111111$

$\frac{2}{9} = 0.2222222$

$\frac{3}{9} = 0.3333333$

$\frac{4}{9} = 0.4444444$

$\frac{5}{9} = 0.5555555$

$\frac{6}{9} = 0.6666666$

$\frac{7}{9} = 0.7777777$

$\frac{8}{9} = 0.8888888$

Talk with the class about the pattern they notice. Also, some students' calculators may produce different last digit for the last four decimals: 0.5555556, 0.6666667, 0.7777778, 0.8888889. Discuss that they are rounding the last digit up because the digit that follows is five or greater. Also tell the students that these decimals are called "repeating decimals" and show them the shortened version for writing them with a line over the part of the decimal that repeats; for example, $\frac{2}{9} = 0.\overline{2}$.

4. Repeat for elevenths, listing the fractions from one-eleventh to ten-elevenths and their decimal equivalents. Talk with the students about the pattern they notice. Discuss the different last digits some may have. Also, show the students how to write these repeating decimals in the shortened form, with a line above the part of the decimal that repeats; for example, $\frac{2}{11} = 0.1818181$ or $0.\overline{18}$.

5. Discuss the decimal equivalents for the fractions one-third and two-thirds. If students have completed the *Benchmarks* lesson (see Chapter 11), then have them compare these results with what they entered on their *Benchmarks* charts for one-third and two-thirds. Discuss why the decimal equivalents for one-third and two-thirds are the same as for three-ninths and six-ninths.

6. For the rest of the class, engage the students in making additional predictions about the decimal equivalents for other fractions. Explain: "I'll write a fraction on the board. Without using your calculator, discuss at your table what decimal you predict you'll get by dividing its numerator by its denominator. We'll talk about your ideas and then we'll all do the division on our calculators and see what we learn."

Teaching Notes

Patterns are key to all of mathematics, and this lesson encourages students to use patterns as a way of making sense of fractions that produce repeating decimals. Not only does looking for patterns help students learn about fraction and decimal equivalents, it also reinforces for students the usefulness of organizing information in orderly ways.

Before teaching this lesson, teach the lesson about relating fractions and decimals (see Chapter 12). The experience from that lesson is useful preparation. Also, this lesson builds on the homework assignment from the previous lesson. If, however, you didn't assign the homework, then give it as a class assignment at the beginning of this lesson.

It's always best to follow students' leads when introducing a new idea. The lesson that follows built on the students' responses from a particular class and doesn't exactly mirror the teaching directions presented. You may want to change the order of introducing elevenths, ninths, and thirds to make the lesson more effective for your students.

As with Chapter 12, this lesson provides only an introductory experience with repeating decimals. It is not sufficient for students' learning and, therefore, don't expect students to understand fully how repeating decimals relate to fractions and to other decimals. Keep in mind that students will encounter this idea in later grades, and that this lesson can serve as a foundation on which further learning can build.

The Lesson

▲▲▲

I began class by having the students compare with the others at their table their homework papers from the *Relating Fractions and Decimals* lesson (see Chapter 12). (If the class hadn't done the assignment, I would have explained the assignment, given them time at the beginning of the class to complete it, and then had them discuss their results.)

I gave the class directions. "See if you chose any of the same fractions and, if you did, check that you got the same results. Also, talk about any results that confused or surprised you. In a moment, we'll have a class discussion about what you learned and what problems you found." When students talk about their homework in small groups, it encourages them to share confusion they might have encountered. It's often hard for students to confess before the entire class about something they don't understand, but in small groups, they learn that others can also be confused. This supports them in contributing their problems for whole-class discussion.

"Who would like to share a result that surprised or confused you?" I began.

"We noticed that some of the decimals kept going," Shannon said.

"How about coming up and recording on the board the fraction and decimal equivalent you tested and explaining your idea?"

As Shannon wrote on the board, she explained, "For instance, the decimal for two-ninths was point two, two, two, two, like that, and the decimal for seven-ninths was point seven, seven, seven, seven." She recorded:

$\frac{2}{9} = .2222222$

$\frac{7}{9} = .7777777$

"Did anyone else try a fraction with a denominator of nine?" I asked.

"I tried five-ninths on the calculator and it came out zero point five, five, five. There were seven fives," Blaire added.

"I did one-ninth and I got zero decimal point one, one, one, one, one, one, one," Chen continued.

"There was a zero first in my decimals, too," Shannon said.

I added the zeros to what Shannon had written and recorded Blaire's and Chen's discoveries underneath:

$\frac{2}{9} = 0.2222222$

$\frac{7}{9} = 0.7777777$

$\frac{5}{9} = 0.5555555$

$\frac{1}{9} = 0.1111111$

I asked, "Based on the pattern you see, can you predict what you think eight-ninths would be as a decimal?"

"It will probably be zero point eight, eight, eight, eight, eight, eight, eight," said Isabella. "It looks like if a fraction has a denominator of nine, then the numerator is the decimal and it goes on and on."

"Try it with your calculator," I instructed.

"Yes, that's what my calculator has," Isabella said. I wrote on the board:

$\frac{8}{9} = 0.8888888$

I explained, "Mathematicians call decimal numbers like these 'repeating decimals.' " I rewrote the decimal equivalents to show the standard shortcut:

$\frac{2}{9} = 0.\overline{2}$

$\frac{7}{9} = 0.\overline{7}$

$\frac{5}{9} = 0.\overline{5}$

$\frac{1}{9} = 0.\overline{1}$

$\frac{8}{9} = 0.\overline{8}$

I explained what I had written, "Mathematicians have a shortcut way of indicating that the repeating continues. Your calculator display ran out of room, but when you divide, the numbers keep repeating. The line above the number tells that it keeps on repeating."

I then asked, "Did anyone get a different repeating decimal when completing your homework?"

Crystal replied, "I got two numbers that repeated."

"Come up and record on the board the fraction you tried and the decimal equivalent you got."

Crystal wrote on the board $\frac{7}{11} = 0.6363636$ and explained, "I didn't know

what to expect so I was really surprised when my display went six, three, six, three, six, three."

Misha said, "I tried four-elevenths, and my decimal was like Crystal's but backwards. It went three, six, three, six, three, six." I wrote on the board:

$\frac{4}{11} = 0.3636363$

"Like this?" I asked. Misha nodded.

"Did anyone else try a fraction with the denominator of eleven?" I asked.

Justin responded, "I did five-elevenths and I got zero point four, five, four, five, four, five." I wrote on the board:

$\frac{1}{11} =$

$\frac{2}{11} =$

$\frac{3}{11} =$

$\frac{4}{11} = .03636363$

$\frac{5}{11} = 0.4545454$

$\frac{6}{11} =$

$\frac{7}{11} = 0.6363636$

$\frac{8}{11} =$

$\frac{9}{11} =$

$\frac{10}{11} =$

I asked, "What do you notice about these repeating decimals?"

"It is always two numbers that repeat," Matthew said.

"The numbers are like the ones in the *Ten-Coin* problem. If you add up the two numbers, you get the sum of nine," Kim replied. Kim was referring to the homework activity she had done for the *Eight-Coin* problem. (See Chapter 14.)

"Four-elevenths and seven-elevenths are the same numbers except in reverse," Patrice added.

"What do you think the decimal equivalent is for six-elevenths? Discuss this with your neighbor first and then try it out on the calculator," I said.

Rory answered, "We got zero point five, four, five, four, five, four. It's the same as five-elevenths but in reverse."

I added this decimal to the chart on the board. "Discuss with your neighbor what you think the rest of the decimal equivalents will be and then test out your conjectures with your calculators." The class quickly began working on the problem. After the students had time to test their predictions, I asked volunteers to record on the board the decimal equivalents they had found.

$\frac{1}{11} = 0.0909090$

$\frac{2}{11} = 0.1818182$

$\frac{3}{11} = 0.2727273$

$\frac{4}{11} = 0.3636363$

$\frac{5}{11} = 0.4545454$

$\frac{6}{11} = 0.5454545$

$\frac{7}{11} = 0.6363636$

$\frac{8}{11} = 0.7272727$

$\frac{9}{11} = 0.8181818$

$\frac{10}{11} = 0.9090909$

"Did any of your solutions surprise you?" I asked.

"We thought three-elevenths would end in a two, but the last number was a three instead," Ian said. I wrote on the board:

$\frac{3}{11} = 0.2727273$

"Like this?" I asked. Ian nodded and so did several others.

Isabella responded, "But ours came out with a two on the end." Students began comparing results from their calculators. In a moment, I asked for their attention.

"Why do you think that calculators give different answers?" I asked.

"My calculator always has a few more numbers on it than Crystal's," said Misha.

"Why do you think Ian's calculator gives a three at the end?" I continued.

The class wasn't sure about the discrepancies. They all agreed that some calculator displays fit more numbers on them, but they weren't sure why Ian's decimal ended with a three instead of a two. I

explained, "Some calculators round the last number up if the digit after it is five or greater. That's why Ian's number ends in a three and not a two. The seven caused the two to round up to a three."

Damon interrupted, "For eight-ninths, I got all eights but the last number is a nine. I guess it rounded up the last eight to a nine."

"Mine is all eights," Jonathan said. I went to the place on the board where I had recorded ninths and rewrote the fractions in order from smallest to largest, also adding $\frac{3}{9}, \frac{4}{9}$, and $\frac{6}{9}$. The students gave alternatives for the last four in the list:

$\frac{1}{9} = 0.1111111$

$\frac{2}{9} = 0.2222222$

$\frac{3}{9} = 0.3333333$

$\frac{4}{9} = 0.4444444$

$\frac{5}{9} = 0.5555555$ or 0.5555556

$\frac{6}{9} = 0.6666666$ or 0.6666667

$\frac{7}{9} = 0.7777777$ or 0.7777778

$\frac{8}{9} = 0.8888888$ or 0.8888889

I then wrote the fractions again, this time recording each decimal equivalent using the standard shortcut:

$\frac{1}{9} = 0.\overline{1}$

$\frac{2}{9} = 0.\overline{2}$

$\frac{3}{9} = 0.\overline{3}$

$\frac{4}{9} = 0.\overline{4}$

$\frac{5}{9} = 0.\overline{5}$

$\frac{6}{9} = 0.\overline{6}$

$\frac{7}{9} = 0.\overline{7}$

$\frac{8}{9} = 0.\overline{8}$

I then pointed to the decimal equivalents for the elevenths and asked, "How do you think a mathematician would write these repeating decimals? Discuss your ideas with your neighbor and raise your hand when you think you have a solution for all of them." After the students had an opportunity to discuss with their partners, I asked volunteers to share their ideas as I wrote them on the board:

$$\tfrac{1}{11} = 0.\overline{09}$$
$$\tfrac{2}{11} = 0.\overline{18}$$
$$\tfrac{3}{11} = 0.\overline{27}$$
$$\tfrac{4}{11} = 0.\overline{36}$$
$$\tfrac{5}{11} = 0.\overline{45}$$
$$\tfrac{6}{11} = 0.\overline{54}$$
$$\tfrac{7}{11} = 0.\overline{63}$$
$$\tfrac{8}{11} = 0.\overline{72}$$
$$\tfrac{9}{11} = 0.\overline{81}$$
$$\tfrac{10}{11} = 0.\overline{90}$$

Matthew protested, "I don't agree with three-elevenths. There were two numbers that repeated, two and seven, so the line should be over both of them, not just the two."

"Yes, you're right, Matthew," I said. I corrected the decimal for three-elevenths. "Did anyone try the fraction one-third?" I asked.

Maria answered, "I did and I got another repeating decimal. It was all repeating threes." A few others had tried it and got the same result. I wrote on the board:

$$\tfrac{1}{3} = 0.3333333$$

"How do you think a mathematician would record that decimal?" I asked. Maria came up and recorded on the board:

$$\tfrac{1}{3} = 0.\overline{3}$$

"Let's think back to our benchmark list. How did we record one-third as a decimal and as a percent?" I asked.

"It was thirty-three and a third hundredths as a decimal and thirty-three and a third percent," Chen said. I wrote on the board:

$$\tfrac{1}{3} = 0.\overline{3} = 0.33\tfrac{1}{3} = 33\tfrac{1}{3}$$

"What about two-thirds?" I asked.

Jonathan had already done the division on his calculator. "I knew it!" he said excitedly. "It's repeating sixes!" I wrote on the board:

$$\tfrac{2}{3} = 0.6666666 \text{ or } 0.6666667$$
$$\tfrac{2}{3} = 0.\overline{6} = 0.66\tfrac{2}{3} = 66\tfrac{2}{3}\%$$

Jose made another discovery. He said, "Look, the decimal for one-third is the same as for three-ninths."

"And two-thirds and six-ninths are the same, too," Madison noticed.

It wasn't immediately clear why this was so, but Misha quickly came up with an explanation. She said, "It has to be because one-third is the same as three-ninths, and two-thirds is the same as six-ninths." I wrote on the board:

$$\tfrac{1}{3} = \tfrac{3}{9} = 0.\overline{3}$$
$$\tfrac{2}{3} = \tfrac{6}{9} = 0.\overline{6}$$

Writing on the board not only described Misha's thinking but also gave time for students who don't think as quickly as she does to think about the equivalent fractions. There was a buzz in the room as students talked about Misha's idea.

I interrupted their conversations. "Can you think of other fractions that will produce the same decimal equivalents?" The room was silent for a moment, then several hands shot up. I called on Frank.

"Four-twelfths. It's the same as one-third," he announced. Students went to their calculators to verify Frank's idea. Then hands shot up and students gave other fractions, more of them equivalent to $\tfrac{1}{3}$ than $\tfrac{2}{3}$ — $\tfrac{10}{30}, \tfrac{20}{60}, \tfrac{7}{21}, \tfrac{5}{15},$ and $\tfrac{8}{12}$. I listed each fraction on the board for students to test.

For the rest of the period I engaged the students in making predictions about the decimal equivalents for other fractions. I said to the class, "I'll write a fraction on the board. Then, without using your calculator, discuss at your table what decimal you predict you'll get by dividing its numerator by its denominator. We'll talk about your ideas and then we'll all do the divisions on our calculators and see what we learn."

Questions and Discussion

▲▲

▲ *What about students who didn't do the homework? How did they participate?*

It's typical to have students who didn't complete a homework assignment, and there are many reasons for this. They might have been absent the day before, ill that evening, had a family commitment that took priority, forgot, or some other reason. I think I've heard them all. But I keep my sights during class on learning. Having them discuss the homework in small groups helps support the learning of all of the students. While the students are discussing among themselves, I circulate and check on who did and didn't complete the assignment. I deal with that later, but keep the emphasis in class on learning. Even students who didn't do the homework can learn from both the small-group and the whole-class discussions based on the assignment.

▲ *Doesn't using different calculators confuse students?*

Calculators are tools that students need to learn to use. Calculators vary, just as do other common tools—tape measures, combination locks, kitchen implements, and so on. It's best not to limit students' experience to just one particular style, but to give them experience with a variety. Students can deal with the differences and will become more flexible, confident, and competent as a result.

CHAPTER FOURTEEN
THE EIGHT-COIN PROBLEM

Overview

This lesson uses money to give students another model for understanding decimals. Students first discuss decimal representations of money and also how money connects with base ten blocks. They then tackle a problem-solving investigation that provides them with additional practice while also involving them in looking for and describing numerical patterns.

Materials

▲ coins: 10 dimes and 10 pennies per pair of students
▲ play $1.00 bills, 5 per pair of students (see Blackline Masters)
▲ place value mats, 1 per pair of students (see Blackline Masters)

Time

▲ one class period

Teaching Directions

1. Write on the board and ask students to read:

$2.50

2.50

Ask the students: "How are these different and how are they alike?"

2. Pose two questions: "How could we show two and fifty-hundredths using the fewest number of base ten blocks possible? How could we show two dollars and fifty cents with the money at our table using the fewest possible number of dollar bills and coins?" Discuss and record on the board:

2 flats	5 rods	0 units
2 dollars	5 dimes	0 pennies

3. Distribute a place value mat to each pair of students and pose a problem: *Using only dimes and pennies, place fifty-three cents on your mat using the fewest possible number of coins.* Ask students for the solution and how to record fifty-three cents. Write on the board the two ways to record:

53¢

$.53

4. Ask the students: "Who can explain why the decimal representation makes sense to represent fifty-three cents?" Lead a class discussion about the value of dimes and pennies and how they are similar to the base ten blocks. Ask the students: "What fraction of a dollar is fifty-three cents? What percent of a dollar is fifty-three cents?"

5. Present another problem: *Clear your mat and this time place seventeen cents on it. Again, use only dimes and pennies, and the fewest number of coins possible.* When the students find the solution, ask them how to record seventeen cents using a decimal representation with the dollar sign. Write on the board:

$.17

6. Introduce the *Eight-Coin* problem to the class. First ask: "How many coins did you use to show fifty-three cents? Seventeen cents?" Once the students realize that they used eight coins for each, present the problem: *Think of other amounts of money you can show with exactly eight coins, using just dimes and pennies. See if you can find all the different amounts possible, then list them from smallest to largest and look for patterns in the list.* Also instruct the students that they can work in pairs, but that each student should individually record each amount with a decimal representation.

7. After the students work on the problem, discuss with the class the largest possible amount, the smallest possible amount, the other possible amounts, and any patterns discovered in their lists.

8. Write a related problem on the board for the students to complete for homework:

Suppose we explored the different amounts of money we could represent with ten coins. Find all the different amounts, list them in order, and then look for patterns in your list. Write down any patterns you find.

Teaching Notes

This lesson is especially useful for students who are still confused about decimal place value, giving them the opportunity to draw from their experiences and knowledge about money to help make sense of decimal place value and notation. At the same time, students whose understanding of decimals is more solid will still benefit from the review and also from the problem-solving investigation.

I prefer to use real coins for lessons that involve money and duplicate play dollar bills. The investment for using real coins is minimal; for this lesson you need ten dimes and ten pennies per pair of students. One way to handle the management of the coins is to distribute them at the beginning of the lesson and let students know that they are to return them at the end of class. This gives you a way to check on them and avoids losing coins and having to replace them for other activities. If you prefer, however, you can purchase play coins.

The Lesson

▲▲

To begin class, I distributed to each pair of students a baggie with ten pennies, ten dimes, and five play one-dollar bills. "Please leave the baggie of money unopened," I said. I then wrote on the board:

$2.50

"Who can read this?" I asked.

Most hands shot up. Rather than call on one student, I said to the class, "Let's read it softly together."

"Two dollars and fifty cents," some students said.

"Two fifty," others said.

I said, "I heard two responses. One was 'two dollars and fifty cents' and the other was 'two fifty.'"

"They're both OK," Ian said.

"Yes," I agreed. "Both are commonly used. It's possible that 'two fifty' could be two hundred fifty dollars instead of two dollars and fifty cents, but generally you wouldn't be confused because you'd know which amount made sense." I then wrote on the board:

2.50

"How does this number differ from what I first wrote?" I asked.

"The dollar sign," several students answered at once.

"How would you read this number?" I asked. I called on Patrice.

"Two and fifty-hundredths," she said.

"Would you say 'two fifty' for this as you did for the other?" I asked.

"No," Misha said, "that would be really easy to mix up with two hundred fifty." Others nodded their agreement.

I asked, "So when I put a dollar sign in front of two and fifty-hundredths, it means two dollars and fifty cents. The two look the same but one has a dollar sign in front. Do the two numbers mean the same?" The students were quiet, not sure how to answer. No one raised a hand.

"How could we show two and fifty-hundredths using base ten blocks?" I then asked. Now hands went up. Before calling on anyone, I added, "How would you show it using the fewest possible number of blocks?" Then I called on Chen.

"You'd use one flat and five rods and no units," he answered.

"And how would you show two dollars and fifty cents with the money at your table? Unzip the baggie and show two dollars and fifty cents using the fewest possible number of dollar bills and coins." It took only a minute for students to show two dollars and five dimes. I wrote on the board:

2 flats	*5 rods*	*0 units*
2 dollars	*5 dimes*	*0 pennies*

Leslee said, "Now I see how they're the same. They both use two wholes and five tenths."

I responded, "I know that a rod is a tenth of a flat because it takes ten rods to cover a flat. Are dimes tenths?"

Matthew said, "They have to be because it takes ten dimes to make one dollar."

"If I have a one-dollar bill, I can exchange it for ten dimes and I still have the same amount I started with," Rebecca said.

"With base ten blocks, when the flat is worth one, the rod is worth one-tenth, and the unit is worth one-hundredth. If you think a dime is a tenth, then what's worth one and what's worth one-hundredth in money?"

"A dollar bill is one whole," Shannon said.

"Ten dimes make a dollar, so each dime is one-tenth of a dollar. And a hundred pennies make a dollar, so each penny is one-hundredth of a dollar," Jonathan added.

Jose said, "It takes ten pennies to make one dime and it takes ten dimes to make one dollar. That's the same as the base ten blocks. It takes ten hundredths to make one-tenth and ten tenths to make one whole."

Elaine said, "And since it takes ten pennies to make a dime and ten dimes to make a dollar, it also means it takes a hundred pennies to make a dollar. Ten pennies ten times equal one hundred pennies. That's the same as for the hundredths and one whole with the base ten blocks."

Kendra said, "The dime is the same as tenths because it takes ten dimes to make one dollar and the penny is the same as hundredths because it takes one hundred pennies to make one dollar."

I then distributed a place value mat to each pair of students. I gave an initial instruction: "Using dimes and pennies, place fifty-three cents on your mat using the fewest possible number of coins." I watched as students easily placed five dimes and three pennies in the correct columns on their mats.

"Who would like to report the coins you used?" I asked. I called on Bryant.

"We have five dimes and three pennies," he said.

"Raise a hand if you used the same coins as Bryant," I said. Most hands went up immediately; the stragglers followed.

"How can I record fifty-three cents?" I asked.

"You can write fifty-three with a cents sign," Tamara suggested. I was interested in relating money to decimals and, therefore, in using a decimal representation to represent fifty-three cents. However, Tamara's suggestion was a correct one and, therefore, I accepted it. I wrote on the board:

53¢

"Like this?" I said. Tamara nodded.

"How else can I record fifty-three cents?" I asked.

"You can do it with a dollar sign," Elaine said. "You write a dollar sign, then point fifty-three." Typically, a student will make the suggestion Elaine did. If not, however, I would introduce this notation. I recorded on the board:

$.53

"Who can explain why Tamara's way makes sense?" I asked.

Crystal answered, "It's fifty-three cents.

That could mean fifty-three pennies, but it's the same amount of money as five dimes and three pennies. They're both the same."

"Let's look at the decimal representation, with the dollar sign," I said, pointing to $.53. "Who can explain why this makes sense to represent fifty-three cents?"

Rory said, "It's fifty-three–hundredths, and that's the same as fifty-three pennies because a penny is a hundredth of a dollar."

Madison added, "You could say it's five-tenths and three-hundredths, and the five-tenths are the five dimes because a dime is one-tenth of a dollar, and the three-hundredths are the pennies."

"What fraction of a dollar is fifty-three cents?" I asked.

"Fifty-three–hundredths," Jonathan answered.

"And what percent of a dollar is fifty-three cents?" I asked.

"It's fifty-three percent," Matthew said.

I then said, "Clear your mat and this time place seventeen cents on it. Again, use only dimes and pennies, and use the fewest possible number of coins." The students quickly placed one dime and seven pennies on their mats.

"Let's say together the coins you used," I said

"One dime and seven pennies," the students replied.

"Who would like to come up and record seventeen cents using a decimal representation with the dollar sign?" I asked. I called on Kendra. She came up and wrote:

> $.17

"What do you think about what Kendra wrote?" I asked.

"It's right," Peter said. "It says one dime and seven pennies, and that's seventeen cents."

INTRODUCING THE EIGHT-COIN PROBLEM

To give students practice using coins to show amounts of money and representing the amounts with decimal notation, I introduced a problem-solving investigation.

"How many coins did you use to show fifty-three cents?" I asked.

"Eight," they chorused.

"And how many for seventeen cents?" I asked.

"Eight," they answered again.

"Your task now is to think of other amounts of money you can show with exactly eight coins, using just dimes and pennies. See if you can find all the different amounts possible. You can work with your partner, but you should each record individually. Record each amount you find with a decimal representation like these." I pointed to $.53 and $.17 on the board. "When you think you have all of the amounts, list them from smallest to largest and look for patterns in the list. When you're all finished, we'll discuss the results as a class." I wrote on the board:

The Eight-Coin Problem

Before they began working, I asked, "Who can explain what you're to do now?" I asked this because it helps for students to hear the directions again.

Kim said, "We look for other amounts of money using eight dimes and pennies, and then we look for patterns."

"Anything else to add?" I asked.

"Put them in order," Martin said.

"Anything else?"

"We can work together, but we each have to write our own paper," Blaire added.

"Anything else?" I asked. There were no other hands.

"Any questions?"

After waiting a moment to be sure no one had a question, I said, "OK, get to work."

The students dove in. Some experimented randomly, putting out an assortment of dimes and pennies, checking to be sure that there were eight coins, recording, and then trying again.

A few students, however, worked in a more orderly way. Kendra, for example, said to her partner, Leslee, "Let's start with all dimes. That's the most we can make, eighty cents." Leslee counted out the dimes and placed them on the mat.

"Then we can do seven dimes and one penny," Kendra said.

"We have to write this one down first," Leslee said.

"OK," Kendra said. Both girls got out paper, wrote *The Eight-Coin Problem* at the top, and recorded *$.80*. Leslee finished first, removed the eight dimes, counted out seven and replaced them to the mat, and added a penny.

When I stopped to see how Ian and Jonathan were doing, they had completed their list. "We forgot thirty-five cents, but then we stuck it in," Ian told me.

"How did you know you had forgotten it?" I asked.

"It was missing from the pattern," Jonathan said. "See, the pennies went eight, seven, six, and down like that. Five was missing." Jonathan showed me their corrected list.

$.08

$.17

$.26

$.35

$.44

$.53

$.62

$.71

$.80

"What other patterns do you see?" I asked.

"The dimes go up—zero, one, two, all the way to eight," Ian said.

"Anything else?" I asked. The boys hadn't found anything else yet.

"Write down the patterns you found so far and then take another look," I said.

Patrice was excited to show me what she and Shannon had found. "There's a seven pattern, too!" she exclaimed.

"Show me what you mean," I said.

"It's like a diagonal pattern," Patrice said. She moved her finger from the zero in $.08 to the seven in $.17. "Zero plus seven is seven," she said. She then moved her finger from the one in $.17 diagonally down to the six in $.26. She said, "One plus six is seven. It works like that all the way down."

I said to the girls, "Write about that pattern on your paper. Then see what other patterns you can find."

"Look, if you add across, you get eight every time," Shannon said.

"Yes, that's another pattern. Write both of those down on your papers," I said.

"I found something weird," Misha came to tell me. I walked back to her seat to talk with her and her partner, Blaire.

"They go up by nine cents each time," Misha said.

"Can you explain what Misha means?" I asked Blaire. I always check to be sure that students understand what their partners claim.

Blaire said, "First I couldn't figure out what she meant, but then I got it. If you add nine cents onto eight cents, you get seventeen cents. And seventeen cents plus nine makes twenty-six cents. And that works all the way down. They get nine cents more each time."

"Why do you think that's weird?" I asked Misha. She shrugged.

"Be sure to write about that discovery," I said. "Also, try to figure out why that happens." I was curious if any of the students would be able to figure out why this pattern made sense. Starting with eight pennies, you get to the next higher amount with eight coins by removing a penny (subtracting one cent) and adding a dime (adding ten cents). The net result of adding a dime and removing a penny is to increase the amount by nine cents.

I interrupted the class when about ten minutes remained in the period. Some had only found the amounts; some had found the amounts and written about one pattern; some had described several patterns.

"Let's talk about what you learned," I said. "What was the largest amount you made with eight coins?"

"Eighty cents," Mark answered. The others agreed.

"And the smallest amount?" I asked.

"Eight cents," Crystal answered.

"What other amounts did you find using eight coins, and what patterns did you notice?" Several of the students reported. A discussion like this can help students see a variety of ways of thinking. Some students found the same patterns, such as the digits changing by one each time. No one else had described what Patrice had noticed, however. And although a few students had noticed the nine-cent difference that Misha discovered, no one was able to explain why that was so. I offered my explanation about adding ten cents and removing one cent each time, but I did so with a light touch, not expecting all of them to understand it immediately.

Homework

For homework, I gave the students a similar problem. "Suppose we explored the different amounts of money we could show using ten coins."

"You could get one dollar," Matthew blurted out.

I didn't respond but instead continued with directions. "Find all the different amounts, list them in order, and then look for patterns in your list. As you did with the eight-coin investigation, write down any patterns you find." Figures 14–1 through 14–3 show how some students solved this problem.

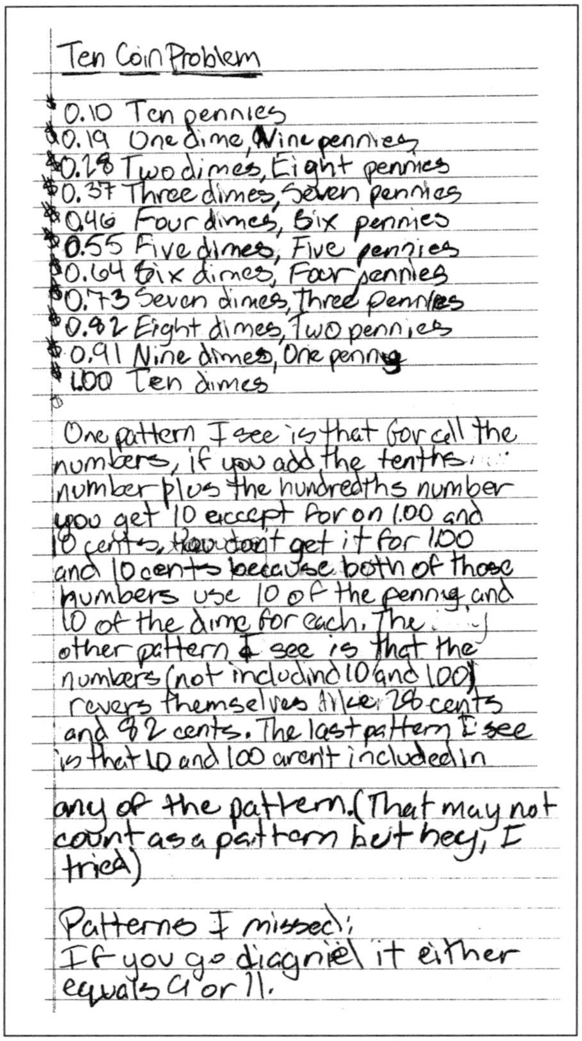
Ten Coin Problem

$0.10 Ten pennies
$0.19 One dime, Nine pennies
$0.28 Two dimes, Eight pennies
$0.37 Three dimes, Seven pennies
$0.46 Four dimes, Six pennies
$0.55 Five dimes, Five pennies
$0.64 Six dimes, Four pennies
$0.73 Seven dimes, Three pennies
$0.82 Eight dimes, Two pennies
$0.91 Nine dimes, One penny
$1.00 Ten dimes

One pattern I see is that for all the numbers, if you add the tenths number plus the hundredths number you get 10 except for on 1.00 and 10 cents. You don't get it for 100 and 10 cents because both of those numbers use 10 of the penny and 10 of the dime for each. The other pattern I see is that the numbers (not including 10 and 100) revers themselves like 28 cents and 82 cents. The last pattern I see is that 10 and 100 aren't included in any of the pattern. (That may not count as a pattern but hey, I tried)

Patterns I missed:
If you go diagniel it either equals 9 or 11.

▲▲▲▲▲**Figure 14–1** *Misha reported several patterns, including that the sum of the digits equals ten.*

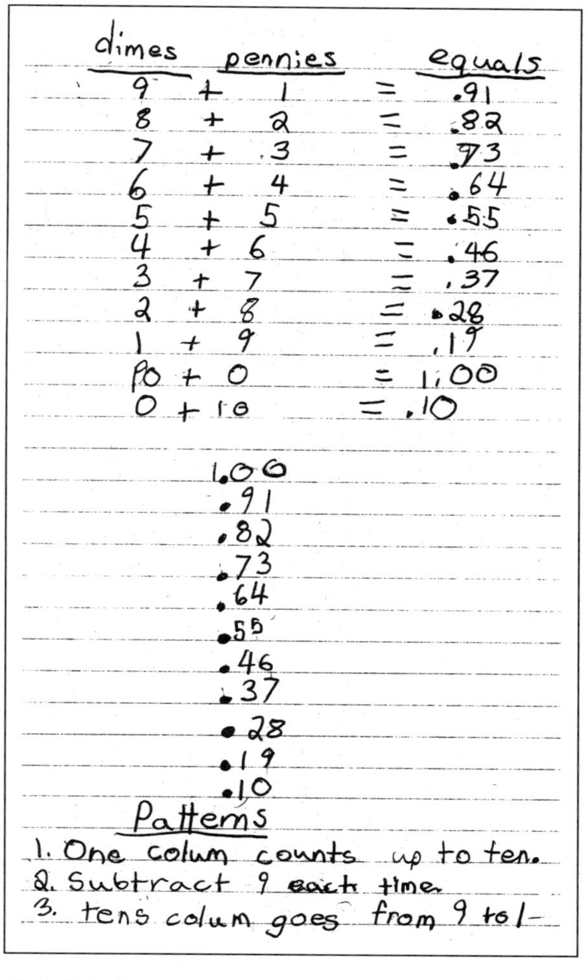

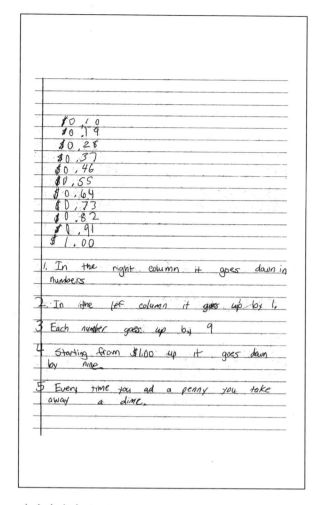

Figure 14–2 *Mark explained that there is a difference of nine between each amount of money in his list.*

Left figure content:

dimes	pennies		equals
9	+ 1	=	.91
8	+ 2	=	.82
7	+ 3	=	.73
6	+ 4	=	.64
5	+ 5	=	.55
4	+ 6	=	.46
3	+ 7	=	.37
2	+ 8	=	.28
1	+ 9	=	.19
10	+ 0	=	1.00
0	+ 10	=	.10

1.00
.91
.82
.73
.64
.55
.46
.37
.28
.19
.10

Patterns
1. One colum counts up to ten.
2. Subtract 9 each time.
3. tens colum goes from 9 to 1

Right figure content:

$0.10
$0.19
$0.28
$0.37
$0.46
$0.55
$0.64
$0.73
$0.82
$0.91
$1.00

1. In the right column it goes down in numbers

2. In the lef column it goes up by 1.

3 Each number goes up by 9

4 Starting from $1.00 up it goes down by nine.

5 Every time you ad a penny you take away a dime.

Figure 14–3 *Kendra noticed that each time a penny is added, a dime is taken away.*

EXTENSIONS

In later classes, have students explore the patterns for other numbers of coins. Up to twenty coins is appropriate.

Also, have students include dollar bills as well as dimes and pennies in the investigation. Instead of eight coins, for example, using any combination of dollars, dimes, and pennies would produce a maximum amount of eight dollars and a minimum amount of eight cents. However, if you include dollar bills in the investigation, there are forty-five different amounts using a total of eight bills and coins, which can make for an investigation that is more tedious than interesting. Limit the total number of bills and coins to five. For three bills and coins, there are ten different amounts; for four, there are fifteen different amounts; for five, there are twenty-one different amounts.

Questions and Discussion

▲▲▲

▲ *When you asked how base ten blocks relate to money, several students answered and offered essentially the same ideas. Why did you have them all answer?*

Even though students have different ways to describe the same idea, I think it's beneficial to give as many as would like the chance to talk. When students explain their ideas, they are cementing their knowledge. Also, others benefit from hearing the same idea expressed in different ways.

▲ *You gave the students the option of working with a partner on the investigation with eight coins, but you had them record individually. Why did you do this?*

While I think it's best for a problem-solving situation for students to have the chance to collaborate and share their ideas, one goal of the lesson was for students to have practice recording amounts of money using decimal representation. It seemed that it would be best for all students to have this practice.

▲ *Didn't the problem of investigating the amounts for eight coins really distract the students from studying decimals?*

The problem-solving investigation provided the vehicle for students to use the decimal notation for money and helped them relate an abstract idea to the concreteness of money. The repeated use in the investigation not only provided students practice with the decimal notation, it also provided the students with a mathematical challenge that was interesting to consider. This was especially useful for students for whom the practice might be trivial.

CHAPTER FIFTEEN
MONEY RIDDLES

Overview

Riddles involving money give students practice representing equivalent fractions, decimals, and percents. Students solve a series of riddles and then, for homework, create and solve several money riddles of their own. In a second class period, they exchange and solve one another's riddles. This lesson provides the students experience computing with decimals.

Materials

▲ coins: 4 quarters, 10 dimes, and 10 pennies for each pair or group of four students
▲ play bills, 10 each of $1.00, $5.00, and $10.00 bills (see Blackline Masters)
▲ *Money Riddles* worksheet, 1 per pair of students (see Blackline Masters)
▲ *More Money Riddles* worksheet, 1 per student (see Blackline Masters)

Time

▲ two class periods

Teaching Directions

1. Distribute coins and play bills to each pair of students. Give the class several warm-up problems, asking students to show the money with the fewest coins possible for various amounts of tenths and hundredths of a dollar. For example: *How much is three-hundredths of a dollar? How much is four-tenths of a dollar?*

2. Next, pose problems that involve fifths: *How much is one-fifth of a dollar? How much is one-fifth of fifty cents?* Again ask students to show the answers with the fewest coins possible and explain their reasoning.

3. Introduce money riddles by writing on the board the first riddle from the *Money Riddles* worksheet:

> *What is the sum of three-hundredths of $1.00, four-tenths of $1.00, and one-fourth of $20.00?*

Instruct the students: "With your partner, use the coins to represent each part of the clue. Then use decimal notation to record the amount of money in each part of the clue and in the answer to the riddle."

4. After the class has time to work on the riddle, ask volunteers to come to the front of the room to explain their answers and to record on the board their solutions. This is an ideal opportunity to introduce the standard way to list decimals for addition, lining up the decimal points. If no student has done so, record the problem on the board:

$$\begin{aligned} \$\ .03 \\ .40 \\ \underline{5.00} \\ \$5.43 \end{aligned}$$

5. Distribute the *Money Riddles* worksheet, one to each pair of students, and explain: "You and your partner should solve all of the riddles on this page, just as we did the first one. Use the money to represent the amount of money in each part of the clue. Make sure you agree on each solution and can explain how you got it. Record the amounts of money for each part of the clue, and for the answer."

6. Give the students the rest of the class time to solve the riddles. Collect their papers at the end of the class.

7. For homework, distribute to each student a copy of the *More Money Riddles* worksheet.

8. Begin the next class by handing back their *Money Riddles* worksheets and asking the students to compare the solutions they came up with yesterday with another pair of students. Tell them: "If there's disagreement, discuss your reasoning with your group and see if you can come to a consensus about the correct solution. Make sure each person in the group is able to explain the answers and how to figure them out." Also, ask the students to compare their solutions from their homework assignment.

9. After the students have time to compare, discuss as a class the solutions to each riddle. Have the students discuss the different strategies they used and write on the board the various ways to record the solutions.

10. For homework, instruct the students to make up five money riddles. Tell them: "Your problems and solutions should not exceed ten dollars, and your clues should include decimals, fractions, and percents." Also tell them to solve each riddle as well and provide an answer key. (Have students exchange riddles for the next day's homework.)

Teaching Notes

The riddles in this lesson are written in such a way as to help the students review and reinforce equivalent representations of decimals, fractions, and percents. Students should have some facility with percents before tackling these riddles. Chapters 9 and 10 provide a good introduction. The lesson also provides the opportunity to talk with students about the usefulness of the convention of lining up decimal points when adding several decimals. In this way, the students see the usefulness of the procedure.

The Lesson

▲▲▲

DAY 1

To begin the period, I distributed a bag of coins and play bills to each pair of students and gave the class a few warm-up problems. I first asked, "How much is three-hundredths of a dollar? Show this amount of money with the fewest coins possible." After I noticed that students had put out three pennies, I called on Chen.

"It's three pennies, or three cents," he said. The other students agreed.

"How much is four-tenths of a dollar?" I next asked. Again, students showed the answer with coins and a student reported.

"How much is thirteen-hundredths of a dollar?" I asked. A few students began to count out thirteen pennies, but others reminded them that they needed to use the fewest number of coins possible.

"How much is one-fifth of a dollar?" I asked. Some students had difficulty at first with this. A few put out four quarters and then realized that this wouldn't help. Most used dimes. After a few minutes, I called on Madison.

"It's two dimes," she said.

"How did you figure that out?" I asked.

"We remembered it from the Benchmarks chart," she said, giggling.

"Can anyone explain Madison's answer another way?" I asked.

Elaine said, "You need ten dimes for a dollar. To make fifths, you need five piles, and there are two in each pile. One-fifth of a dollar is twenty cents."

"Is there another way to explain this?" I asked.

Misha said, "I counted five numbers to get to one hundred—twenty, forty, sixty, eighty, one hundred. Twenty is one-fifth of a hundred."

"How much is one-fifth of fifty cents?" I then asked. A few hands shot up. I reminded them to talk with their partners and show the answer with the fewest coins possible. Then I called on Ian.

"Fifty is half of a hundred, so instead of two dimes, you have just one dime," he said.

Patrice said, "Five dimes make fifty cents, and one-fifth of five dimes is one dime, and that's ten cents."

Introducing Money Riddles

I gave the class a money riddle to solve. I wrote on the board the first riddle from the worksheet that I planned to distribute:

What is the sum of three-hundredths of $1.00, four-tenths of $1.00, and one-fourth of $20.00?

I said, "With your partner, use the coins to represent each part of the clue. Then use decimal notation to record the amount of money in each part of the clue and in the answer to the riddle." The room got noisy as the students went to work. I circulated and watched. After most of the students had time to solve the riddle, I called the class back to attention. Even though some weren't finished, I thought that a discussion would be helpful to them, especially if they were having difficulty.

Rebecca and Blaire came to the front of the room to present their solution. Rebecca explained and Blaire recorded on the board. Rebecca said, "We think the answer is five dollars and forty-three cents. We figured that three-hundredths of a dollar is three pennies and four-tenths of a dollar is forty pennies. That's a total of forty-three cents. We weren't sure about one-fourth of twenty dollars, but Elaine showed us if we count by fives—five, ten, fifteen, twenty—that's four numbers. The first number is five, so one-fourth of twenty dollars would be five dollars. We added five dollars to forty-three cents." Blaire wrote:

$.03 + $.40 + $5.00 = $5.43

The girls sat down. "Does anyone else have something to share?" I asked.

"We did the same thing, except we thought four-tenths of a dollar was four dimes, not forty pennies," Susan said. "We took out three pennies and four dimes from our bag and also got forty-three cents."

Kendra continued, "Then we tried to make twenty dollars with four piles. We finally figured out that each pile would have five dollars in each, so we knew that one-fourth of twenty dollars was five dollars."

"Do you agree with how Blaire recorded?" I asked.

"Yes, but we wrote them up and down," Susan said.

"Come up and show us how your recorded," I said. Susan came up and wrote:

$.03
$.40
+$5.00
$5.43

I wondered for a moment what to do about Susan's recording. I knew that one reason students add decimals incorrectly is because they don't line up the decimal points. This error is often because students rely on following a procedure rather than reasoning about what the numbers mean. In this case, Susan and Kendra had reasoned correctly, but still I felt it was an ideal opportunity to introduce the standard way to list decimals for adding.

I said, "The answer you got is correct, but I have a suggestion for how you recorded. When decimals are listed in a column, as you've done, it's common to write them so that all of the decimal points are lined up. That way, the numbers in the same place are directly underneath one another. Also, you only need to put the dollar sign next to the first amount in the list and in the answer. What you did is fine, but you'll generally see the problem written this way." I recorded:

$ .03
  .40
+ 5.00
$5.43

I then said to the class, "Check your papers. If you wrote the numbers in a column, be sure that you lined up the decimal points. Also, write the dollar sign only for the first addend and for the answer."

As students checked their papers, Blaire said, "Did I write the dollar sign too many times?" She was referring to what she had recorded on the board.

"No," I responded. "When you write the problem horizontally, you can include all of the dollar signs." These instructions didn't focus on students' reasoning but rather on a few of the conventions for representing money symbolically.

I then distributed the activity sheet, *Money Riddles,* one to each pair of students. I explained, "You and your partner should solve all of the riddles on this page, just as we did this first one. Use the coins to help you figure out the answer from the clues. Make sure you agree on each solution and can explain how you got it. Also, record the amounts of money for each part of the clue, and for the answer. The first riddle is the one you just tried, so you can record the answer easily. Then try the others."

The class used most of the class period to work on the riddles. For homework, I had duplicated *More Money Riddles*, a worksheet with three additional riddles. I planned to give a worksheet to each student who finished early.

Homework

At the end of the class, I collected the original sheets of riddles and distributed *More Money Riddles* to students who didn't yet have one. A few students still hadn't completed all of the original riddles and I asked them to finish them that night for homework. "Tomorrow, we'll go over the riddles you were working on today. Also, be prepared tomorrow to discuss these three extra riddles."

DAY 2

I handed back their papers from the day before and said to the class, "Before we discuss our solutions together, I'd like you to compare the solutions you and your partner came up with yesterday with another pair of students. If there's disagreement, discuss your reasoning with the group and see if you can come to consensus about the correct solution. Make sure each person in the group is able to explain the answers given and how to figure them out. When you've done this, then compare the solutions from your homework." I organized the class so that students knew who would work together. Then, while the students got started, I talked briefly with Martin, who had been absent the day before, and then had him join a group.

After about ten minutes, I called the students to attention to begin a class discussion. There wasn't any disagreement among the students for the first five riddles, but they reported the difficulties they had with riddle 6: *How much money is there altogether in three groups if each group has two-hundredths of $1.00 and seven-tenths of $1.00?*

Rory began, "This one took a little more time. It was easy to find two-hundredths of a dollar and seven-tenths of a dollar but then we had to make more groups."

"So what did your group come up with?"

"Well, two-hundredths of a dollar is two pennies and seven-tenths of a dollar is seven dimes, so we put together seventy-two cents. But then the riddle said to make three groups, so we made two more groups of seventy-two cents. We added on paper to get the answer. We got two dollars and sixteen cents." I recorded $2.16 on the board.

"We did the same thing except we did it in our heads," Jonathan said. "We added seventy cents three times to get two dollars and ten cents. Then we added two cents three times, which equals six cents. We then did them together. We got the same as Rory."

Crystal reported another way to find the answer. She said, "We made three groups, too, but we did multiplication. We wrote the problem on the paper. Can I come up and show?" I agreed and Crystal came up and wrote:

$$.72$$
$$\times 3$$
$$\overline{216}$$

Crystal continued explaining, "When we multiplied the numbers we got two hundred sixteen, but we weren't sure what to do with the decimal. But then Misha said that if we put it between the one and the six, the answer would be twenty-one dollars and sixty cents, and that's too much.

And before the two gives only twenty-one cents and something extra. It didn't make sense. So we put the decimal point between the two and the one. It was the best answer. Oh, and we put in the dollar sign." Crystal inserted the decimal point and the dollar sign.

.72
×3
$2.16

Riddle 8 had also given students some difficulty: *If 40% of $1.00 and three-hundredths of $1.00 are subtracted from $2.00, how much money is left?*

Lena was eager to report. "This was cool. We knew we had to subtract for this one, so we started with two dollars since the clues were subtracted from two dollars. Then we figured out what each part was and subtracted it from two dollars to get our answer."

I asked, "Can you explain what are forty percent of a dollar and three-hundredths of a dollar?"

Lena's partner, Madison, chimed in, "Three-hundredths of a dollar is just three pennies, so we knew we had to subtract three cents. So we exchanged one of the two dollars for nine dimes and ten pennies and took away three pennies so we had one dollar and ninety-seven cents. We actually did that in our heads, but you told us we had to use the money, too." I recorded on the board what Madison reported:

$2.00 − $.03 = $1.97

Madison continued, "The forty percent confused us a little, so we looked at it as forty out of one hundred instead, which is forty cents. That made it much easier for us. We then took four dimes away because four dimes is the same thing as forty cents. We were left with one dollar and fifty-seven cents." I recorded:

$1.97 − $.40 = $1.57

"Did anyone do it another way?" I asked.

Kendra explained, "We knew three-hundredths was three pennies, too, and we didn't like the forty percent either. We changed it to a decimal since we were using money anyway."

"What is the decimal equivalent of forty percent?" I asked.

"It's point forty, and that's easy to see is forty cents," Kendra answered. I wrote on the board:

40% = .40

Kendra continued, "OK, we started with two dollars and then we added the forty cents and the three cents together first to get forty-three cents. Then we took forty-three cents away from the two dollars at the same time instead of doing it in separate steps."

"So you did this?" I asked. I recorded on the board:

$2.00 − $.43

Kendra nodded. "How did you do this subtraction?" I asked.

Kendra answered, "Two dollars minus forty is one dollar and sixty cents, and then minus three more cents makes a dollar fifty-seven, just like Madison got." I recorded:

$2.00 − $.43 = $1.57

We continued discussing the last two riddles. The class had quite a debate as to what was the correct solution for riddle 10: *If three-tenths of $1.00, two-hundredths of $1.00, and one-fifth of $10.00 is subtracted from $5.00, how much is left?*

Adam responded first, "We think you will have two dollars and sixty-eight cents left over."

Hunter's hand shot up. "We think it's three dollars and thirty-two cents," he said.

"We disagree," Miles said. "We think you won't have any money left over. It was a trick question." I wrote the three suggestions on the board:

$2.68

$3.32

$0

"Adam, can you and Ian explain your answer?" I asked.

Adam said, "Three-tenths of a dollar and two-hundredths of a dollar is easy. That's thirty-two cents. One-fifth of ten dollars is two dollars, because if I make five equal groups, I have two dollars in each. So we took out a five-dollar bill and then subtracted two dollars. That left us with three dollars." Adam held up the money as he explained, and I recorded to keep track of his thinking:

$5.00 – $2.00 = $3.00

Adam continued, "Then we had to subtract our thirty-two cents, so we exchanged one of the dollars for dimes and took away three of them. Then we needed to subtract two pennies."

I interrupted Adam and asked, "When you subtracted three dimes, what did you have left then?"

Adam said, "Two dollars and seventy cents." Adam paused as I recorded:

$3.00 – $.30 = $2.70

Adam continued, "Then we exchanged one dime for ten pennies, subtracted two of them, and were left with a total of two dollars and sixty-eight cents." I recorded the rest of Adam's explanation:

$2.70 – $.02 = $2.68

Hunter explained next what he and Luis did. "We did the same thing except we did the subtraction on paper instead. We knew we were starting with five dollars, so we wrote that on our paper. We also figured out we were subtracting two dollars and thirty-two cents, so we wrote that under the five dollars. We subtracted the two numbers and got three dollars and thirty-two cents." I recorded:

$5.00
$- 2.32$
$3.32

"That doesn't make sense," Marcus said. "If you have five dollars and take away two dollars, you have three dollars left. Then if you subtract thirty-two cents, how can you have more than three dollars?"

"I don't think you borrowed," Shannon suggested. "It looks like you just brought down the three and the two instead of subtracting."

"Oh, I see what we did," Hunter said. "Yeah, we agree with Adam. The answer is two dollars and sixty-eight cents."

"What about Miles and Rory's solution?" I asked.

"Never mind," Rory said. "We thought one-fifth of ten dollars was five dollars. I think we saw the five in one-fifth and thought in halves. One-half of ten dollars is five dollars, so we thought if we were subtracting five dollars, from five dollars you would have nothing left. But now we agree with Adam."

Homework

"For homework, make up five money riddles. Your problems and solutions should not exceed ten dollars, and make sure to include clues with decimals, fractions, and percents. Solve each riddle as well and provide an answer key. We'll exchange them tomorrow." I planned to have students exchange their riddles for the next homework. See Figures 15–1 and 15–2 for two students' riddles.

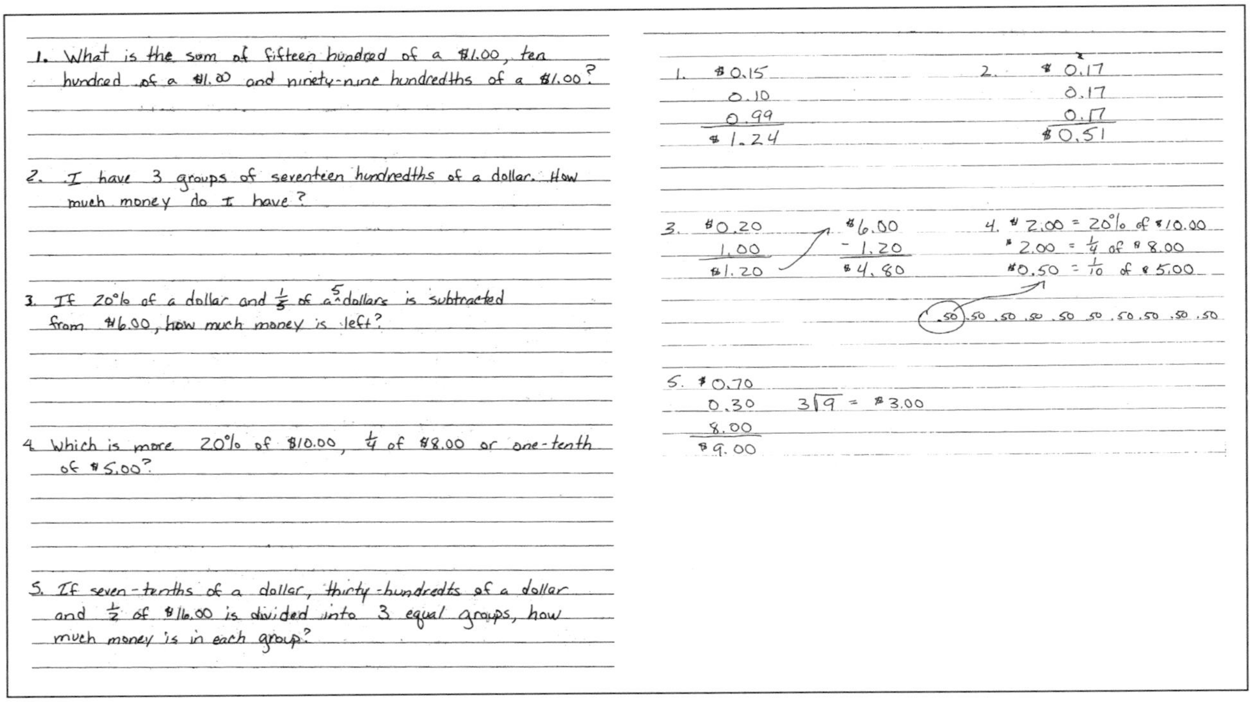

1. What is the sum of fifteen hundred of a $1.00, ten hundred of a $1.00 and ninety-nine hundredths of a $1.00?

2. I have 3 groups of seventeen hundredths of a dollar. How much money do I have?

3. If 20% of a dollar and $\frac{1}{5}$ of a $5 dollars is subtracted from $6.00, how much money is left?

4. Which is more 20% of $10.00, $\frac{1}{4}$ of $8.00 or one-tenth of $5.00?

5. If seven-tenths of a dollar, thirty-hundredths of a dollar and $\frac{1}{2}$ of $16.00 is divided into 3 equal groups, how much money is in each group?

1. $0.15
      0.10
      0.99
     $1.24

2. $0.17
      0.17
      0.17
     $0.51

3. $0.20 $6.00
      1.00   - 1.20
     $1.20 $4.80

4. $2.00 = 20% of $10.00
   $2.00 = $\frac{1}{4}$ of $8.00
   $0.50 = $\frac{1}{10}$ of $5.00
   .50 .50 .50 .50 .50 .50 .50 .50 .50 .50

5. $0.70
      0.30   3)9 = $3.00
      8.00
     $9.00

▲▲▲▲▲▲Figure 15–1 *Except for saying "hundred" for hundredths in riddle 1, Blaire's riddles are clear and the answers are correct.*

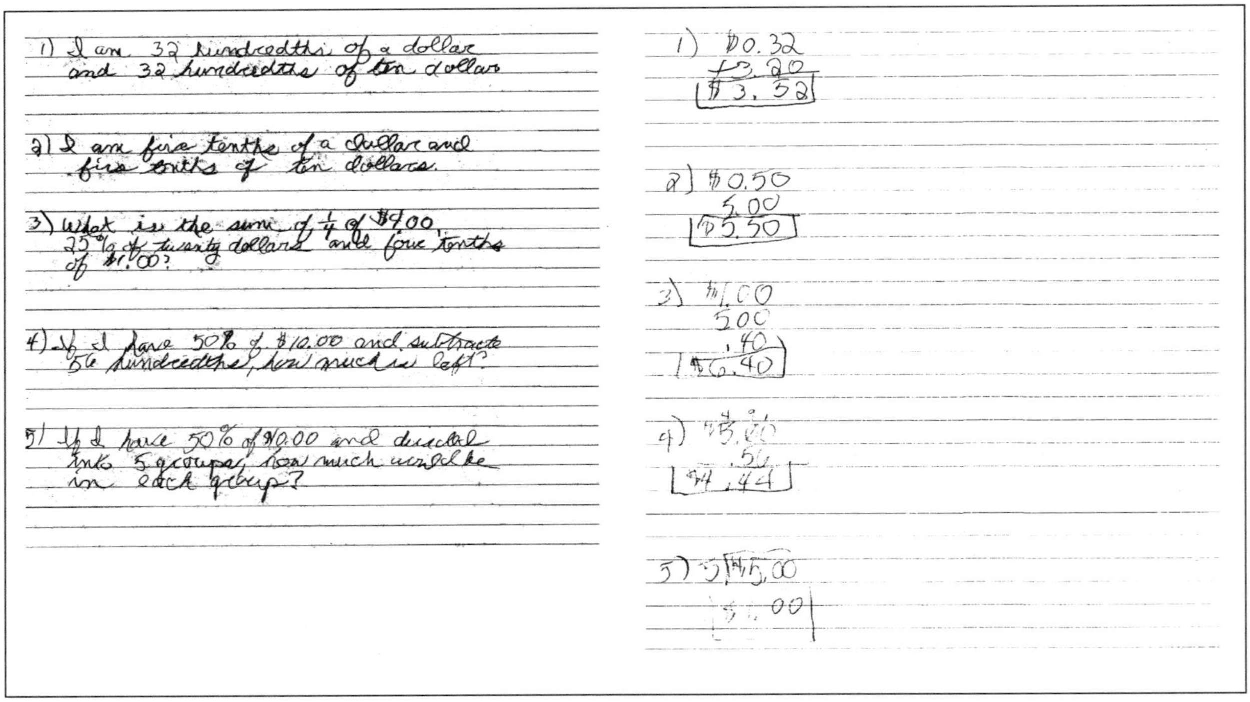

1) I am 32 hundredths of a dollar and 32 hundredths of ten dollars

2) I am five tenths of a dollar and five tenths of ten dollars.

3) What is the sum of $\frac{1}{4}$ of $4.00, 22% of twenty dollars and four tenths of $1.00?

4) If I have 50% of $10.00 and subtract 56 hundredths, how much is left?

5) If I have 50% of $9.00 and divided into 5 groups, how much will be in each group?

1) $0.32
      $3.20
     $3.52

2) $0.50
      5.00
     $5.50

3) $1.00
      5.00
       .40
     $6.40

4) $5.00
       .56
     $4.44

5) 5)$5.00
     $1.00

▲▲▲▲▲▲Figure 15–2 *Madison mixed fractions, decimals, and percents in her riddles.*

Questions and Discussion

▲▲

▲ *Why did you use the first riddle from the sheet as a sample?*

That way, the students would have a guarantee of success for at least the first one they had to do independently. I find that getting started on worksheets is difficult for some students, and this helped to ease them into working on the assignment.

▲ *What if the opportunity hadn't come up to show the class the correct way to write decimals in a column with the decimal points lined up?*

This is a good question. If the situation hadn't come up, I might have taken the opportunity at this time to show the class the correct way to record. However, if I felt with a particular class that the attention to the recording would distract from the emphasis on their reasoning, I wouldn't have necessarily done so in this lesson. There are many opportunities to teach this convention in this collection of lessons.

▲ *Sometimes you have students come up and record and sometimes you record for them. How do I know which to do?*

I have no hard-and-fast rule for this. My goal is for students to have as many opportunities as possible to see ways to record mathematical thinking. At times, it's good for students to come up and record as they explain, as Rebecca and Blaire did, and then Susan. But at times, I find it useful to do the recording as a model for others or to be sure that I understand what a student is explaining. When Adam explained, for example, his words came out in quite a rush, and I wanted to model for the class how recording calculations is helpful for examining and checking them. Then, Hunter and Luis's explanation gave me another opportunity to reinforce writing decimals in a column correctly. It's helpful to the students' learning to record how they reason, whether you or the students do it.

CHAPTER SIXTEEN
FOREIGN EXCHANGE AND ROUNDING

Overview

Investigating the value of foreign currencies in relation to U.S. dollars gives students experience rounding decimals and seeing how decimals are used in a real-world context. Also, from discussing the information on a foreign currency exchange table, the students learn that the U.S. dollar is not always worth one dollar in other countries and that when traveling internationally it's important to think about exchanging currency.

Materials

▲ table of foreign currency exchange rates, 1 per student (print from an Internet source; search for "currency exchange rates")

Time

▲ one class period

Teaching Directions

1. Begin by telling the students they will be comparing the U.S. dollar to other currencies from around the world. Then distribute to each student a table of foreign currency exchange rates.

2. Lead a class discussion about other countries' monetary systems. Ask the students to examine the table. Ask: "Which other countries also call their unit of money a dollar? If countries don't have dollars, what do they call their monetary units?"

3. Talk with the students about reading the foreign exchange table. Write the number on the board that indicates the number of Mexican pesos we could purchase with one U.S. dollar. Ask someone to read the number.

4. Instruct the students to find Mexico on the list and the number you wrote on the board. Tell them: "Discuss with your partner what you think that number means." Have volunteers explain their thinking to the class. Discuss the value of the U.S. dollar in pesos and talk about approximating the value. For example, if the table indicates that 9.4079 pesos are worth one dollar, we could say that a dollar is worth about 9 pesos, or 9.4 pesos, or 9.5 pesos. If students don't come up with these ideas, write on the board 9.00, 9.50, and 10.00 and discuss which is closest to 9.4079. (Adjust these numbers to fit the actual data on the table you copied.)

5. Draw on the board a row of squares equal to the number of pesos worth one dollar. To the left of the row, write: *Mexican Pesos*. Above the row, write *What $1.00 Is Worth*.

What $1.00 Is Worth

Mexican Pesos   ⬚⬚⬚⬚⬚⬚⬚⬚⬚

6. Repeat for Hong Kong. Write on the board the number of Hong Kong dollars worth one U.S. dollar. Ask students to read the number, locate it on their tables, and explain its meaning. Have them agree on an approximate amount to represent the number of Hong Kong dollars we could purchase with one U.S. dollar. Represent this amount with a row of squares and to the left of the row, write: *Hong Kong Dollars*.

What $1.00 Is Worth

Mexican Pesos
Hong Kong Dollars

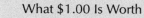

7. Continue with several other countries, discussing the currency, rounding the number in the chart to an approximation, and comparing the value to the United States dollar.

Teaching Notes

Often when studying decimal numbers that extend past the hundredths column, many students fail to see the relevance for such numbers or the need to learn to work with them. Giving students experience with decimals in a real-world situation such as thinking about foreign currencies can help them see the importance of using decimals and interpreting numbers in the thousandths and ten thousandths.

Also, students have traditionally learned rules for rounding and then applied the rules to textbook or worksheet exercises. Often, the numbers appear without any contexts, resulting in abstract practice that's unrelated to real-world applications. The approach in this lesson shifts the focus from memorizing rules to building students' decimal number sense. For example, by asking students if a number is closer to zero, one-half, or one focuses their attention away from learning a rule to making sense of the numbers they are considering.

The Lesson

▲▲▲

To begin the lesson, I said, "Today we'll compare the worth of the U.S. dollar to other money around the world." Students began sharing traveling stories, as some of the students were fortunate enough to have traveled outside of the United States. I also brought in coins that I've collected over the years from several different countries. Many of the students expressed surprise that the U.S. dollar is not always worth one dollar in other countries.

I then distributed to each student a table of foreign currency exchange rates that I had printed from the Internet. The one I printed listed countries alphabetically, named their currency unit, and then had two columns, one listing the value of the foreign currency unit in relation to our dollar, and the other listing how many of the foreign units were worth one U.S. dollar.

"Look over the list and see which other countries also call their unit of money a dollar," I said. The students called out the names of the countries—Australia, Bahamas, Barbados, Bermuda, Canada, and so on.

"Countries that don't call their money dollars have many other names—pesos, schillings, francs, pounds, rubles." Students searched the list and called out other names.

I said, "Every country has its own monetary system and its own currency. And for countries that do use dollars, their dollars don't look the same as ours."

"They probably don't have a picture of George Washington," Misha said.

"He was our president, not theirs," Bryant added.

"That's right. Other countries' dollars look different from ours, and they're worth different amounts, too. In this table, the first column of numbers tells how much the other country's unit of money is worth here, and the second column tells how much we could buy in that country with one of our own dollars. Find Mexico on the list and look just at the number in the second column."

I chose Mexico because of its proximity to California and because some of my students either have traveled to Mexico or have relatives living there. I asked, "Can someone read the number in the second column?" I wrote the number on the board:

9.4079

Shannon read, "Nine and four thousand seventy-nine–ten thousandths."

I then said, "Discuss with your partner what you think that number means in terms of dollars and pesos." After several minutes, a few students were eager to explain.

Chen reported for him and Frank. He said, "We think it means that in Mexico, the peso is worth about nine of our American dollars."

"Please explain your thinking to the class," I probed.

"Even though it has all of those numbers behind the nine, we were really interested in the whole number. The nine has a four behind it, so we didn't round up. We left it alone."

Misha's hand was waving. "I think that Chen has it backwards," she said. "We think that one American dollar is worth about nine pesos, that you would get nine pesos if you gave a dollar to a Mexican person."

"That's what we said," Chen defended.

"Tell us again what you mean, Chen," I said.

"You get about nine pesos for a dollar," he said. Chen now agreed with Misha even though his original statement didn't express this idea.

"That's what I think," Misha confirmed.

To represent this relationship graphically, I drew a row of nine squares and to the left of the row I wrote *Mexican Pesos*. Above the row of squares, I wrote *What $1.00 Is Worth*. In this way, I began constructing a bar graph that I could extend to compare the value of one U.S. dollar to other currencies.

What $1.00 Is Worth

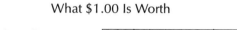

Mexican Pesos

"Does someone have another idea?" I asked.

Maria added, "We think that about nine and a half Mexican pesos are worth an American dollar."

"Can you explain?"

"Well, for every one American dollar, we could get nine and a half Mexican dollars . . . I mean, pesos . . . to equal the same thing," Maria explained.

I responded, "Can you explain why you thought nine and a half was a better amount to use than nine?"

"Since we're working with money, we figured we only needed a number showing dimes and cents, so that would be a number up to the hundredths place. So, in the number, we only need the nine and the forty after the decimal point. And we thought that nine dollars and forty cents

was closer to nine dollars and fifty cents, so we rounded up."

"We came up with something more exact," Jenny said. "We thought the same thing about dollars and cents, so we eliminated the last two numbers, the seven and the nine. Our number was like Maria's, but we noticed a seven after the zero so we rounded the zero to a one. We think the Mexican peso is worth nine dollars and forty-one cents of our dollars."

Alex objected, "That can't be right! It's the other way around. You need nine pesos and forty-one cents to get one dollar."

"Oh yeah," Jenny said, after thinking a moment.

"They're centavos, not cents," Luis corrected.

Underneath the 9.4079 I had written on the board, I wrote:

> 9.00
>
> 9.50
>
> 10.00

"Which of these numbers is closest to the number of pesos worth one dollar?" I asked.

Kim answered, "Probably closer to nine fifty because if we get rid of the two digits we don't use in money, we're left with nine forty, and that's closest to nine dollars and fifty cents."

I added half a square to the row of nine squares I had drawn to represent the number of Mexican pesos that were worth one U.S. dollar.

What $1.00 Is Worth

Mexican Pesos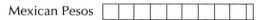

I then directed the students to look at the information about Hong Kong currency. "Hong Kong uses dollars, but their own dollars. Look at the number in the second column for Hong Kong." I wrote on the board:

7.7964

"About how many Hong Kong dollars are worth one U.S. dollar?" I asked.

"Almost eight," Damon said.

"What if we wanted a more exact answer?"

"It would probably be around seven Hong Kong dollars and eighty Hong Kong cents," Rory said.

"Can you explain?" I prompted.

"We only need the two numbers after the decimal point since it's in money, and I rounded the seventy-nine cents up and got seven dollars and eighty cents," replied Rory.

"I got the same thing but did it a different way," Crystal said. "I knew I would only need the seven and nine, but I noticed the six after the nine. So I rounded up the nine, which changed the seven, too."

On the board, underneath 7.7964, I listed three numbers:

7.00

7.50

8.00

"Which of these is closest to how many Hong Kong dollars are worth one of our dollars?"

"Definitely the eight," Justin said.

Next to the row of nine and half squares I had drawn to show how many Mexican pesos were worth one dollar, I drew a row of eight squares. To the left of the row I wrote *Hong Kong Dollars*.

What $1.00 Is Worth

Mexican Pesos									
Hong Kong Dollars									

"What do the eight squares represent?" I asked.

"It means that you could buy something that costs eight Hong Kong dollars with only one American dollar," Blaire said.

"What country would you like to look at next?" I asked.

"Egypt!" Jenny said. Jenny was especially interested in Egypt and all things Egyptian. We all looked at the table.

"What are pounds?" Maria asked.

I explained, "Our unit of currency is the dollar, but in Egypt the unit of currency is the pound. It's not like the pound you think about when you weigh things. It's a name for their basic unit of money."

This seemed to satisfy the class. I asked them to talk with their partners. "Figure out how many Egyptian pounds are worth one of our dollars," I said. The chart indicated 3.7170. After a few moments, I called the class to attention.

"Who would like to report?" I asked.

Peter said, "We think it takes about four of their pounds to make one of our dollars."

Patrice had another idea. "We think it's closer to three and a half."

"What's closer to three and a half?" I asked.

"About three and a half Egypt pounds is the same as one dollar," Patrice answered. I wrote on the board:

3.7170

4.0

3.5

"Which is closer?" I asked the class. Discussion broke out. I quieted the class and called on Martin.

"It's almost in the middle but a little closer to three and a half pounds," he said.

Elaine added, "In our money, three dollars and seventy-five cents is in the middle of three fifty and four dollars. It's only a little less."

"Who would like to come up and draw a row of squares for Egyptian pounds?" I asked. I wrote *Egyptian Pounds* on the board and Leslee came up to draw a row of three and a half squares.

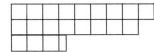

We continued with several other countries, discussing the currency, rounding the number in the chart to an approximation, and comparing the value to the United States dollar. For some, we didn't have the space to add a row of squares to our graph. In Italy, for example, more than 1,600 lire were worth the same as one U.S. dollar!

Questions and Discussion

▲ *When Misha challenged Chen, he claimed that he agreed with what she had said. But that wasn't what he first reported. How do you deal with this sort of confusion?*

It's true that Chen's second statement wasn't what his original statement had implied. But it seemed to me that Chen was clear about his understanding once he heard what Misha said, and even thought he had initially stated it correctly. If, however, Misha hadn't corrected Chen, I would have done so to check that his confusion had to do with the language, not the monetary value.

▲ *Although the students are estimating and rounding, the standard rule for rounding was never mentioned. Shouldn't the students be taught this procedure?*

In many instances in our everyday lives, we find ourselves needing to estimate, where an exact answer isn't necessary and an approximation will suffice or even be preferable. What's important isn't following a rule, but making sense of the information in the particular context. This lesson aims at focusing the students' attention to the meaning of the numbers rather than on a rule or a specific procedure.

CHAPTER SEVENTEEN
PIGS WILL BE PIGS

Overview

The book *Pigs Will Be Pigs*, by Amy Axelrod, is the springboard for giving students experience using decimal notation to represent and compute with money. Students figure out how much money the Pig family has and how much they spend for dinner at the Enchanted Enchilada restaurant. They then decide how they might spend the same amount of money to order dinner for four. The lesson gives students practice representing calculations symbolically and lining up and placing decimal points correctly. Also, the lesson provides students with practice estimating as they figure out how they might spend the allotted money.

Materials

▲ *Pigs Will Be Pigs*, by Amy Axelrod (Simon & Schuster, 1994)
▲ Enchanted Enchilada menu, 1 per group (see Blackline Masters)
▲ 12-by-18-inch white paper, 1 sheet per group of four students

Time

▲ two class periods

Teaching Directions

1. Read aloud the book *Pigs Will Be Pigs*, by Amy Axelrod. After reading the book, ask: "About how much money do you think the Pigs collected when they searched the house?" Read the book again and ask the students record the amount of money each Pig found.

2. Ask the students to figure out the exact amount of money the Pigs collected. Ask student who finish more quickly to check their calculations with a neighbor.

3. Discuss with the students how they added. As the students report the money each of the Pigs found, model recording the amounts on the board, writing them in a column and lining up the decimal points. (The total should be $34.67.)

4. Present a problem for students to figure out in their heads: *How much do four specials cost if each costs $7.99?* Have the students report their answers and how they got them; record their methods and solutions on the board. **Note:** If no student multiplied, present this method, writing a multiplication problem on the board, multiplying out loud, and recording the answer without a decimal point:

$7.99

× 4

3196

Lead a class discussion about how when multiplying decimals, you have to be sure to think about where it makes sense to put the decimal point in the answer.

5. Ask the students: "How much money did the Pigs have left over from the thirty-four dollars and sixty-seven cents after spending thirty-one dollars and ninety-six cents on the four specials? What else could they order?"

6. Present the menu problem: *Pretend that you're the Pig family eating at the Enchanted Enchilada restaurant and you have the same amount to spend as they had. Decide what you'd like to eat and estimate how much it will cost. Then figure out exactly what your choices cost and how much change you have left.* Distribute to each group a list of the menu items.

7. After the groups finish, ask groups to share what they ordered, the total for their meals, and how much change they had remaining.

8. Begin the second day with a second menu problem: *You have $40.00 to spend for four people and you must order for the table at least one appetizer, one special, and four drinks. Spend as much of the $40.00 as possible. Record what you order, including the prices of each item and show your calculations.* Distribute to each group a sheet of 12-by-18-inch white paper. After the students finish, lead a class discussion for groups to present their solutions.

Teaching Notes

In *Pigs Will Be Pigs*, by Amy Axelrod, the Pig family would like to go out to dinner, but they don't have enough money. Mrs. Pig forgot to go to the bank, and Mr. Pig has only one dollar in his wallet. They search the house looking for loose change and forgotten bills. First Mr. Pig finds his lucky two-dollar bill in his sock drawer, then Mrs. Pig searches her bedroom and finds two nickels, five pennies, and a quarter. In their room, the Piglets find six dimes, a dollar bill, and two hundred pennies in their penny collection. Altogether the family finds $34.67. They collect the money they find in a shoebox, head for their favorite restaurant, the Enchanted Enchilada, and eat until they're stuffed.

Along with providing students practice with computing mentally and estimating, the problems in this lesson present the opportunity to model for students the standard convention for writing computational problems, thus connecting their numerical reasoning to conventional representations.

The Lesson

▲▲

DAY 1

To begin the lesson, I read aloud the book *Pigs Will Be Pigs*, by Amy Axelrod. When I finished reading, I asked the class, "About how much money do you think the Pigs collected when they searched the house?" I gave all who volunteered the chance to report their estimates.

"Please take out paper and pencil," I then said. I gave the students time to do this, and then continued, "I'll read the beginning of the book again. This time, take notes about the money each of the Pigs finds."

When I finished reading about all of the money found, I said to the class, "Now, working with your group, figure out the exact amount the Pigs collected." Students organized their work on their papers in various ways. Some combined the dollars first and then added on the cents. Some lined all of the amounts up in a column and then added. (See Figures 17–1 through 17–3.)

Some groups finished more quickly and I asked them to compare their work with another group that was also finished. Finally, I interrupted the class, had students report the money each of the Pigs found, and modeled recording the amounts, writing them in a column and lining up the decimal points. We agreed that the Pigs had found a total of $34.67.

I then said, "Let's figure out how much the Pigs spent on the specials. Who remembers how much the specials cost?"

Crystal answered, "They were seven dollars and ninety-nine cents." I wrote on the board:

$7.99

I said, "Without using pencil and paper, figure out how much four specials cost. When you think you have an answer, check it with the person next to you. Then raise a hand when you're ready to report your answer and how you got it." I gave the students time to do this.

Jose reported first. "I knew it was close to thirty-two dollars because eight times four is thirty-two. But it was one penny less for each, so I subtracted four cents. The answer is thirty-one ninety-six."

Misha figured another way. She explained, "I knew it was twenty-eight whole dollars. Then I had to add on ninety-nine cents four times, so I thought of it as four more dollars but take away a penny for each. So it was thirty-two minus four pennies. I got the same as Jose."

No one else had a different idea. I said, "Watch as I record Jose's idea and see if it describes how he figured. First, Jose rounded and multiplied eight dollars times four." I wrote:

$8.00
<u>×   4</u>
$32.00

I looked at Jose and he nodded his agreement. "Then I subtracted four cents," Jose said. I wrote:

$32.00
<u>−   .04</u>
$31.96

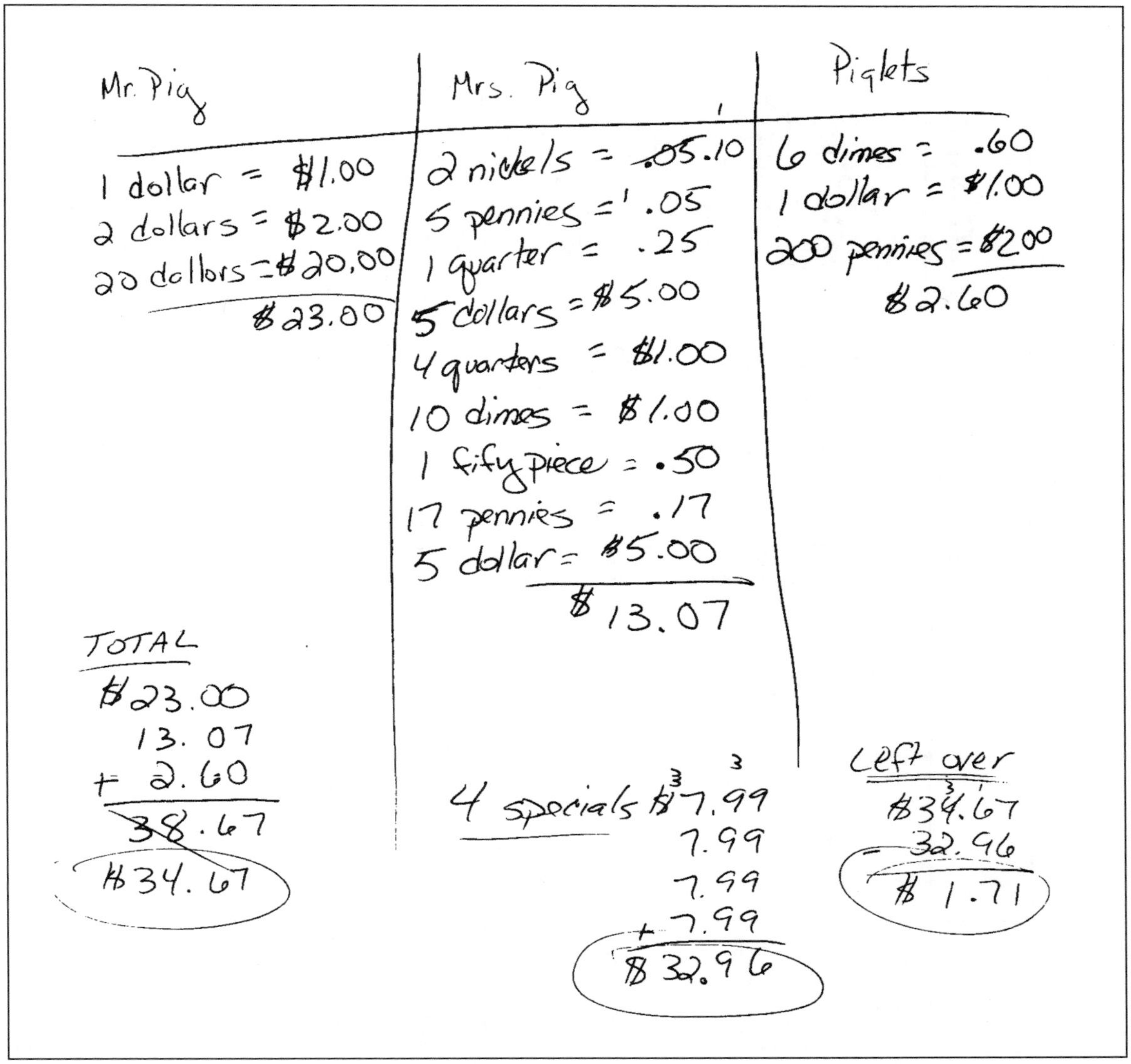

Mr. Pig | Mrs. Pig | Piglets

Mr. Pig
1 dollar = $1.00
2 dollars = $2.00
20 dollars = $20.00
$23.00

Mrs. Pig
2 nickels = .05 .10
5 pennies = .05
1 quarter = .25
5 dollars = $5.00
4 quarters = $1.00
10 dimes = $1.00
1 fifty piece = .50
17 pennies = .17
5 dollar = $5.00
$13.07

Piglets
6 dimes = .60
1 dollar = $1.00
200 pennies = $2.00
$2.60

TOTAL
$23.00
13.07
+ 2.60
38.67
$34.67

4 specials $7.99
7.99
7.99
+ 7.99
$32.96

Left over
$34.67
-32.96
$1.71

▲▲▲▲▲▲**Figure 17–1** *Nicholas's group recorded the amounts using words and then converted the totals to monetary notation.*

I then said, "Now I'll record Misha's way. Misha, remind me what you did first."

She said, "I added the dollars." I began to list four $7.00 in a column, but Misha interrupted me.

"I really multiplied," she said.

"I'll write it both ways," I said. I continued:

$7.00 $7.00
 7.00   ×   4
 7.00 $28.00
+ 7.00
$28.00

"Then I added on four more dollars and took away the four pennies," Misha explained. I recorded:

$28.00
+ 4.00
$32.00

$32.00
− .04
$31.96

"I know another way to do it," Shannon said.

"Tell us," I said.

Pigs Will Be Pigs 137

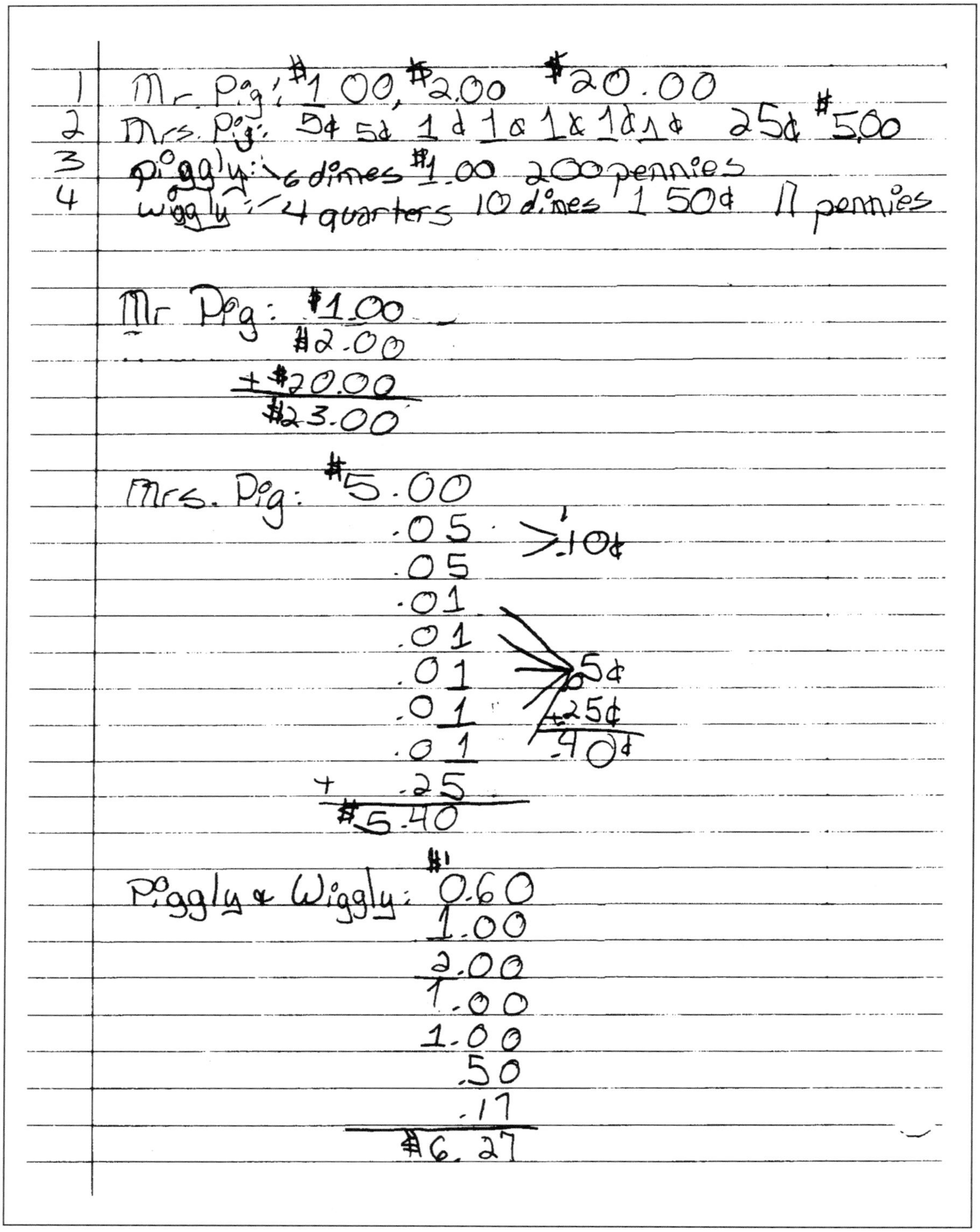

1 | Mr. Pig: $1.00, $2.00 $20.00
2 | Mrs. Pig: 5¢ 5¢ 1¢ 1¢ 1¢ 1¢ 1¢ 25¢ $5.00
3 | Piggly: 6 dimes $1.00 200 pennies
4 | Wiggly: 4 quarters 10 dimes 1 50¢ 17 pennies

Mr Pig: $1.00
              $2.00
          + $20.00
            $23.00

Mrs. Pig: $5.00
               .05   ⟩10¢
               .05
               .01
               .01
               .01   5¢
               .01   +25¢
               .01   40¢
           +   .25
             $5.40

Piggly & Wiggly: $1 0.60
                        1.00
                        2.00
                        1.00
                        1.00
                         .50
                         .17
                       $6.27

▲▲▲▲▲▲Figure 17–2 *Misha's group correctly lined up the decimals. For Mrs. Pig, they use a unique way of adding.*

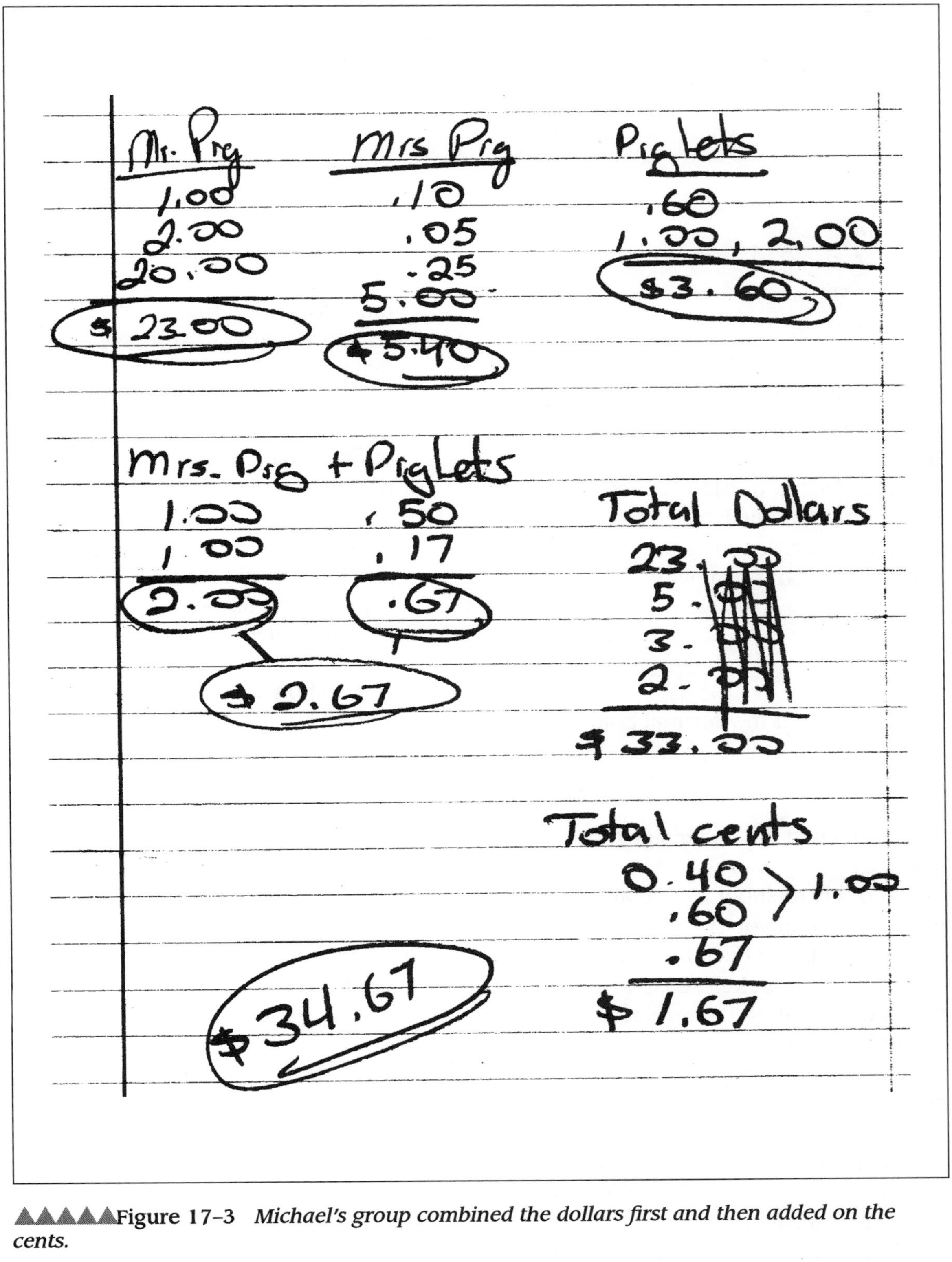

Mr. Prg   Mrs Prg   Piglets

```
Mr. Prg          Mrs Prg          Piglets
 1.00             .10              .60
 2.00             .05             1.00, 2.00
20.00             .25            ⎯⎯⎯⎯⎯⎯⎯
⎯⎯⎯⎯⎯⎯           5.00             ($3.60)
($ 23.00)       ⎯⎯⎯⎯⎯⎯
                 ($5.40)


Mrs. Prg + Piglets
 1.00      .50              Total Dollars
 1.00      .17               23. 00
⎯⎯⎯⎯⎯    ⎯⎯⎯⎯⎯                5. 00
(2.00)    (.67)               3. 00
    ⎲_____⎳                2. 00
      ($ 2.67)              ⎯⎯⎯⎯⎯⎯⎯
                            $ 33.00


                         Total cents
                          0.40 ⟩ 1.00
                           .60
                           .67
                         ⎯⎯⎯⎯⎯⎯
   ($34.67)              $ 1.67
```

▲▲▲▲▲▲Figure 17–3   *Michael's group combined the dollars first and then added on the cents.*

"Can I come up and show?" she asked. I nodded. Shannon came up and wrote $7.99 four times in a column, carefully lining up the decimal points. Then she added, indicating where she had carried. She wrote:

$$
\begin{array}{r}
\scriptstyle 3\ 3 \\
\$\ 7.99 \\
7.99 \\
7.99 \\
+\ 7.99 \\
\hline
\$31.96
\end{array}
$$

If Shannon hadn't volunteered this idea, I would have suggested it and recorded. No one had another suggestion, so I offered one more method. "Here's another way," I said. I wrote on the board, multiplied out loud, and recorded the answer without a decimal point or dollar sign.

$$
\begin{array}{r}
\$7.99 \\
\times\ \ \ \ 4 \\
\hline
3196
\end{array}
$$

"You left out the decimal point," Lena said.

"Put it after the thirty-one," Matthew added.

"And put in the dollar sign," Kendra said.

I did this to show $31.96 and commented, "When you multiply and decimals are involved, you have to be sure to think about where it makes sense to put the decimal point in the answer. And if the problem involves money, be sure to include the dollar sign with the first amount in the problem and in the answer."

I then said to the class, "These are all correct ways to figure and correct ways to record the calculations. I have a question that I'd like you to think about. Sometimes I wrote the number four by itself." I pointed to the instances where I had multiplied by four. "But sometimes I wrote 'point zero

four' or 'four point zero zero.'" I pointed to where I had subtracted $.04 or added $4.00. "Talk with your neighbor about why I did this."

The room got noisy as students talked. When I called them back to attention, many of them wanted to report. I called on Francesca first.

"When it's money, you have to use the decimal point. But the other four just meant times four," she said.

Martin added, "You only use the decimal points for the money numbers."

I said, "I agree with you both, that with the decimal point I wrote either four cents or four dollars. But what did the fours mean when I wrote them by themselves?"

"It's when you were multiplying," Blaire noticed.

"Because there were four people in the Pig family," Damon said.

Luis added, "You multiplied by four because all four ordered the special."

"So how much money did the Pigs find in their hunt?" I then asked the class.

"Thirty-four sixty-seven," students responded.

"How much money did they have left over after paying for the four specials?" I asked. Most of the students lowered their heads to do the calculation on their papers. A few figured mentally.

"They had two seventy-one left," Rory reported. I recorded on the board:

$$
\begin{array}{r}
\$34.67 \\
-31.96 \\
\hline
\$\ 2.71
\end{array}
$$

I then held up the menu from the book. "What else could they have ordered?" I asked. The students in front were able to read the menu.

"They can get two coffees for one dollar each," Chen said.

"Or they can get one sopaipilla for two dollars and split it," Maria added.

"They can get any of the desserts since they are all two fifty or less," Frank said.

A Menu Problem

I then presented a problem for the students to work on in groups. "Pretend that you're a family of four eating at the Enchanted Enchilada restaurant, and you have the same amount to spend as the Pig family had. Decide what you'd like to eat and estimate how much it will cost. Try to spend as much of $34.67 as possible. Then figure out exactly what your choices cost and how much change you have left."

I distributed to each group a list of the menu items. The students were interested in this problem and quickly got to work. As the groups discussed their possible meals, I walked around the room listening to their conversations. One group's estimation strategy in particular caught my attention.

"If we have thirty-four sixty-seven to spend, that means we can spend about eight fifty each," said Frank.

"How do you know?" Kim asked.

"Well, I rounded thirty-four sixty-seven to thirty-five dollars. I knew that four doesn't go evenly into thirty-five but four times eight is thirty-two, and four times nine is thirty-six. Thirty-four sixty-seven is in between thirty-two and thirty-six, so I estimated something between eight dollars and nine dollars and got eight fifty," Frank answered.

"How about we figure out exactly how much money we each can spend since we need to spend as much of the thirty-four sixty-seven as possible," Luis suggested.

"I think it's eight dollars and sixty-six cents each," said Jenny, after figuring with paper and pencil. "That uses up thirty-four dollars and sixty-four cents, so there's three cents left over."

Kim said, "I know! Let's each choose what we want to eat if we can spend up to eight sixty-six. Then we can add up what we each spent."

Another group used an entirely different method for deciding what to order. "I love stuffed jalapeños," Leslee said.

"Me, too! Let's order some of those for everyone," Marcus suggested.

"But I don't like jalapeños. They're too hot," Chen protested. "I'd rather get nacho chips for a dollar fifty."

Patrice said, "OK, how about we get two appetizers for everyone to share and then we each get a dinner and a drink. Most of the dinners are about five dollars and the drinks are around one dollar. So that's six times four people, which is twenty-four dollars so far."

Leslee said, "If we each get a dinner and a drink and then two appetizers for the group, our total will only be about twenty-eight dollars. I think we can each get either a side dish, a dessert, or a salad. Most of the side dishes, desserts, and salads are about two dollars each."

Chen said, "Let's start with one order of nachos for one fifty and one order of stuffed jalapeños for two dollars. That uses up three fifty so far. Why don't each of you call out what you want for dinner and I'll add it to our list. Then we can go around again and call out drinks, and then keep going around saying what we want until everyone has had a chance to order something else."

Marcus said, "We have to estimate first, so call out what you want first and about how much it costs." This group exceeded their budget, so they decided to share desserts.

After the groups finished, each shared what they ordered, the total for their meals, and how much change they had remaining. (See Figures 17–4 and 17–5.)

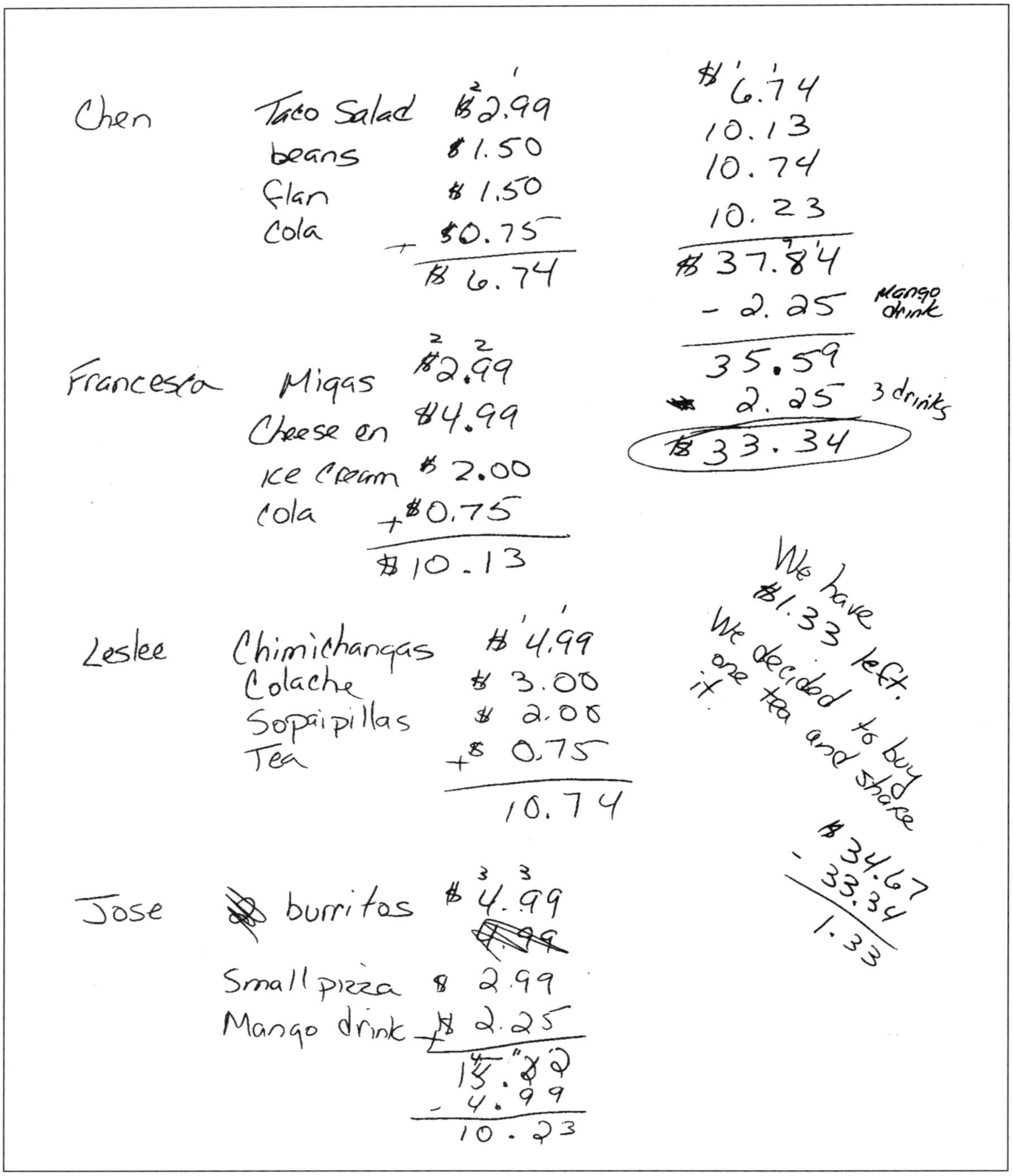

▲▲▲▲▲▲Figure 17–4 *Chen's group didn't predict first, so they had to go back and delete some food and drink items.*

DAY 2

I gave the class another problem to solve in groups. I explained, "You have forty dollars to spend for four people, and you must order for the table at least one appetizer, one special, and four drinks." I wrote on the board:

1 appetizer

1 special

4 drinks

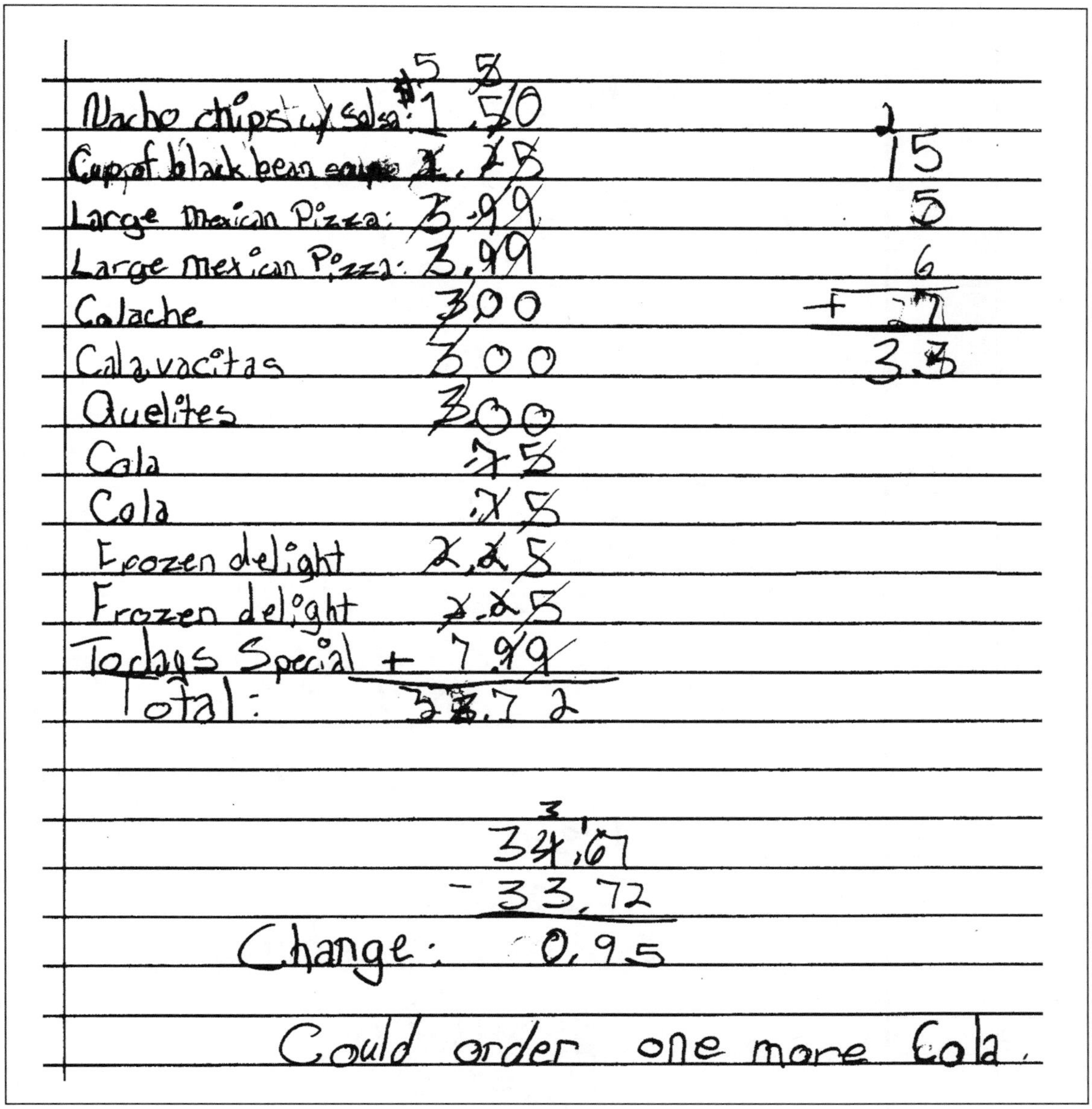

```
                   $5  5
Nacho chips w/ salsa: 1.50
Cup of black bean soup: 1.75            15
Large Mexican Pizza: 3.99                5
Large mexican Pizza: 3.99                6
Calache           300               +  7
Calavacitas       300                  3.3
Quelites          300
Cola               .75
Cola               .75
Frozen delight    2.25
Frozen delight    2.25
Tachos Special  +  7.99
   Total:          33.72


                        3
                      34.67
                    - 33.72
          Change:     0.95


         Could order one more Cola.
```

▲▲▲▲▲▲Figure 17–5 *Misha's group estimated first by adding up the dollars and then rounding the cents to make sure they would have enough money.*

I distributed a 12-by-18-inch sheet of white paper to each group and told them, "Spend as much of the forty dollars as possible. Record what you order, including the prices of each item, and show your calculations."

When the students had finished, I led a class discussion for groups to present what they ordered, how much money they spent, how they recorded, and the strategies they

used to solve this problem. (See Figure 17–6 for an example.)

EXTENSION

Repeat the last problem, this time telling the students that they have to figure in a 15 percent tip and still not exceed the forty-dollar total amount.

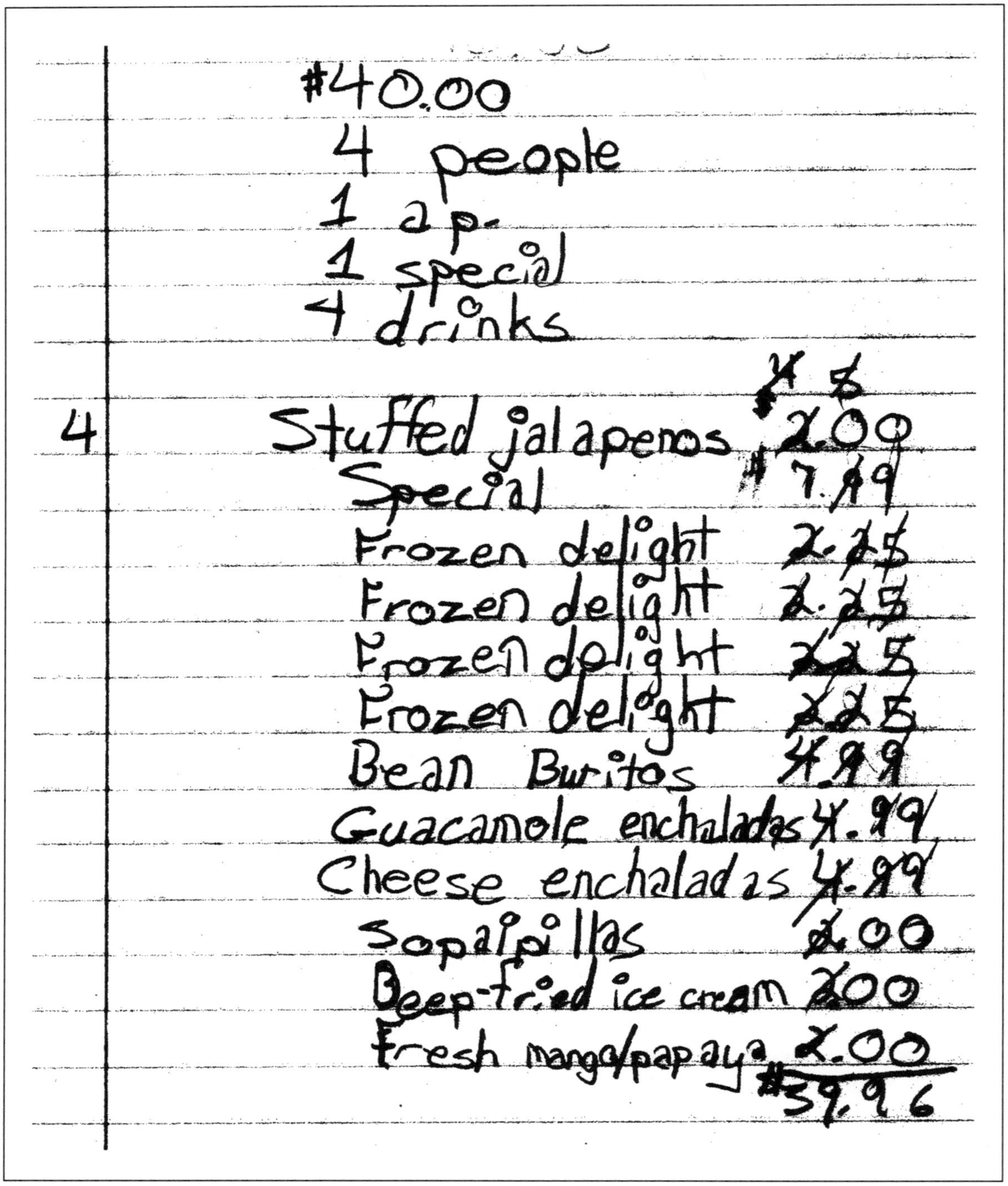

#40.00
4 people
1 a p.
1 special
4 drinks

4   Stuffed jalapenos $2.00
    Special $7.99
    Frozen delight   2.25
    Frozen delight   2.25
    Frozen delight   2.25
    Frozen delight   2.25
    Bean Buritos   4.99
    Guacamole enchaladas 4.99
    Cheese enchaladas 4.99
    Sopapillas   2.00
    Deep-fried ice cream 2.00
    Fresh mango/papaya 2.00
                     $39.96

▲▲▲▲▲Figure 17–6   *Marcus's group spent almost all of the $40.00.*

144   **Lessons for Decimals and Percents**

Questions and Discussion

▲▲

▲ *Why did you record Jose's and Misha's methods on the board?*

By representing students' methods, I'm modeling for the class how to use paper and pencil to keep track of numerical reasoning. Also, I can model some of the standard ways we record decimals when calculating. Finally, I can talk about placing the decimal point in the product through connecting to the context of the problem, emphasizing the importance of the answer making sense rather than focusing on a rule for placing it.

▲ *Why did you ask the students about the difference between the 4 and $.04 or $4.00?*

When students are computing, it's important for them to be able to explain what numbers mean. Often when the context of the problem isn't evident, students focus on computational procedures and lose track of why they've used particular numbers. It's in those situations that students place decimal points incorrectly, or record answers that don't make sense, or make other errors. It's helpful as often as possible to focus students on the meaning of numbers in problems.

CHAPTER EIGHTEEN
ALEXANDER, WHO USED TO BE RICH LAST SUNDAY

Overview

This lesson gives students experience subtracting decimal numbers. The lesson begins with reading aloud the story *Alexander, Who Used to Be Rich Last Sunday*, by Judith Viorst. During a second reading, the students calculate the amount each of Alexander's brothers has and how much is left each time Alexander spends money. Each of these calculations provides the opportunity to model for the students how to represent problems with standard decimal notation. Finally, the students write and illustrate their own versions of *Alexander, Who Used to Be Rich Last Sunday*. They share their published books with the class for others to do the calculations.

Materials

▲ *Alexander, Who Used to Be Rich Last Sunday*, by Judith Viorst (Atheneum, 1978)

Time

▲ two to three class periods

Teaching Directions

1. Read aloud the book *Alexander, Who Used to Be Rich Last Sunday*, by Judith Viorst.

2. Then begin again reading the book aloud. The first page states: "It isn't fair that my brother Anthony has two dollars and three quarters and one dime and seven nickels and eighteen pennies." Ask the students how much money each part represents and how to record it. On the board, record the amounts in a column with the decimal points lined up and then ask the students to figure out the answer:

$2.00
.75
.10
.35
+ .18
$3.38

3. Read the second page of the book and repeat Step 2 for Alexander's other brother, Nicholas.

4. Continue reading. Each time Alexander spends money, stop for the students to calculate how much he has left.

5. Reread Alexander's transactions, this time assuming that Alexander has his brother Anthony's money as well as the $1.00 from his grandparents, a total of $4.38. Ask the students to subtract each time Alexander spends money. As you read the transactions, write them on the board:

Bubble gum	$.15
Bets	$.15
Rent a snake	$.12
Fine	$.10
Flush down toilet	$.03
Fell through crack	$.05
Ate chocolate	$.11
Nick's magic trick	$.04
Kicked Anthony	$.05
Deck of cards	$.20

6. Reread Alexander's transactions again, this time assuming that Alexander has his brother Nicholas's money as well as the $1.00 from his grandparents, a total of $3.38. Ask the students to subtract each time Alexander spends money.

7. The next day, tell the students that they will write their own versions of *Alexander, Who Used to Be Rich Last Sunday*. Ask: "What do you think is a realistic amount of money to begin with?" Decide on an amount for everyone to use.

8. Ask students to brainstorm story ideas in groups and then work individually on rough drafts. Have students edit one another's work and check their computations.

9. Finally, invite students to present their stories to the class. The students listening do the calculations as they did with the original story.

Teaching Notes

Alexander, Who Used to Be Rich Last Sunday, by Judith Viorst, is a comical story about how Alexander spends the dollar his grandparents gave him when they came to visit on Sunday. He couldn't resist many temptations during the week and, by the end of the book, he winds up with only a deck of cards, a one-eyed bear, a melted candle, and some bus tokens.

When first subtracting decimals as part of their school learning, students benefit from solving problems in the contexts of real-life situations so that they can utilize their prior experience. Since students have most likely had experiences subtracting with money in the context of real-life situations, it's a useful context to use. The problems from this book are accessible to students since they generally think of subtracting different amounts of cents as subtracting whole numbers. For example, subtracting fifteen cents from eighty-five cents doesn't necessarily call on decimal understanding. The benefit of using this book is that it offers the opportunity to connect the computations, $.85 – $.15, for example, to decimal notation.

The Lesson

▲▲

DAY 1

I began the lesson by reading aloud to the class the book *Alexander, Who Used to Be Rich Last Sunday*, by Judith Viorst. Even though the reading level of this book was quite simple for most of the students, they enjoyed the book. The students found Alexander's emotions, reactions, and sibling relationships to be very realistic, and they thought that the story was comical.

I then read the book again, this time stopping each time there was an opportunity for the students to do a calculation. The first page, for example, stated that Alexander's brother, Anthony, "has two dollars and three quarters and one dime and seven nickels and eighteen pennies." I asked the students how much money each part represented and how to record it. On the board, I recorded the amounts in a column with the decimal points lined up:

$2.00
.75
.10
.35
+ .18

I then asked, "How much money does Anthony have? Figure this out, compare your answer with your neighbor, and raise a hand when you're ready to report." I gave the students time to do this and then I called on Frank.

"He has three dollars and thirty-eight cents," he answered. The others agreed. I recorded *$3.38* on the board.

I asked Frank, "How did you add?"

Frank answered, "The two dollars and three quarters make two seventy-five. A dime more makes two eighty-five. Then I knew that fifteen cents more would make it three dollars, so I took fifteen cents from the thirty-five cents. Now I had twenty cents left in nickels and eighteen cents more. That's twenty plus ten plus eight. That's thirty-eight. So it's three dollars and thirty-eight cents."

Blaire raised a hand. "I got the same answer, but I did it differently," she said.

"Tell us how," I said.

Blaire explained how she added the numbers in each column. She began, "Five and five is ten and eight is eighteen, so you write down the eight and carry one." Blaire continued with the other columns, also arriving at an answer of $3.38.

The next page of the book tells how much money Anthony's brother Nicholas had—one dollar, two quarters, five dimes, five nickels, and thirteen pennies. This time I had the students record on their own papers, and then had Elaine and Chen explain how they figured out that Nicholas had $2.38.

The class laughed when I read the next page, where Alexander complains that all he has are bus tokens.

When I got to the part of the book where Alexander begins to spend his money, I stopped again for the students to do the calculations. Alexander first spends fifteen cents on bubble gum. The students quickly figured out in their heads that he was left with eighty-five cents. I recorded on the board:

$1.00
− .15
$ .85

I said to the class, "As I continue, figure out the answers and also record each problem." Next Alexander lost three bets and had to pay Anthony, Nicholas, and his mom each five cents. I circulated as the students did the problem. Then I recorded on the board:

$ .85
− .15
$ .70

I reminded the class, "Notice how I line up the decimal points in the problem and write the dollar sign." I proceeded through the book until Alexander had spent all of his money.

Retelling the Story

I said to the class, "At the beginning of the story, Alexander's brother, Anthony, had three dollars and thirty-eight cents. Suppose he gave that money to Alexander."

"Then Alexander would have four dollars and thirty-eight cents," Crystal said.

"Yes, that's right," I confirmed. "So if Alexander then spent the money the same way, he'd still have money left over."

Misha raised a hand. "He'd have the three dollars and thirty-eight cents that he started with," she said.

"Let's try it and see if that works," I said. I read the story again, this time having the students begin with $4.38 and subtract each amount. For the first transaction, I modeled the recording on the board:

$4.38
− .15
$3.23

As I read, I noted each transaction on the board so that the students could use it for the next problem:

Bubble gum	$.15
Bets	$.15
Rent a snake	$.12
Fine	$.10
Flush down toilet	$.03
Fell through crack	$.05
Ate chocolate	$.11
Nick's magic trick	$.04
Kicked Anthony	$.05
Deck of cards	$.20

We verified at the end that if Alexander had started with $4.38, he would have wound up with $3.38. (See Figure 18–1.)

I next presented the students with the same problem, but this time told them to pretend that Alexander started with Nicholas's $2.38 plus the dollar from his grandparents. I gave the students time to do the calculations independently. "Check with a neighbor to see if you agree," I told them. (See Figure 18–2.)

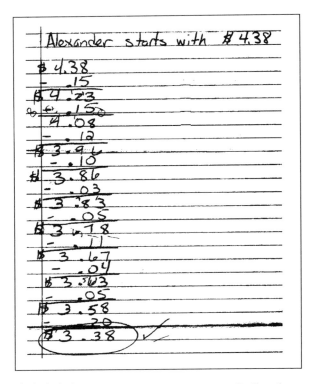

▲▲▲▲▲Figure 18–1 *Rory correctly lined up the decimal points and showed how Alexander would be left with $3.38.*

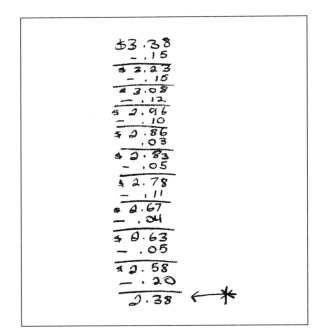

▲▲▲▲▲Figure 18–2 *Jose subtracted correctly to figure out how much would be left if Alexander started with Nicholas's $2.38 plus the dollar from his grandparents.*

DAY 2

I began class by telling the students how they were going to write their own stories. "Now you'll write your own versions of *Alexander, Who Used to Be Rich Last Sunday,*" I told the students. "What do you think is a realistic amount of money to begin with?" The students were in agreement that the book was a bit outdated as far as the cost of items. And they agreed that in order to update the prices of items, they would need to start with more money in the beginning of the book. Ten dollars seemed about right.

The students then worked in groups and brainstormed different scenarios and items they would buy. They especially enjoyed in the original book how Alexander lost his money because of his behavior or irresponsibility, and they tried to come up with similar situations that were realistic yet comical.

After brainstorming in their groups, students worked individually on rough drafts. "Be sure to include how much money the character spent and how much money was left," I told them. They worked on the stories for two days. After students finished their drafts, they participated in several peer-editing conferences to add, delete, and revise their stories. The peer editors also checked the computations. By the end of the week, the students were ready to publish and bind their individual books.

Many students volunteered to sit in the author's chair and read aloud their published work. As each student author read aloud his or her book, the other students recorded the amounts spent and did the subtractions as they had done with the original book. I then placed their books in the school library for other students to read and enjoy. Figures 18–3 and 18–4 show two students' stories.

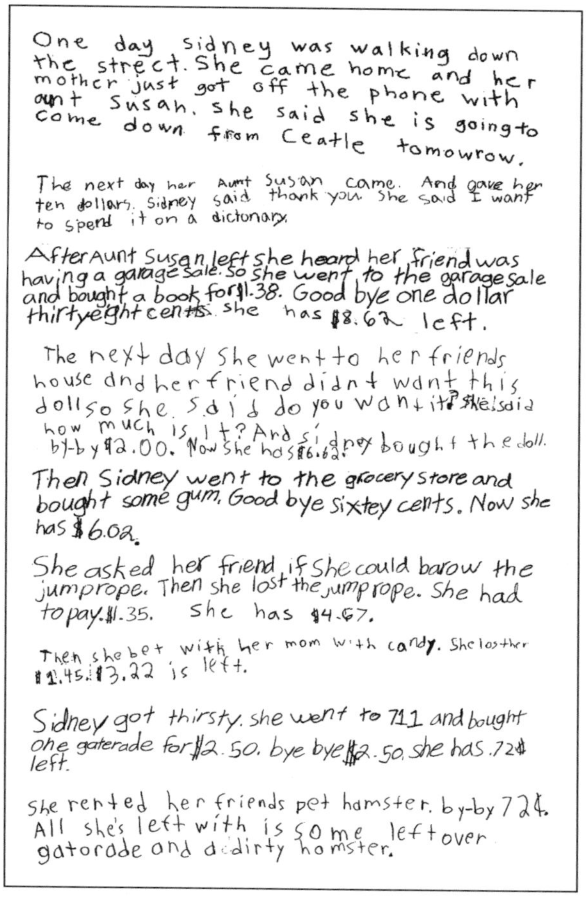

One day sidney was walking down the street. She came home and her mother just got off the phone with aunt Susan. she said she is going to come down from Ceatle tomowrow.

The next day her Aunt Susan came. And gave her ten dollars. Sidney said thank you she said I want to spend it on a dictionary.

AfterAunt Susan left she heard her friend was having a garage sale. so she went to the garage sale and bought a book for $1.38. Good bye one dollar thirtyeight cents. she has $8.62 left.

The next day she went to her friends house and her friend didnt want this doll so she. s.d I do you want it? she said how much is it? And sidney said by-by $2.00. Now she has $6.62. sidney bought the doll.

Then Sidney went to the grocery store and bought some gum. Good bye sixtey cents. Now she has $6.02.

She asked her friend if she could barow the jumprope. Then she lost the jumprope. She had to pay $1.35. she has $4.67.

Then she bet with her mom with candy. She los ther $1.45. $3.22 is left.

Sidney got thirsty. she went to 711 and bought one gaterade for $2.50. bye bye $2.50. she has .72¢ left.

she rented her friends pet hamster. by-by 72¢. All she's left with is some leftover gaterade and a dirty hamster.

▲▲▲▲▲▲Figure 18-3 Elaine retold the story using modern situations.

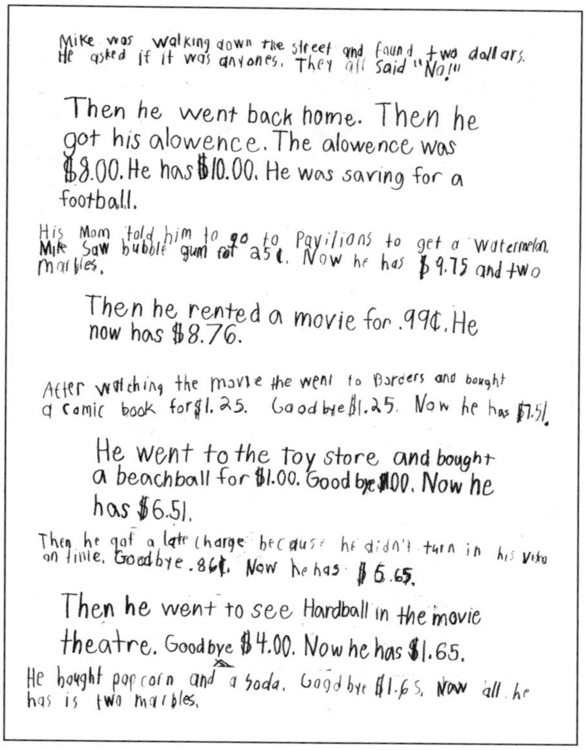

Mike was walking down the street and found two dollars. He asked if it was anyones. They all said "No!"

Then he went back home. Then he got his alowence. The alowence was $3.00. He has $10.00. He was saving for a football.

His Mom told him to go to Pavilions to get a watermelon. Mike saw bubble gum for a 5¢. Now he has $9.75 and two marbles.

Then he rented a movie for .99¢. He now has $8.76.

After watching the movie the went to Borders and bought a comic book for $1.25. Good bye $1.25. Now he has $7.51.

He went to the toy store and bought a beachball for $1.00. Good bye $1.00. Now he has $6.51.

Then he got a late charge because he didn't turn in his video on time. Goodbye .86¢. Now he has $6.65.

Then he went to see Hardball in the movie theatre. Goodbye $4.00. Now he has $1.65.

He bought popcorn and a soda. Goodbye $1.65. Now all he has is two marbles.

▲▲▲▲▲▲Figure 18-4 In his version of the story, Chen used up-to-date prices.

Questions and Discussion

▲▲

▲ *Why did you have the students do the calculations starting with $4.38 or $3.38 if they already knew the answer?*

In this situation, my goal was to give the students practice performing subtractions and representing the problems. Already knowing the answer gave them a way to check on their final result, providing a clear goal for their calculations. But while the students knew the final answer, they didn't know the specific differences that preceded them.

CHAPTER NINETEEN
$1.00 WORD RIDDLES

Overview

This lesson provides students addition practice with decimals. Using a monetary value for each letter of the alphabet—a = $.01, b = $.02, c = $.03, and so on—the students add the values of each letter in words to find their value. They then search for words with the value of exactly one dollar. *The $1.00 Word Riddle Book*, by Marilyn Burns, aids the students in their search for one-dollar words by presenting students with riddles whose solutions are words worth exactly one dollar.

Materials

▲ *The $1.00 Word Riddle Book*, by Marilyn Burns (Math Solutions Publications, 1995)
▲ Values of Letters chart (enlarge from Blackline Masters)

Time

▲ two class periods, plus additional time for students to search for more words

Teaching Directions

1. Post a chart of the values of the letters of the alphabet—a = $.01, b = $.02, c = $.03, and so on. Ask: "What do you notice about the monetary values of the letters?" Be sure the students all understand that the values of the letters continue to z = $.26.

2. Give the following direction: "If you use these values to figure out the total of the letters in your first name, raise a hand if you estimate that your name would be worth more than one dollar." Continue with other questions: "Do you think your name will be worth more than five dollars? Less than fifty cents? Less than a quarter? Who thinks their first and last names together would be more than one dollar? Less than one dollar? More than five dollars?"

3. Instruct the students: "Calculate the values of the letters in your first name, then exchange papers with your neighbor and check each other's computation."

4. After students have completed this, ask: "How did the value of your name compare with your prediction?" Have students report and model on the board how to list the values of the letters in a column and add. Discuss with the class why some people have names of the same length but different values.

5. Give the students time to figure the total cost of their first and last names and then to figure the values of names of other family members.

6. For the rest of the class period, give the following direction: "Search for words with letters that total exactly one dollar."

7. For homework, challenge the students to continue searching for words that equal exactly one dollar. Write on the board clues to several possible solutions:

    a day of the week

    a Halloween word

    a United States coin

    a number < 100 that's divisible by 5

    someone who stole from the rich to give to the poor

    a sea creature

    what you wear on your hands in cold weather

8. Begin the next day's lesson by having the students share the words they found that equaled exactly one dollar.

9. For the rest of the class period, present riddles from *The $1.00 Word Riddle Book*. Read the clues aloud, show the pictorial clues, and give students time to figure out the solutions.

10. Encourage the students to continue searching over the next several days for words worth exactly one dollar. Explain: "When you discover one, ask a classmate to check your computation, generate a riddle for which the new word is the answer, and write the riddle on an index card." Make the riddles available for others to solve.

Teaching Notes

Most students have had prior experience adding with money. They know about adding or subtracting dollars to dollars and cents to cents, and they've seen money written in columns, with the decimal points lined up underneath each other. Rather than introduce a rule to students about lining up decimals in a column, it's better to help them make connections through real-life applications and their prior knowledge.

This lesson makes a connection between mathematics and language arts. As students search for one-dollar words, some start to develop strategies. For example, the letter s is worth $.19, so a word that is worth $.81 may produce a $1.00 word by making it plural. This strategy can be extended to the values of other suffixes: -ing, -ed, -ly, and so on. There are well over five hundred one-dollar words in the English language, so the search is a reasonable one to present to students. Some students will become more interested than others, of course, but with the clues from riddles in the *$1.00 Word Riddle Book*, all can participate and experience success.

The Lesson

▲▲

DAY 1

I began the lesson by focusing the students' attention on a chart posted at the front of the class. On the chart were the letters of the alphabet listed in alphabetical order, with each letter assigned a monetary value: a = $.01, b = $.02, c = $.03, and so on.

"What do you notice about the information on the chart?" I inquired.

"It's the alphabet," Rory responded.

"Each letter is worth something," Madison added.

"What do you notice about the monetary values of the letters?" I asked.

Shannon answered, "The first letter of the alphabet is worth one cent, b is worth two cents, and each letter value increases by one cent down the list, so z is worth 26 cents."

I then said, "If you used these values to figure out the total of the letters in your first name, raise your hand if you estimate that your first name would be worth more than

one dollar." I waited a moment for students to decide.

Then I asked, "Who thinks that his or her name would be worth more than five dollars?" Again, I waited, and then continued posing other amounts and waiting for responses. "Less than fifty cents?" "Less than a quarter?" "Who thinks your first and last names together would be more than one dollar?" "Less than one dollar?" "More than five dollars?"

I then directed the students to calculate the value of their first names. "Add the values of the letters, and then exchange papers with your neighbor and check each other's addition to be sure you're right."

"Do I use Jeff or Jeffrey?" Jeff wanted to know.

"It's your choice," I answered.

I gave the students time to figure the values of their first names and then asked, "How did the value of your name compare with your prediction?"

Ian answered, "I definitely thought my

name would be less than one dollar, and it was. It's worth only twenty-four cents."

"What did you add?" I asked.

"Nine cents, one cent, and fourteen cents," Ian answered. I recorded on the board to model how to list the values in a column and show the dollar sign for the first number and for the answer:

$.09
.01
+.14
$.24

Kim added, "I thought so, too. My name was only thirty-three cents. I added eleven plus nine plus thirteen." I recorded this as well:

$.11
.09
+.13
$.33

"Why did you think your names would be worth less than one dollar?" I asked.

"We only have three letters," Ian answered.

"Mine's worth thirty cents, and it has four letters," Chen said. I had Chen report the numbers he added and, as I had done for Ian and Kim's values, listed them and showed the total.

"I have four letters, but mine is worth forty-nine cents," Jose said.

"I have four letters, and my name is seventy-six cents," Rory added.

"Mine has eight letters, and it's worth only sixty-one cents," Isabella exclaimed.

"Mine has eight letters, too, but it's worth eighty-three cents," Jonathan said.

"My name has nine letters and it's only seventy cents," Francesca added.

All of the students were eager to share their values. I directed their thinking by saying, "So Francesca has a name that's longer than Jonathan's, but it's worth less. And some people have names of the same

length, but they have different values. What matters when you figure the value of your name?"

Rory said, "What matters is what the letters are. Like I have only four letters, but I have letters that are worth a lot—the y and the two rs. So my name is seventy-six cents."

Chen added, "If you have letters like a, b, c, d, or e, like mine, then it will be cheaper."

"Did anyone have a name close to one dollar?" I asked.

"Mine is ninety cents," Matthew said.

"Mine is ninety-eight cents," Crystal said.

"Figure out the total of your first and last names combined. Again, have your neighbor check your work and then we'll compare those values," I said. The students went back to work. We then discussed the values of their first and last names combined.

"Try figuring the values of names of other people in your family and see what you find out," I said.

After a few minutes, Kendra called out, excitedly, "Suzanne is worth one dollar! My sister, Suzanne, is worth a dollar!" Others added the values of the letters in Suzanne to verify Kendra's discovery. No one else found a one-dollar name.

I then gave another direction, asking the students to look for any words with letters that totaled exactly one dollar. "Your task now is to search for words that equal one dollar. Suzanne is the only name we've found so far, but now let's broaden our search. The words don't have to be names; they can be any words."

The students quickly began searching. Most used a guess-and-check strategy, picking a word and figuring out its value. When they found a word close to one dollar, they would start exchanging and rearranging letters to try to find a word worth exactly one dollar. Sometimes when I've done this activity, some students have success. But by the end of the period for this class, even though they had been working furiously, no one had found a one-dollar word.

Homework

I ended the class by giving the students a homework assignment. "For homework you have the challenge of finding some words that equal exactly one dollar. I'll give you clues for some words that I know work, but see if you can find others as well." I wrote several clues on the board:

a day of the week

a Halloween word

a United States coin

a number < 100 that's divisible by 5

someone who stole from the rich to give to the poor

a sea creature

what you wear on your hands in cold weather

(The words are *Wednesday, pumpkin, quarter, thirty, Robin Hood, starfish,* and *mittens*.) Figures 19–1 and 19–2 show how two students worked on this challenge.

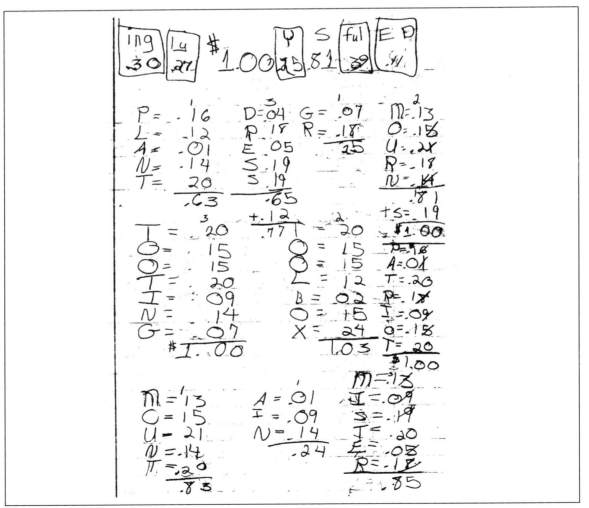

▲▲▲▲▲▲**Figure 19–1** *Misha searched for her own $1.00 words for homework. She began by guessing and checking, but then used the values of common endings to apply to words close to $1.00.*

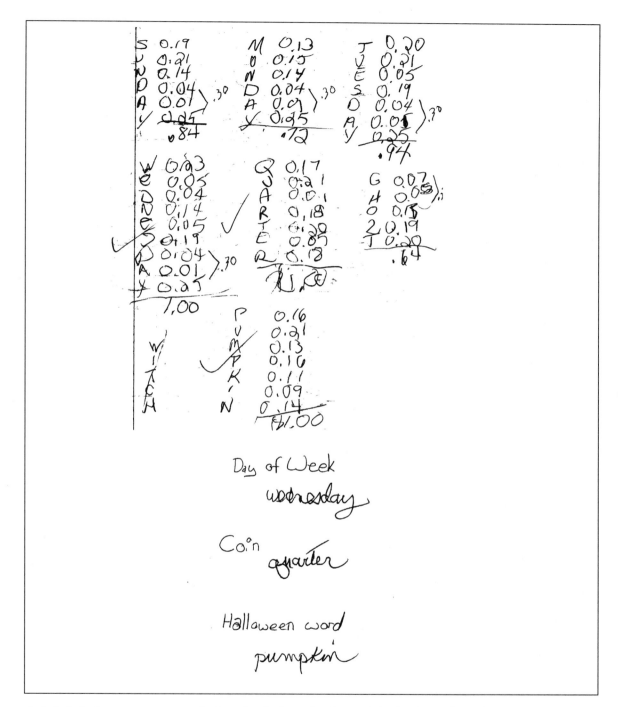

▲▲▲▲▲▲Figure 19–2 *Frank found solutions for four of the homework riddles.*

DAY 2

I began the next day's class by asking students to share the words they found that equaled one dollar and the strategies they used. Aside from using the clues I had given, students found several other words that equaled exactly one dollar.

For the rest of the class, I presented riddles from *The $1.00 Word Riddle Book*, reading the clues aloud, showing the class the pictorial clues, and giving them time to figure out the solutions.

Throughout the week, the students continued searching for one-dollar words. When someone discovered one, after having someone else check that the arithmetic was correct, he or she would generate a riddle for which the new word was the answer and write it on an index card. I collected the cards and later put them out so that the riddles were available for students to try. (See Figures 19–3 and 19–4.)

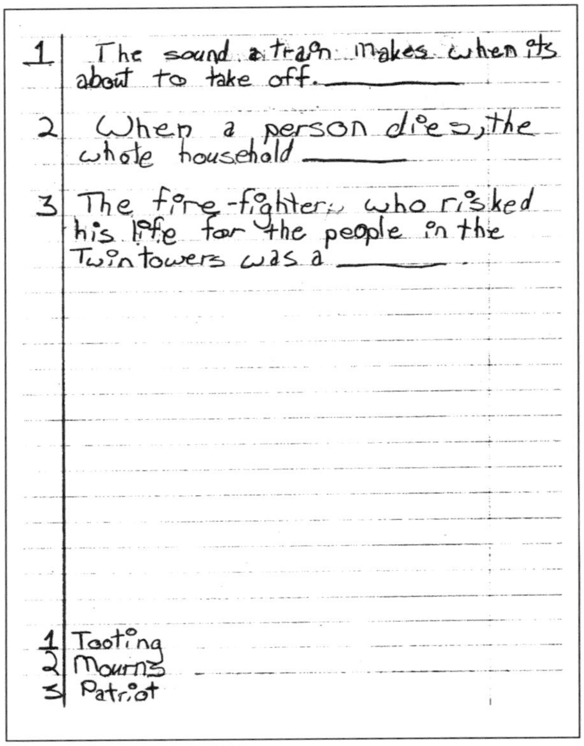

1. The sound a train makes when its about to take off. _____

2. When a person dies, the whole household _____

3. The fire-fighter who risked his life for the people in the Twin towers was a _____.

1. Tooting
2. Mourns
3. Patriot

▲▲▲▲▲▲Figure 19–3 *Misha used one of her homework $1.00 words and two others to create $1.00 word riddles.*

1. Past tense of volley.

2. Means out of hundred

1. volleyed   2. Percents

▲▲▲▲▲▲Figure 19–4 *During the week, Ian was able to find two $1.00 words.*

Questions and Discussion

▲▲

▲ *When you record on the board, do you explain about lining up the decimal points?*

Whether or not I explain about lining up decimal points depends on whether or not this is the first time that I've modeled this sort of recording for students. If I've already done the *Money Riddles* lesson (see Chapter 15), then recording at this time revisits what I've previously introduced to the students. However, if this is the first time I'm showing the convention of lining up decimal points, or if I think students need more reinforcement, I may choose to explain what I'm doing and why.

▲ *Do you expect students to record as you did when they are figuring out the values of words?*

First of all, I'm aware that writing the values in columns isn't necessarily essential to figuring out correct totals. Rather than require it, I do as much modeling as possible of recording in columns. I find that the more recording I model for the students, the more quickly they become comfortable recording as I've modeled and naturally use the standard convention of lining up decimal points. Also, if I see students recording in columns but not lining up decimal points, I call their attention to what they've written, point out the potential for careless errors, and ask that they take care to line them up. I try to handle this issue by encouraging students, helping them see the benefit of recording carefully and in an orderly way.

ADDITIONAL ACTIVITIES

The seven activities described in this section extend the lessons from the previous chapters and offer additional ideas for classroom instruction. Each activity presents an overview, the materials and time required, teaching directions, and samples of student work. Four of the activities, *Broken Calculator, Getting to One, Knockout,* and *From Here to There*, use calculators to provide students additional experiences estimating and calculating with decimals. *Target Practice* also provides experience with estimating and calculating, but students do not rely on calculators. The other two activities, *Cover Up* and *Pursuit of Zero*, are games that students can play in pairs or in small groups.

Broken Calculator

OVERVIEW

Broken Calculator is a version of a computer program. The students are instructed that their calculators are "broken" and the only keys that work are the 2, 6, +, −, ×, ÷, and = keys. Using only these keys and at most ten keystrokes, they investigate possible ways to get specified numbers on the their displays.

MATERIALS

▲ calculators, 1 per student

TIME

▲ one class period, plus additional time for repeat experiences

TEACHING DIRECTIONS

1. Tell the students that for this activity, the only keys that they can use on their calculators are the 2, 6, +, −, ×, ÷, and = keys. They are to assume that the rest of the keys are "broken."

2. Try a sample with the class. Write *8.5* on the board. Ask the students for ideas about how to make 8.5 appear on the display using just the keys mentioned in Step 1. On the board, write the steps used to model for students how to record. For example:

$6 \div 2 = 3$

$3 \div 6 = 0.5$

$0.5 + 2 = 2.5$

$2.5 + 6 = 8.5$

3. Give the students the following numbers to make appear on their calculator displays:

0.16

6.4

0.003

For each, they should keep track of what they did with the calculators.

4. Ask students to compare solutions and see if there are different ways to solve each.

Getting to One

OVERVIEW

The students investigate different ways to get a 1 on the displays of their calculators by adding two or more of the same number. The exploration gives students a way to use calculators to stretch their thinking about decimals.

MATERIALS

▲ TI-30 calculators or calculator with constant function, 1 per student

TIME

▲ one class period

TEACHING DIRECTIONS

1. Present an example that shows the students how to use the calculator to add the same number over and over again. Direct them: "Press two, then the plus key, and then the equals key." Be sure they all see a 2 on their displays. Then direct them: "Press the equals key again." Be sure they all have a 4 on their displays. Have them continue to press the equals key and verify that their calculators continue to add two each time.

2. Present a simple problem: *What number would you press so that when you press the plus key and then the equals key over and over again, you will get the number 6 on your display?* Give students time to try this. Typically, students will solve the problem in one of the following ways:

> 3, +, =, =
>
> 2, +, =, =, =

Record these solutions as follows:

> 3 + 3 = 6
>
> 2 + 2 + 2 = 6

Ask them to try to reach 6 starting with 1 (1, +, =, =, =, =, =, =) and then with 1.5 (1.5, +, =, =, =, =). Record the solutions:

> 1 + 1 + 1 + 1 + 1 + 1 = 6
>
> 1.5 + 1.5 + 1.5 + 1.5 = 6

Ask students for any other solutions.

3. Present this problem: *Find all of the ways to get a 1 on the calculator display by adding equal addends.* If you'd like, give them the hint to think about money. Students typically find that 0.5 works as an addend.

Target Practice

OVERVIEW

This activity builds students' estimation and computation skills as they try to get as close as possible to a target number. Students can do the activity individually or in pairs or small groups.

MATERIALS

▲ dice, 2 per student, pair, or small group of students
▲ deck of 36 cards, with 4 cards of each number from 1 to 9, 1 per student, pair, or small group of students (**Note:** You can use a standard deck of playing cards with only the ace through 9 cards or ask students to make the decks using index cards.)

TIME

▲ one class period to introduce, plus additional time for playing

TEACHING DIRECTIONS

1. Draw the following on the board:

___ ___ . ___ . ___ − ___ . ___ + 0 . ___ ___ = ___

2. Explain: "First roll the two dice and multiply the numbers to determine your target number. Then deal seven cards to determine the seven numbers you can place in the seven spaces in the problem. Your goal is to place numbers so that the answer you calculate is as close as possible to the target number."

3. Do a sample with the class to be sure that the students understand.

Knockout

OVERVIEW

This lesson gives students practice reading, representing, and subtracting decimals and reinforces their understanding of the importance of the places in the numbers.

MATERIALS

▲ calculators, 1 per student
▲ optional: overhead calculator

TIME

▲ one class period

TEACHING DIRECTIONS

1. Explain to the students: "I'll give you a number to enter into your calculator, and then I'll ask you to change one digit at a time without clearing your calculator."

2. Give a first number: "Enter decimal point, one, two, three." If you have an overhead calculator, press .123 and project it for the students to see. If not, write .123 on the board. (Most calculators will display 0.123.)

3. Ask a student to read the number.

4. Present the "knockout" challenge: "Without changing any of the other digits or clearing your calculator, knock out the digit two so that there's a zero in its place." Ask the students to talk about their ideas among themselves and then have volunteers present solutions. Typically, someone in the class will suggest subtracting .02, resulting in 0.103 on the display. If not, present this solution and then present another problem.

5. Ask: "Without changing any of the other digits or clearing your calculator, how can you knock out the digit one so that there's a zero in its place?" Again, have a student suggest a solution and explain how he or she figured it out.

6. Repeat Step 5 for the digit 3.

7. Repeat Steps 2 through 6 for another number: .1234.

8. Continue the activity for other numbers.

From Here to There

OVERVIEW

This activity helps reinforce students' estimation skills. Students figure out missing numbers in numerical sentences. They use calculators to test their predictions, refine their estimates, and verify their answers.

MATERIALS

▲ calculators, 1 per student
▲ optional: overhead calculator

TIME

▲ one class period to introduce, and additional time for repeat experiences

TEACHING DIRECTIONS

1. Write a sample problem on the board:

$12 \times \underline{\hspace{1cm}} = 135$

Ask for an estimate of the missing number. For each estimate, do the multiplication (the overhead calculator is good for this) and record the answer. Then, if the answer isn't correct, ask for another estimate. Continue until students solve the problem. For example:

$12 \times \underline{12} = 144$
$12 \times \underline{11} = 132$
$12 \times \underline{11.5} = 138$
$12 \times \underline{11.4} = 136.8$
$12 \times \underline{11.3} = 135.6$
$12 \times \underline{11.2} = 134.4$
$12 \times \underline{11.25} = 135$

2. Give the students problems to try such as the following. Choose problems that match the abilities of your students:

$$2.56 + \underline{} = 2.561$$
$$24 \div \underline{} = 10$$
$$15 \times \underline{} = 79.5$$

Cover Up

OVERVIEW

Cover Up is a game that students can play in pairs or in groups of three or four. The game is an appropriate follow-up for building, naming, recording, and comparing decimals with base ten blocks. The object of the game is to be the first player to cover one whole (a flat) with ten tenths (ten rods). Students may put only rods on the flat, not units—thus, when they have ten hundredths, they exchange for one tenth.

MATERIALS

▲ base ten blocks, at least 10 units, 10 rods, and 1 flat per student
▲ dice, 2 per pair or group of students
▲ optional: overhead base ten blocks
▲ optional: *Cover Up* directions, 1 per pair of students (see Blackline Masters)

TIME

▲ twenty minutes to introduce, and additional time to play

TEACHING DIRECTIONS

1. Explain the rules. Either project an overhead transparency of the directions, write the directions on the board, or distribute a copy to each pair of students.

Cover Up

You Need:
    a partner or group of three or four students
    base ten blocks
    2 dice

Rules

1. Each player takes one whole (one flat).

2. On a turn, a player rolls the dice and adds the numbers. The sum tells the number of hundredths the player can take. When a player has ten hundredths, he or she exchanges it for one tenth. If the player has one tenth (a rod), the player may place it on the flat. When a player has completed his or her turn, the next player takes the dice.

3. Play continues with each player following Rule 2.

4. If a player rolls a number that results in covering the flat with extra hundredths, the player skips that turn and passes the dice. At any time, a player may roll just one of the dice instead of both.

5. The winner is the first player to completely cover the whole without having any extra hundredths.

2. Play the game with you as one player and either a student or the whole class as the other.

3. When you feel the students understand how to play, have them play in pairs or in groups of three or four.

Pursuit of Zero

OVERVIEW

Pursuit of Zero is a game that students can play in pairs or in groups of three or four. The game is an appropriate activity to reinforce building, naming, recording, and comparing decimals with base ten blocks. It is best introduced after students have learned to play *Cover Up* (see page 166). The object of the game is to be the first player to get completely rid of all blocks.

MATERIALS

▲ base ten blocks, at least 10 units, 10 rods, and 1 flat per student
▲ dice, 2 per pair or group of students
▲ optional: overhead base ten blocks
▲ optional: *Pursuite of Zero* directions, 1 per pair of students (see Blackline Masters)

TIME

▲ twenty minutes to introduce, plus additional time to play

TEACHING DIRECTIONS

1. Explain the rules. Either project an overhead transparency of the directions, write the directions on the board, or distribute a copy to each pair of students.

Pursuit of Zero

You Need:
    a partner or group of three or four students
    base ten blocks
    2 dice

Rules

1. Each player takes one whole (one flat).

2. On a turn, a player rolls the dice and adds the numbers. The sum tells the number of hundredths the player can remove from the whole. Before removing any blocks, the player may make any equivalent exchange; for example, changing the whole for ten tenths or some combination of tenths and hundredths. When a player has completed his or her turn, the next player takes the dice.

3. Play continues with each player following Rule 2.

4. If a player rolls a number that calls for removing more than the player has, the player skips that turn and passes the dice. At any time, a player may roll just one of the dice instead of both.

5. The winner is the first player to get completely rid of all blocks.

2. Play the game with you as one player and either a student or the whole class as the other.

3. When you feel the students understand how to play, have them play in pairs or in groups of three or four.

ASSESSMENTS

Overview

This section contains nine assessments that are useful for assessing what students are learning as they study decimals and percents. The first six, *Which Is Larger*, *Where Does the Decimal Point Belong?*, *Closest to 0, .5, or 1?*, *Putting Decimals in Order*, *Putting Decimals and Fractions in Order*, and *Which Answer Makes Sense?*, ask students to think about fractions and decimals that are presented abstractly. *Selling Plants* presents students with a problem in a real-world context. *What Do You Know About Decimals?* and *What Do You Know About Percents?* ask students to explain what they understand about decimals and percents.

Teaching Notes

Assessing what students are learning is a continual process. Teachers learn about what students understand from listening to what they say during class discussions, from observing and listening to them as they work on independent activities, and from reading their written work. But not all children contribute regularly in class discussions and, therefore, whole-class discussions don't necessarily provide sufficient information about every student. Also, when students work on activities, they often work with partners or in small groups and, therefore, a child's knowledge or lack of knowledge can be masked. For these reasons, it's useful, and important, to assess students periodically with assignments that they complete individually and in writing.

The assessments presented in this section are similar to the instructional activities in the book in that they are opportunities for students to continue their learning about decimals. Writing requires thinking, and any opportunity to focus on a topic can enhance learning. Also, not only do such papers provide valuable information about individual students, class sets of responses provide useful information about the overall effectiveness of the instruction provided.

It's important, however, to realize that these particular assessments won't provide all the information necessary for a complete and comprehensive picture of each student's understanding. The work that students do on all of the activities in the book is also useful for tracking their strengths, weaknesses, and growth. One way that I've found particularly helpful to facilitate assessment is to set up file folders for the students and keep in them a copy of all the work they do that provides insights into their thinking. This sometimes requires making copies of papers they've worked on collaboratively or would like to take home to share, but it's well worth the effort to have a chronological record of each child's progress.

Which Is Larger?

PROMPT

Which is larger, 0.9 or 0.13? Explain your reasoning.

Ask students to compare pairs of decimals often, changing the difficulty of the problem by increasing the number of decimal places, or showing one number as a fraction and the other as a decimal. To push students' thinking further, ask them to explain their reasoning in more than one way.

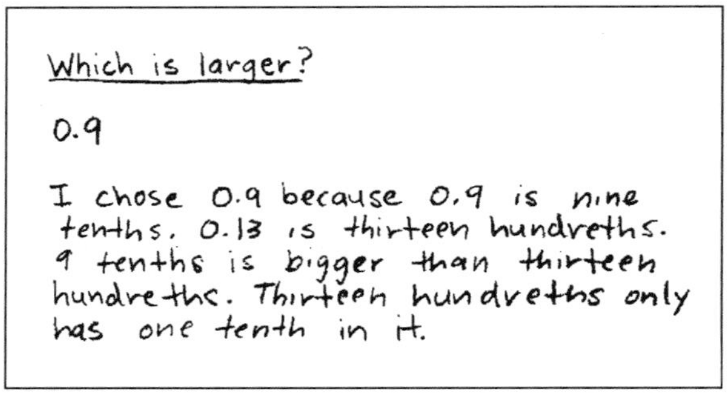

Which is larger?

0.9

I chose 0.9 because 0.9 is nine tenths. 0.13 is thirteen hundreths. 9 tenths is bigger than thirteen hundreths. Thirteen hundreths only has one tenth in it.

▲▲▲▲▲▲**Figure 1** *To compare 0.9 and 0.13, Ian compared the number of tenths in each.*

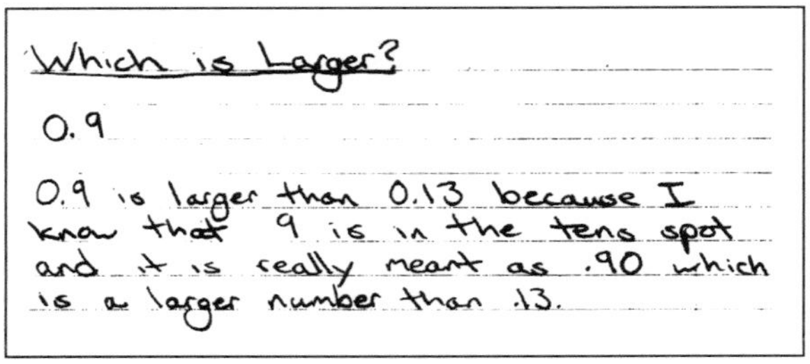

Which is Larger?

0.9

0.9 is larger than 0.13 because I know that 9 is in the tens spot and it is really meant as .90 which is a larger number than .13.

▲▲▲▲▲▲**Figure 2** *Patrice incorrectly described the tenths place as the "tens" place, but understood how to compare the two decimals.*

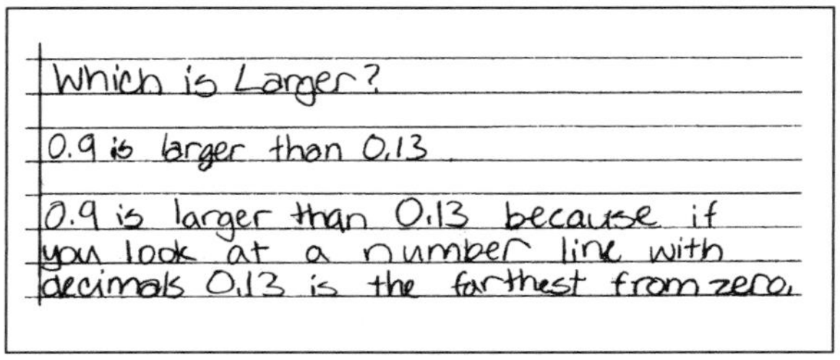

Which is Larger?

0.9 is larger than 0.13

0.9 is larger than 0.13 because if you look at a number line with decimals 0.13 is the farthest from zero.

▲▲▲▲▲▲**Figure 3** *Rebecca correctly identified the larger decimal, but her explanation showed her lack of understanding.*

Where Does the Decimal Point Belong?

PROMPT

Place the decimal point in the given set of digits to form a number that is between the given two numbers: 4107. Explain your reasoning.

  a. Create a number between 4 and 5.

  b. Create a number between 400 and 500.

  c. Create a number between 40 and 50.

  d. Create a number less than one.

This assessment is appropriate after students have had experience building and naming decimals (see Chapter 1). You can repeat this assessment from time to time, increasing or decreasing the number of digits in the number you give, and/or changing the directions. For instance, for the example above, you could ask the students to place the decimal point to create a number that has seven hundredths.

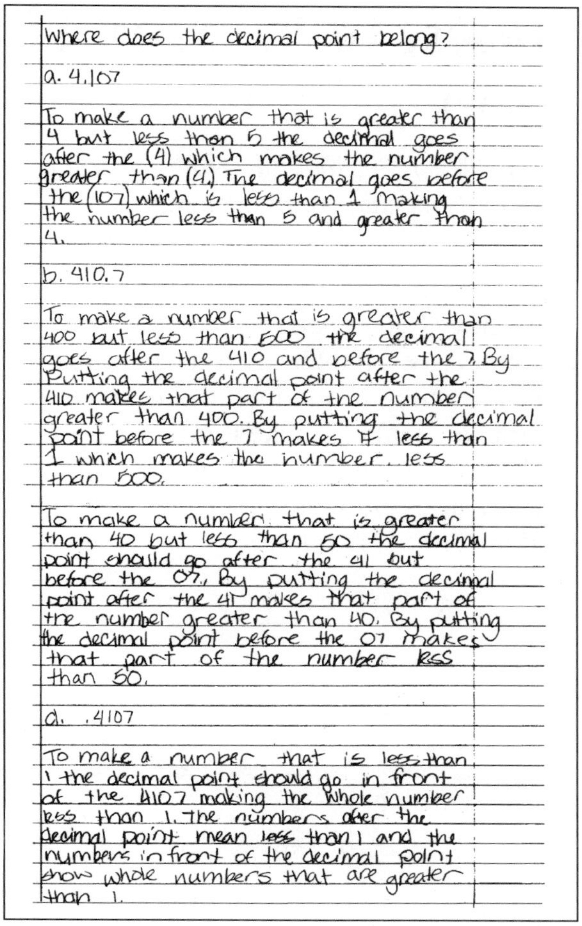

Where does the decimal point belong?

a. 4.107

To make a number that is greater than 4 but less than 5 the decimal goes after the (4) which makes the number greater than (4.) The decimal goes before the (107) which is less than 1 making the number less than 5 and greater than 4.

b. 410.7

To make a number that is greater than 400 but less than 500 the decimal goes after the 410 and before the 7. By putting the decimal point after the 410 makes that part of the number greater than 400. By putting the decimal point before the 7 makes it less than 1 which makes the number less than 500.

To make a number that is greater than 40 but less than 50 the decimal point should go after the 41 but before the 07. By putting the decimal point after the 41 makes that part of the number greater than 40. By putting the decimal point before the 07 makes that part of the number less than 50.

d. .4107

To make a number that is less than 1 the decimal point should go in front of the 4107 making the whole number less than 1. The numbers after the decimal point mean less than 1 and the numbers in front of the decimal point show whole numbers that are greater than 1.

▲▲▲▲▲▲**Figure 4** *Rebecca placed the decimal point correctly in each number and explained her reasoning.*

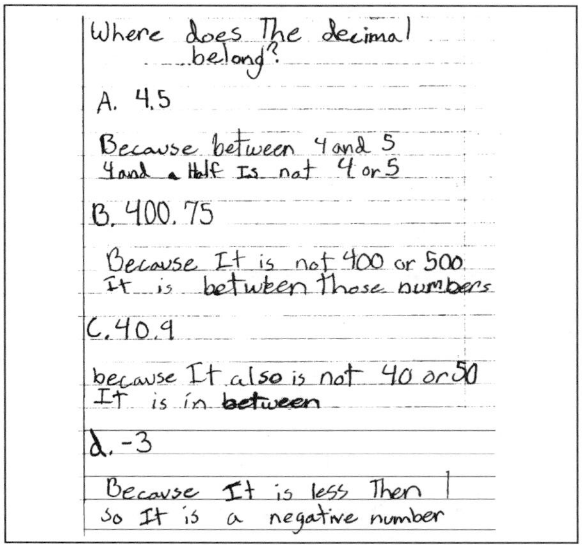

Where does The decimal belong?

A. 4.5

Because between 4 and 5 4 and a Half Is not 4 or 5

B. 400.75

Because It is not 400 or 500. It is between those numbers

C. 40.9

because It also is not 40 or 50 It is in between

d. -3

Because It is less Then 1 So It is a negative number

▲▲▲▲▲▲**Figure 5** *Rory didn't use the decimals in the prompt but instead created his own numbers.*

Closest to 0, .5, or 1?

PROMPT

Decide if each decimal numeral is closest to 0, .5, or 1. Explain your reasoning.

    0.4   .15   0.7   .8   0.33

This assessment is appropriate after students have had experience comparing decimals (see Chapter 4). You can repeat this assessment from time to time, changing the decimals to make it more or less challenging. Including four or five decimals in each assessment is sufficient for gauging students' understanding.

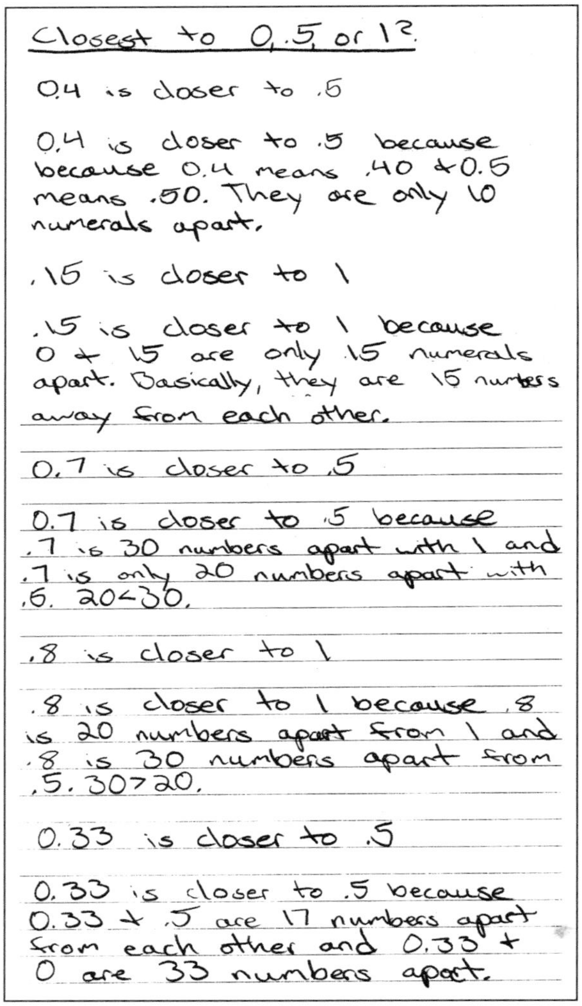

Closest to 0.5 or 1?

0.4 is closer to .5

0.4 is closer to .5 because because 0.4 means .40 & 0.5 means .50. They are only 10 numerals apart.

.15 is closer to 1

.15 is closer to 1 because 0 & 15 are only 15 numerals apart. Basically, they are 15 numbers away from each other.

0.7 is closer to .5

0.7 is closer to .5 because .7 is 30 numbers apart with 1 and .7 is only 20 numbers apart with .5. 20<30.

.8 is closer to 1

.8 is closer to 1 because .8 is 20 numbers apart from 1 and .8 is 30 numbers apart from .5. 30>20.

0.33 is closer to .5

0.33 is closer to .5 because 0.33 & .5 are 17 numbers apart from each other and 0.33 & 0 are 33 numbers apart.

▲▲▲▲▲▲Figure 6 *Patrice's responses showed that she had difficulty comparing these decimals.*

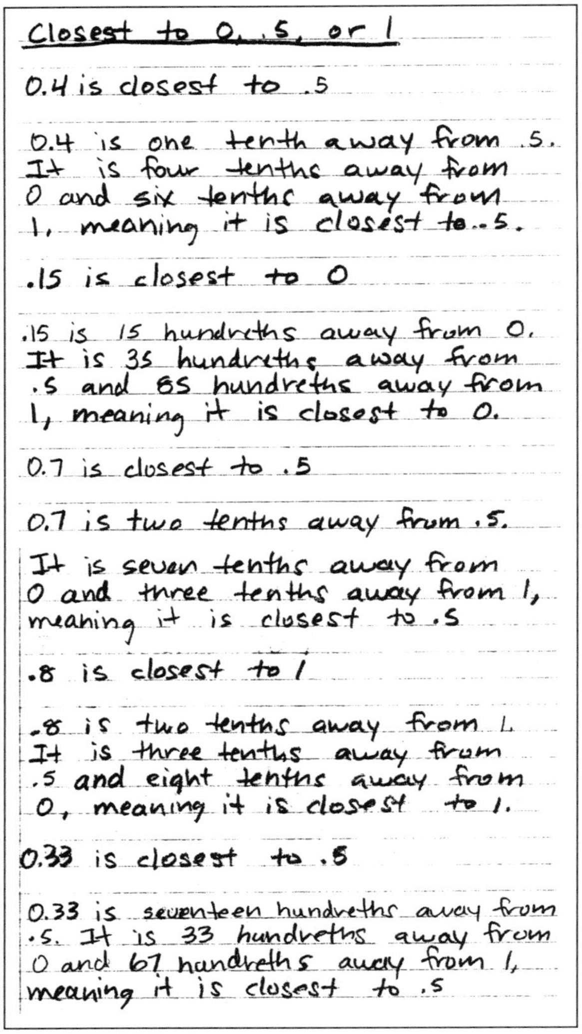

Closest to 0, .5, or 1

0.4 is closest to .5

0.4 is one tenth away from .5. It is four tenths away from 0 and six tenths away from 1, meaning it is closest to .5.

.15 is closest to 0

.15 is 15 hundredths away from 0. It is 35 hundredths away from .5 and 65 hundredths away from 1, meaning it is closest to 0.

0.7 is closest to .5

0.7 is two tenths away from .5. It is seven tenths away from 0 and three tenths away from 1, meaning it is closest to .5

.8 is closest to 1

.8 is two tenths away from 1. It is three tenths away from .5 and eight tenths away from 0, meaning it is closest to 1.

0.33 is closest to .5

0.33 is seventeen hundredths away from .5. It is 33 hundredths away from 0 and 67 hundredths away from 1, meaning it is closest to .5

▲▲▲▲▲▲Figure 7 *Ian's answers are correct and his explanations are clear.*

Putting Decimals in Order

PROMPT

Put each set of decimal numerals in order from smallest to largest. Explain your reasoning.

> 0.5, .27, 0.68
>
> 0.3, 0.03, .04
>
> 2.5, 3.4, 3.05

This assessment gives students the same sort of challenge they have in the *Comparing Decimals* lesson (see Chapter 4). You can repeat this assessment from time to time, changing the decimals to make it more or less challenging. Including four or five decimals in each set can also make the assessment more challenging.

Putting decimals in order

A. .27, .5, .68

.27 looks bigger than .5 because it's got more digits but it really isn't, and .68 is more than .5, because the 6 is a place higher

B 0.03, 0.3, 0.4

0.03 is only 3 off of 0 and 0.3 is more than it but less than 0.4

C. 2.5, 3.05, 3.4

2 is a whole number less than 3 so it's less, and 3.05 is less than 3.4

▲▲▲▲▲▲**Figure 8** *Blaire's paper showed her partial understanding.*

Putting Decimals in Order

.27, .5, .68

I know that this is right because .5 = .50. So .27 is less than 50, but .68 is greater than 50. .27 is least, .68 is th

greatest, and .5 is in the middle.

0.03, 0.04, 0.3

I know that this is right because .3 = .30, .03 = .300, and .04 = .400. .3 is 3 out of 10, .03 is 3 out of 100, and .04 is 4 out of 100. So, .3 is the greatest and .03 is the least.

2.5, 3.05, 3.4

I know this is right because if you look at the whole numbers 2 is less than 3. then I looked at the 3's and 2.05 is 5 out of 100 and 3.4 is 4 out of 10, 3.4 is then greater. 2.5 is the least and 3.4 is the greatest.

▲▲▲▲▲▲**Figure 9** *It's important to assess students in a variety of ways. In this assessment, Patrice ordered the decimals correctly, while her work on a previous assessment was incorrect.*

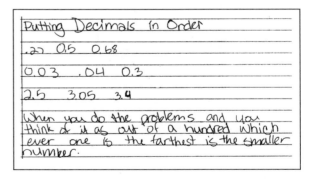

Putting Decimals in Order

.27   0.5   0.68

0.03   .04   0.3

2.5   3.05   3.4

When you do the problems and you think of it as out of a hundred which ever one is the farthest is the smaller number.

▲▲▲▲▲▲**Figure 10** *Crystal ordered the decimals correctly and gave one explanation for all three sets.*

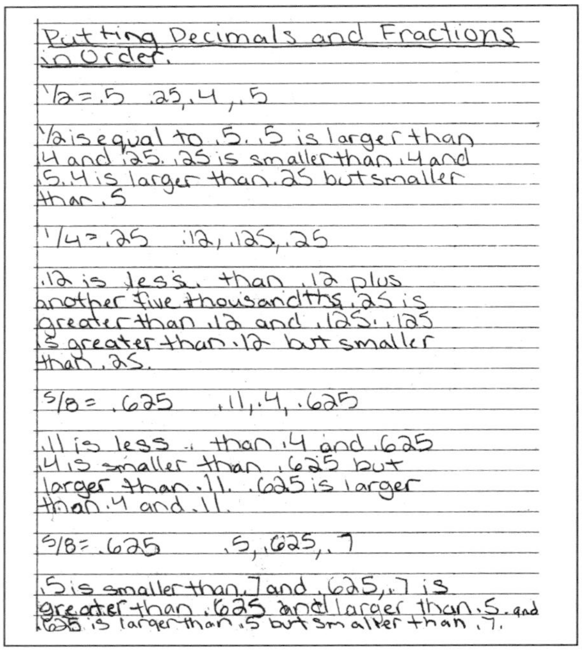

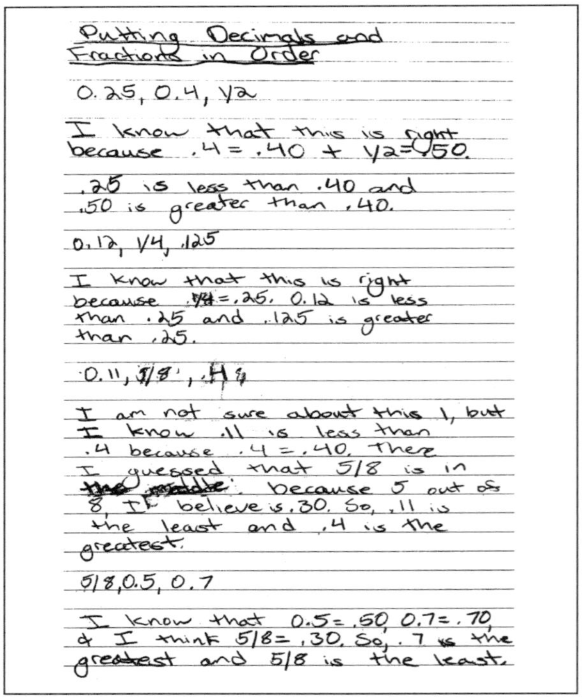

Putting Decimals and Fractions in Order

PROMPT

Put each set of fractions and decimal numerals in order from smallest to largest. Explain your reasoning.

$\frac{1}{2}$, 0.25, 0.4

.125, 0.12, $\frac{1}{4}$

$\frac{5}{8}$, 0.4, 0.11

$\frac{5}{8}$, 0.5, 0.7

There are a variety of ways students can approach this assessment. They could convert the fractions to decimals, convert the decimals to fractions, or do neither and still reason correctly. For example, in the third set, knowing that $\frac{5}{8}$ is greater than $\frac{1}{2}$ is sufficient for figuring out how to order the third set. The last set, however, presents more of a challenge, and you might think this is too difficult for your students. Use your best judgment and adjust as you see fit. (A student verified that 0.7 was larger than $\frac{5}{8}$ by comparing them both to one whole. She reasoned that 0.7 was $\frac{3}{10}$ from a whole while $\frac{5}{8}$ was $\frac{3}{8}$ from a whole and, therefore, since $\frac{3}{10}$ was less than $\frac{3}{8}$, 0.7 was closer to 1.)

Putting Decimals and Fractions in Order.
1/2=.5 .25, .4, .5
1/2 is equal to .5. .5 is larger than .4 and .25. .25 is smaller than .4 and .5. .4 is larger than .25 but smaller than .5
1/4=.25 .12, .125, .25
.12 is less than .12 plus another five thousandths. .25 is greater than .12 and .125. .125 is greater than .12 but smaller than .25.
5/8=.625 .11, .4, .625
.11 is less than .4 and .625 .4 is smaller than .625 but larger than .11. .625 is larger than .4 and .11.
5/8=.625 .5, .625, .7
.5 is smaller than .7 and .625, .7 is greater than .625 and larger than .5. and .625 is larger than .5 but smaller than .7.

Figure 11 *Misha converted the fractions to decimals and correctly ordered the numbers.*

Putting Decimals and fractions in order
0.4, 0.25, 1/2
because 0.4 is less then 0.25 and 1/2 is greater then 0.25
0.12, 1/4, .125
Becaus 0.12 is less then 1/4, and .125 but 1/4 is less then .125
0.4, 0.11, 5/8
0.4 is smaller then 0.11 and 5/8 and but 5/8 is larger then 0.11
0.5, 0.7, 5/8
Because 0.5 is also less than 0.7 and 5/8 but 0.7 is less than 5/8

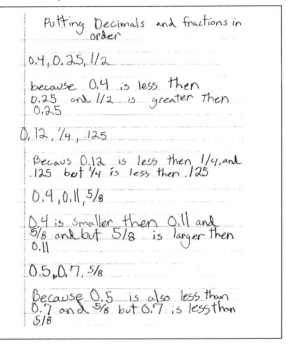

Figure 12 *Rory's paper showed his lack of understanding.*

Putting Decimals and Fractions in Order
0.25, 0.4, 1/2
I know that this is right because .4 = .40 + 1/2 = .50.
.25 is less than .40 and .50 is greater than .40.
0.12, 1/4, .125
I know that this is right because 1/4 = .25. 0.12 is less than .25 and .125 is greater than .25.
0.11, 5/8, .4
I am not sure about this 1, but I know .11 is less than .4 because .4 = .40. Then I guessed that 5/8 is in ~~the middle~~. because 5 out of 8, I believe is .30. So, .11 is the least and .4 is the greatest.
5/8, 0.5, 0.7
I know that 0.5 = .50 0.7 = .70 & I think 5/8 = .30. So, .7 is the greatest and 5/8 is the least.

Figure 13 *In her explanations, Patrice identified where she wasn't sure about her own understanding.*

Which Answer Makes Sense?

PROMPT

Select the correct answer from those listed. Explain your reasoning.

5.16 × 3.4

    a.   *1.7544*

    b.   *17.544*

    c.   *175.44*

    d.   *1754.4*

    e.   *none of the above*

This assessment is similar to an item that appeared on a former National Assessment of Educational Progress (NAEP) test. Students too often focus on rules for placing decimal points in computation problems, rather than reasoning to determine answers. Change the operations and the numbers for other similar problems. Giving students problems like this one from time to time helps students focus on reasoning when computing and also helps prepare them for the kinds of test items they will face.

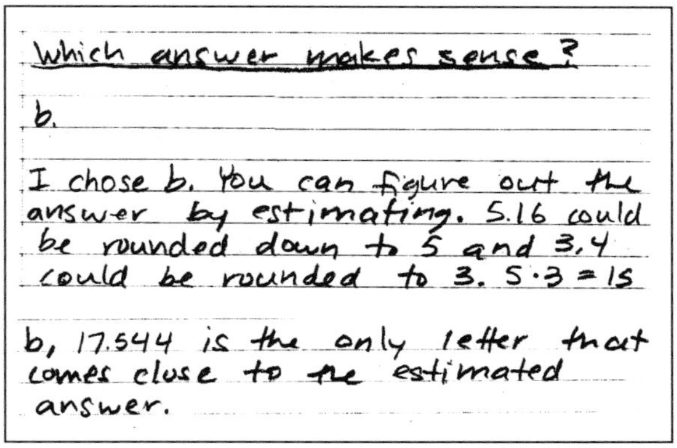

> Which answer makes sense?
>
> b.
>
> I chose b. You can figure out the answer by estimating. 5.16 could be rounded down to 5 and 3.4 could be rounded to 3. 5·3 = 15
>
> b, 17.544 is the only letter that comes close to the estimated answer.

▲▲▲▲▲▲**Figure 14** *Ian chose the correct answer and explained his reason clearly.*

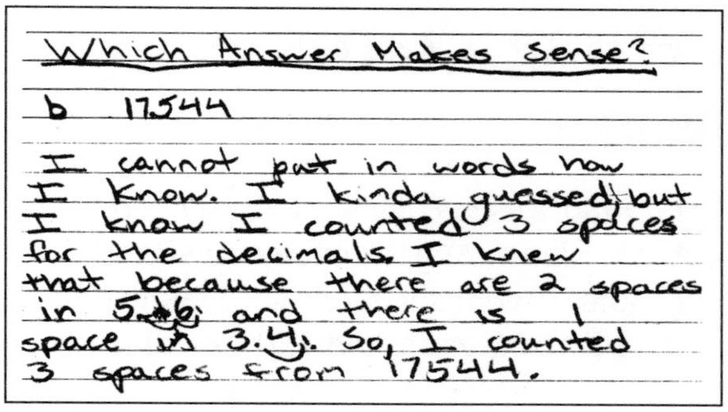

> Which Answer Makes Sense?
>
> b   17.544
>
> I cannot put in words how I know. I kinda guessed, but I know I counted 3 spaces for the decimals. I knew that because there are 2 spaces in 5.16; and there is 1 space in 3.4. So, I counted 3 spaces from 17544.

▲▲▲▲▲▲**Figure 15** *Patrice's explanation demonstrates how a correct answer by itself can mask misunderstanding.*

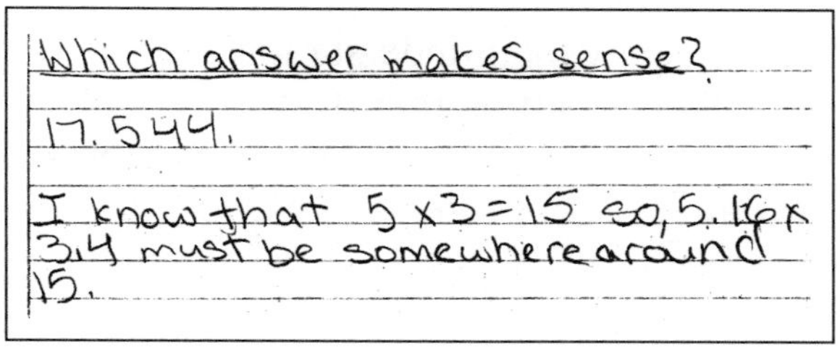

> Which answer makes sense?
>
> 17.544.
>
> I know that 5 × 3 = 15 so, 5.16 × 3.4 must be somewhere around 15.

▲▲▲▲▲▲**Figure 16** *Misha's answer is correct and her reasoning is sound.*

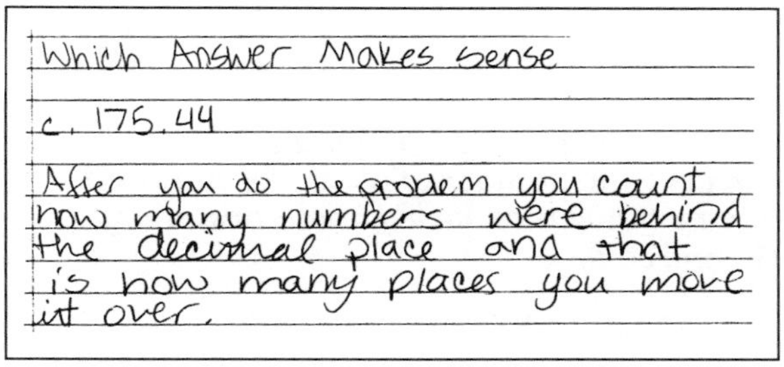

> Which Answer Makes Sense
>
> c. 175.44
>
> After you do the problem you count how many numbers were behind the decimal place and that is how many places you move it over.

▲▲▲▲▲▲**Figure 17** *Crystal's answer shows the danger of following a rule rather than reasoning to find an answer.*

Selling Plants

PROMPT

For a fund-raiser, each student pledged to sell a dozen plants. Amy claimed that she sold only 50% of what she pledged. Jeremy, however, claimed that he sold 150% of what he pledged. George said he sold 75% of his pledge. How many plants did each person sell? Explain your reasoning.

Most students can easily figure out 50 percent of a quantity. In this problem, they also have to show their understanding of percents that are larger than 100 percent as well as show whether they can figure out how much is 75 percent of twelve.

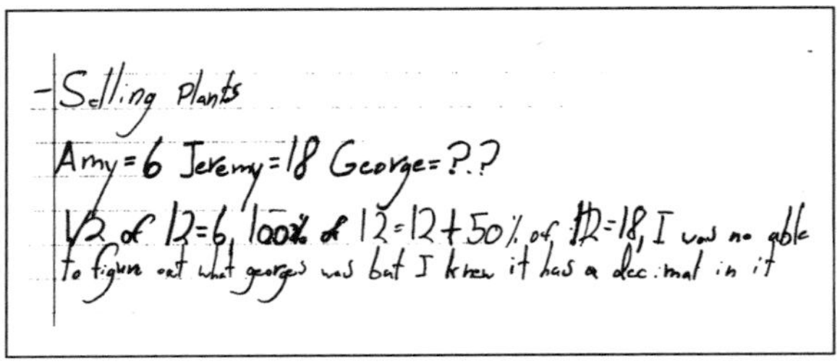

> -Selling Plants
>
> Amy = 6 Jeremy = 18 George = ?.?
>
> 1/2 of 12 = 6, 100% of 12 = 12 + 50% of 12 = 18, I was no able to figure out what george was but I knew it has a decimal in it

▲▲▲▲▲▲**Figure 18** *Jonathan figured correctly the number of plants for Amy and Jeremy but was confused about how many George sold.*

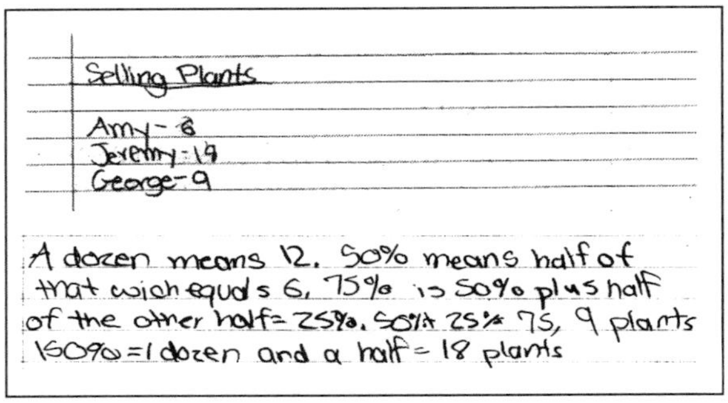

> Selling Plants
>
> Amy - 6
> Jeremy - 18
> George - 9
>
> A dozen means 12. 50% means half of that wich equals 6, 75% is 50% plus half of the other half = 25%. so it 25% is 75, 9 plants 150% = 1 dozen and a half = 18 plants

▲▲▲▲▲▲**Figure 19** *Blaire was able to figure the number of plants each student sold and explained her reasoning clearly.*

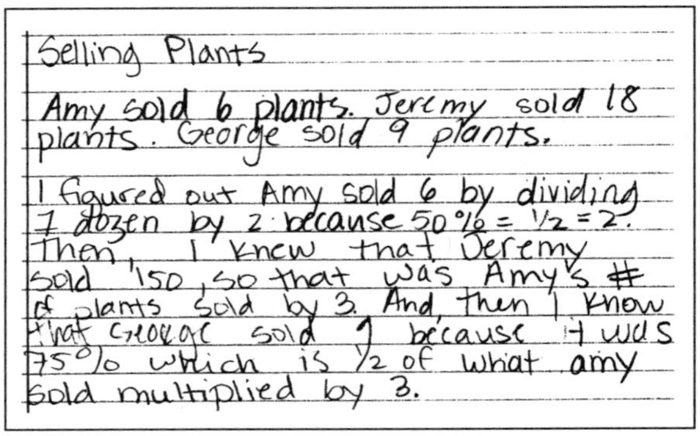

> Selling Plants
>
> Amy sold 6 plants. Jeremy sold 18 plants. George sold 9 plants.
>
> I figured out Amy sold 6 by dividing 1 dozen by 2 because 50% = 1/2 = 2. Then, I knew that Jeremy sold 150, so that was Amy's # of plants sold by 3. And, then I know that George sold 9 because 4 was 75% which is 1/2 of what amy sold multiplied by 3.

▲▲▲▲▲▲**Figure 20** *Francesca had a unique way of figuring out the number of plants that George sold.*

What Do You Know About Decimals?

PROMPT

Write all that you know about decimals. Provide details, including real-world examples and drawings. Also include information about anything you find confusing about decimals.

Give this assignment early in the students' study of decimals as a pre-assessment, after students have had the opportunity to study decimals, or both times so that you and the students can assess the progress they've made. When you give this assignment, encourage students to write as much as possible to give you a way to assess what they understand and what they still need to learn. Also, encourage students to include any ideas about decimals that they're not sure about or that confuse them.

I know that decimals can also be determined as dollars. Decimals (from left to right) are 0. tens 100s thousandth's ten thousandths and so on. Decimals are also used as fractions. Example of that would be $\frac{1}{2}$ = 0.5 in decimals. They both are equal to 1 half.

You might see those decimals at a grocery store. They mean - 0.369 = 0 holes and three hundred and sixty-nine ten-thousandths. 1.78 = 1 hole and seventy-eight hundredths. 0.5 = 1 half or 0 holes and five tenths.

I have seen decimal numbers at my mom's work, at grocery stores, in math class, and in reciepts from many different places.

Figure 21 ***Madison described what she knew about decimals in general and gave some specifics as well.***

This is what I know about decimals. Decimals are used in many things and not just math. They are used as a measurement money and baseball batting average. On the right side of the decimal it starts with tenths and all the numbers have "ths" at the end. On the left side ones is closest to the decimal. All the numbers end in "s." I know each place like "Where is the 2 in 0.01322?" It is in the ten-thousandths place. That is what I know.

You might see 0.369 as a baseball batting average. You might see $1.78 as the cost for something. You might see 0.5 on a calculator.

I have seen decimal numbers in measurements too.

Figure 22 ***Frank described the values of the places and also gave examples of where you might see decimals used.***

What Do You Know About Percents?

PROMPT

Write all that you know about percents. Provide details, including real-world examples and drawings. Also include information about anything you find confusing about percents.

Give this assignment early in the students' study of percents as a pre-assessment, after students have had the opportunity to study percents, or both times so that you and the students can assess the progress they've made. When you give this assignment, encourage students to write as much as possible to give you a way to assess what they understand and what they still need to learn. Also, encourage students to include any ideas about percents that they're not sure about or that confuse them.

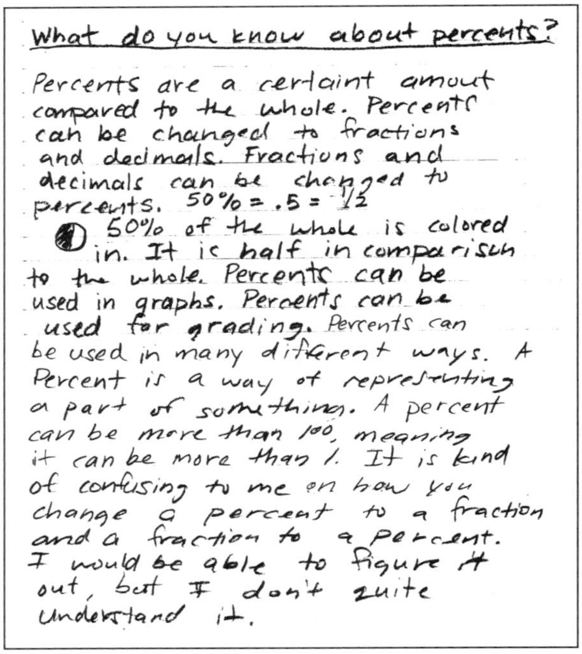

What do you know about percents?

Percents are a certaint amout compared to the whole. Percents can be changed to fractions and decimals. Fractions and decimals can be changed to percents. 50% = .5 = 1/2

50% of the whole is colored in. It is half in comparison to the whole. Percents can be used in graphs. Percents can be used for grading. Percents can be used in many different ways. A Percent is a way of representing a part of something. A percent can be more than 100, meaning it can be more than 1. It is kind of confusing to me on how you change a percent to a fraction and a fraction to a percent. I would be able to figure it out, but I don't quite understand it.

Figure 23 *Ian explained both what he understood about percents and what confused him.*

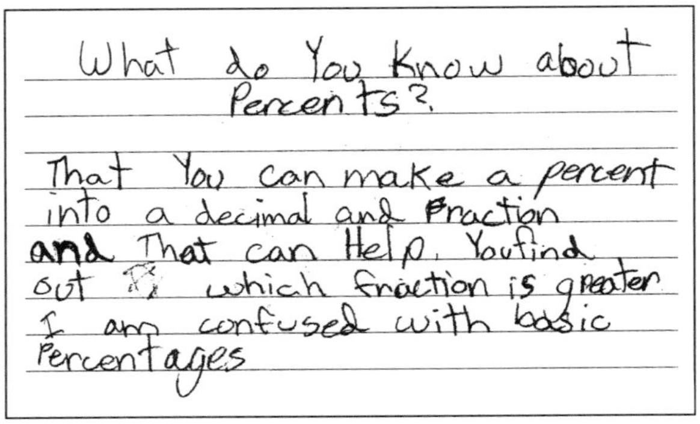

What do You Know about Percents?

That You can make a percent into a decimal and Fraction and That can Help. You find out which fraction is greater I am confused with basic Percentages

Figure 24 *Kendra expressed that she was confused about percents.*

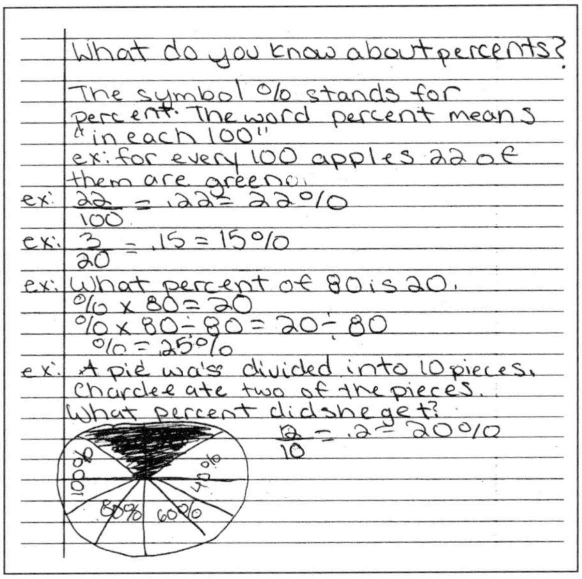

What do you know about percents?

The symbol % stands for percent. The word percent means "in each 100"

ex: for every 100 apples 22 of them are green.

ex: 22/100 = .22 = 22%

ex: 3/20 = .15 = 15%

ex: What percent of 80 is 20.

% x 80 = 20

% x 80 ÷ 80 = 20 ÷ 80

% = 25%

ex: A pie was divided into 10 pieces. Chardee ate two of the pieces. What percent did she get?

2/10 = .2 = 20%

Figure 25 *Misha provided examples to show what she understood about percents.*

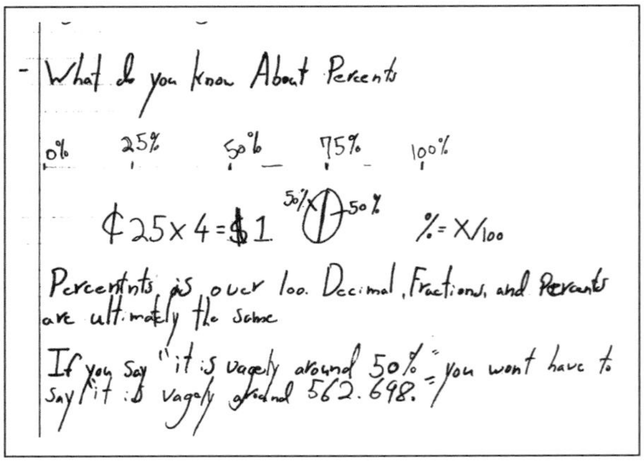

What do you Know About Percents

0% 25% 50% 75% 100%

¢25 x 4 = $1 50% 50% % = X/100

Percentnts is over 100. Decimal, Fractions, and Percents are ultimately the Same

If you Say "it is vaguely around 50%" you wont have to Say it is vaguely around 562.698.

Figure 26 *Jonathan also provided examples to show what he understood about percents.*

BLACKLINE MASTERS

Place Value Mat
Donna's Decimals
Decimal Riddles
The Greatest Wins
Decimal Nim
Target
Race to Zero
Target II
Sam and Sally
The Sum and Difference Game
Place Value Spinner Directions
10-by-10 Grids
Percent Designs
Percent Grids
T Design
Large 10-by-10 Grid
$1.00 Bills
$5.00 Bills
$10.00 Bills
Money Riddles
More Money Riddles
Enchanted Enchilada Menu
Values of Letters
Cover Up
Pursuit of Zero

Donna's Decimals

To show seventy-two–hundredths, Donna placed on her place value mat six rods and twelve units. She then wrote:

$.6 + .12 = .72$

$$\frac{6}{10} + \frac{12}{100} = \frac{72}{100}$$

Donna's classmate, Garrett, told her that she was wrong. Donna responded, "No, I'm right, and I could also build and write seventy-two–hundredths in other ways."

Find as many other ways as you can to represent seventy-two–hundredths with base ten blocks. Draw each solution and label with fractions and decimals.

Decimal Riddles

1. I have 2 ones, 12 tenths, and 6 hundredths. What's the number?

2. I have 30 hundredths and 3 tenths. What's the number?

3. The number is 45 hundredths. I have 25 hundredths. How much more do I need?

4. I have 13 tenths, 2 ones, and 21 hundredths. What's the number?

5. If you add 3 more tenths, the total would be worth 1 whole and 7 tenths. What's the number?

6. I have 16 hundredths. I added some tenths and now I have more than 3 tenths and less than 4 tenths. What's the number?

 From *Lessons for Decimals and Percents* by Carrie De Francisco and Marilyn Burns. © 2002 Math Solutions Publications

The Greatest Wins

You Need:
  1 die
  a partner or group of four

Rules

1. Each player makes a recording sheet as shown.

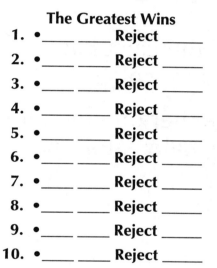

2. Players take turns rolling the die, writing the number in a space in the first line, and passing the die to the next player. Continue until all players have filled in the first line. **Note:** Once a number is recorded, its position can't be changed.

3. Each player reads aloud his or her number. The group agrees on who has the largest number and wins the round.

4. Continue playing for nine more rounds. The overall winner is the player who wins the most rounds.

Variation

Add a third line to create a thousandths place. Play the game same way.

Decimal Nim

You Need:
  1 calculator
  a partner

Rules

1. Player 1 clears the calculator so that zero appears on the calculator display.

2. Player 1 adds either one-tenth or two-tenths by pressing on the calculator one of the following:

    +, .1, =

    +, .2, =

    Player 1 then gives the calculator to Player 2.

3. Player 2 also adds either one-tenth or two-tenths. Player 2 then gives the calculator back to Player 1.

4. Play continues in this way. The winner of the game is the player who causes 1 to appear on the display.

From *Lessons for Decimals and Percents* by Carrie De Francisco and Marilyn Burns. © 2002 Math Solutions Publications

Target

You Need:
   1 calculator
   1 die
   a partner

Rules

1. Player 1 clears the calculator so that zero appears on the calculator display and rolls the die to determine the target number.

2. Player 1 adds either one-tenth or two-tenths by pressing on the calculator one of the following:

   +, .1, =

   +, .2, =

   Player 1 then gives the calculator to Player 2.

3. Player 2 also adds either one-tenth or two-tenths. Player 2 then gives the calculator back to Player 1.

4. Play continues in this way. The winner of the game is the player who causes the target number to appear on the display.

Race to Zero

You Need:
   1 calculator
   a partner

Rules

1.   Player 1 clears the calculator and presses the number 1 so that a 1 appears on the calculator display.

2.   Player 1 subtracts either one-tenth or two-tenths by pressing on the calculator one of the following:

   −, .1, =

   −, .2, =

   Player 1 then gives the calculator to Player 2.

3.   Player 2 also subtracts either one-tenth or two-tenths. Player 2 then gives the calculator back to Player 1.

4.   Play continues in this way. The winner of the game is the player who reaches exactly zero on the display.

Target II

You Need:
  1 calculator
  a partner

Rules

1. Player 1 clears the calculator so that zero appears on the calculator display and rolls the die to determine the target number.

2. Player 1 adds either one-tenth, two-tenths, one-hundredth, or two-hundredths by pressing on the calculator one of the following:

    +, .1, =

    +, .2, =

    +, .01, =

    +, .02, =

    Player 1 then gives the calculator to Player 2.

3. Player 2 also adds either one-tenth, two-tenths, one-hundredth, or two-hundredths. Player 2 then gives the calculator back to Player 1.

4. Play continues in this way. The winner of the game is the player who causes the target number to appear on the display.

From *Lessons for Decimals and Percents* by Carrie De Francisco and Marilyn Burns. © 2002 Math Solutions Publications

Sam and Sally

Sam and Sally were playing the *Sum and Difference* game.

Sam's two numbers were .3 and .1.
Sally's numbers were .3 and .2.

Sam flipped the coin and it came up heads, so the larger sum and difference score. Sally's sum won, but Sam's difference won.

Figure out other numbers that would split the score. Do this for at least three rounds.

 From *Lessons for Decimals and Percents* by Carrie De Francisco and Marilyn Burns. © 2002 Math Solutions Publications

The Sum and Difference Game

You Need:
   a place value spinner
   a die
   a coin
   a partner

Rules

1.   Player 1 rolls the die and spins the place value spinner. The spin determines the value of the number rolled. (For example, if you roll a 3 and spin "hundredths," then your number is .03.) Record the first number.

2.   Player 1 repeats Step 1 to create a second number.

3.   Player 2 follows Steps 1 and 2 to generate two numbers.

4.   Using their numbers, players write two problems—an addition problem and a subtraction problem. Players solve both problems and check each other's answers.

5.   One player flips a coin to determine which answers score a point. Heads means the larger sum and difference win; tails means the smaller sum and difference win.

6.   Continue playing for a total of ten rounds.

From *Lessons for Decimals and Percents* by Carrie De Francisco and Marilyn Burns. © 2002 Math Solutions Publications

Place Value Spinner Directions

1. Cut a 5-by-8-inch index card in half. Cut a circle, about 3 inches in diameter, from one half of the card. Divide and label it as shown.

2. Mark a dot in the center of the other piece of card. Draw a line from the dot to one corner of the card.

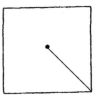

3. Bend up the outside of a paper clip. This part should point straight up when the paper clip is lying flat on the desk.

4. Poke a hole in the center of the circle (be exact) and another hole in the dot on the card.

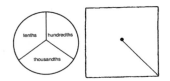

5. Push the bent end of the paper clip through the hole in the card. Tape the rest of the paper clip to the bottom of the card. Make sure the side of the card with the line is facing up.

6. Put the ¼-inch length of plastic straw and then the spinner face on the paper clip.

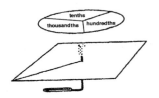

7. Cover the tip of the paper clip with a piece of tape.

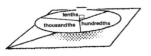

 From *Lessons for Decimals and Percents* by Carrie De Francisco and Marilyn Burns. © 2002 Math Solutions Publications

10-by-10 Grids

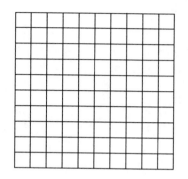

Percent Designs

From *Lessons for Decimals and Percents* by Carrie De Francisco and Marilyn Burns. © 2002 Math Solutions Publications

Percent Grids

T Design

From *Lessons for Decimals and Percents* by Carrie De Francisco and Marilyn Burns. © 2002 Math Solutions Publications

From *Lessons for Decimals and Percents* by Carrie De Francisco and Marilyn Burns. © 2002 Math Solutions Publications

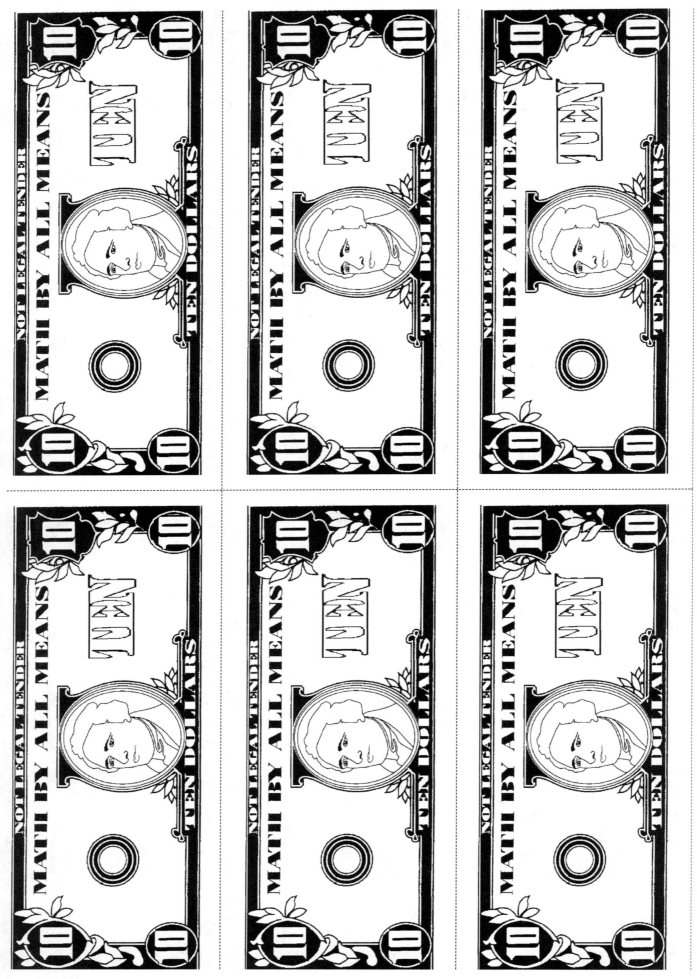

From *Lessons for Decimals and Percents* by Carrie De Francisco and Marilyn Burns. © 2002 Math Solutions Publications

Money Riddles

1. What is the sum of three-hundredths of $1.00, four-tenths of $1.00, and one-fourth of $20.00?

2. What is the sum of six-tenths of $1.00, fifty-five hundredths of $1.00, and one-tenth of $10.00?

3. What is the sum of seven-hundredths of $1.00, one-hundredth of $10.00, and one-tenth of $20.00?

4. What is the sum of nine-hundredths of $1.00, one-tenth of $5.00, and 50% of $10.00?

5. What is the sum of one-hundredth of $1.00, one-fourth of $1.00, and 20% of $10.00?

6. How much money is there altogether in three groups if each group has two-hundredths of $1.00 and seven-tenths of $1.00?

7. How much money is there altogether in five groups if each group has one-hundredth of $1.00 and one-hundredth of $10.00?

8. If 40% of $1.00 and three-hundredths of $1.00 are subtracted from $2.00, how much money is left?

9. If one-tenth of a dime, one-tenth of $1.00, and one-tenth of $10.00 are subtracted from $4.00, how much money is left?

10. If three-tenths of $1.00, two-hundredths of $1.00, and one-fifth of $10.00 are subtracted from $5.00, how much money is left?

More Money Riddles

1. What is the sum of twelve-tenths of $1.00, seven-hundredths of $1.00, and 50% of $2.50?

2. What is the sum of 120% of $4.00, one-fourth of $4.00, and one-hundredth of $4.00?

3. What is thirteen-hundredths of $10.00?

 From *Lessons for Decimals and Percents* by Carrie De Francisco and Marilyn Burns. © 2002 Math Solutions Publications

Enchanted Enchilada Menu

APPETIZERS
Nacho chips with salsa	$1.50
Stuffed jalapeños	$2.00

EGG DISHES
Huevos rancheros	$2.99
Migas	$2.99

SOUPS
Black bean	*Cup*	$1.25
	Bowl	$2.25
Chef's special	*Cup*	$2.00
	Bowl	$3.00

SALADS
Salad bar	*with dinner*	$1.99
	salad bar only	$2.99
Taco salad		$2.99

TORTILLA SPECIALTIES
Cheese enchiladas	$4.99
Guacamole enchiladas	$4.99
Bean burritos	$4.99
Chimichangas	$4.99

MEXICAN PIZZA
Large	$3.99
Small	$2.99

SIDE DISHES
Colache	$3.00
Calavacitas	$3.00
Quelites	$3.00
Texas caviar	$1.50
Frijoles refritos	$1.50

DESSERTS
Flan	$1.50
Biscochitos	$1.50
Natillas	$2.50
Deep-fried ice cream	$2.00
Fresh mango/papaya	$2.00

BEVERAGES
Cola	*glass*	$ .75
	pitcher	$2.00
Frozen delight		$2.25
Mexican coffee		$1.00
Regular coffee		$1.00
Tea		$ .75

TODAY'S SPECIAL $7.99

Values of Letters

a = $ .01	n = $ .14
b = $ .02	o = $ .15
c = $ .03	p = $ .16
d = $ .04	q = $ .17
e = $ .05	r = $ .18
f = $ .06	s = $ .19
g = $ .07	t = $ .20
h = $ .08	u = $ .21
i = $ .09	v = $ .22
j = $ .10	w = $ .23
k = $ .11	x = $ .24
l = $ .12	y = $ .25
m = $ .13	z = $ .26

 From *Lessons for Decimals and Percents* by Carrie De Francisco and Marilyn Burns. © 2002 Math Solutions Publications

Cover Up

You Need:
    a partner or group of three or four students
    base ten blocks
    2 dice

Rules

1. Each player takes one whole (one flat).

2. On a turn, a player rolls the dice and adds the numbers. The sum tells the number of hundredths the player can take. When a player has ten hundredths, he or she exchanges it for one tenth. If the player has one tenth (a rod), the player may place it on the flat. When a player has completed his or her turn, the next player takes the dice.

3. Play continues with each player following Rule 2.

4. If a player rolls a number that results in covering the flat with extra hundredths, the player skips that turn and passes the dice. At any time, a player may roll just one of the dice instead of both.

5. The winner is the first player to completely cover the whole without having any extra hundredths.

Pursuit of Zero

You Need:
   a partner or group of three or four students
   base ten blocks
   2 dice

Rules

1.   Each player takes one whole (one flat).

2.   On a turn, a player rolls the dice and adds the numbers. The sum tells the number of hundredths the player can remove from the whole. Before removing any blocks, the player may make any equivalent exchange; for example, changing the whole for ten tenths or some combination of tenths and hundredths. When a player has completed his or her turn, the next player takes the dice.

3.   Play continues with each player following Rule 2.

4.   If a player rolls a number that calls for removing more than the player has, the player skips that turn and passes the dice. At any time, a player may roll just one of the dice instead of both.

5. The winner is the first player to get completely rid of all blocks.

 From *Lessons for Decimals and Percents* by Carrie De Francisco and Marilyn Burns. © 2002 Math Solutions Publications

INDEX

Ten-Coin problem, 106, 116–17
tenths
    adding, 23, 25–26, 57–59
    benchmark equivalents, 83–84, 86–87,
        88–89
    comparing, 170
    decimal notation, 16–19
    money riddles using, 119, 120, 121–25
    predictions for adding, 49–52
    relating to percents, 66
    representing with base ten blocks, 1–8
    understanding decimals through, 16–19,
        97–100
    writing as decimals, 13
thirds
    benchmark equivalents, 85, 92
    repeating decimals, 104, 108
thousandths
    adding, 58–60
    explaining to students, 48
    finding, between hundredths, 42–48
    predictions for adding, 50, 53–54
    representing with base ten blocks, 1–4
time, for learning, xviii–xix
Time section, xviii

units. *See also* base ten blocks
    decimal notation for, 13
    explaining percents with, 66
    relating to money, 113

understanding decimal notation with, 16–19
value of, 1–4

Values of Letters chart, 152, 154, 202
Viorst, Judith, 146, 148

weights, understanding decimals through, xiv, 28,
    44–48
What Do You Know About Decimals? assessment,
    169, 177
What Do You Know About Percents? assessment,
    169, 178
Where Does the Decimal Point Belong?
    assessment, 169, 171
Which Answer Makes Sense? assessment, 169, 175
Which is Larger? assessment, 169, 170
word endings, monetary value of, 154, 156
writing
    assessment through, 169
    on decimal equivalents of fractions, 96
    on prior knowledge about decimals, xiii
    student retellings of *Alexander, Who Used to Be*
        Rich Last Saturday, 150–51
    on whether one-tenth or one-hundredth is
        greater, 3, 7–8

zeros
    in decimal calculations, 105–6
    before decimal point, xvii, 13, 16, 20
    to right of decimal point, 15, 31, 50, 67